C. R Sail

Farthest East, and South and West

Notes of a Journey Home Through Japan, Australasia and America

C. R Sail

Farthest East, and South and West

Notes of a Journey Home Through Japan, Australasia and America

ISBN/EAN: 9783744798273

Printed in Europe, USA, Canada, Australia, Japan

Cover: Foto ©Andreas Hilbeck / pixelio.de

More available books at **www.hansebooks.com**

FARTHEST EAST, AND SOUTH AND WEST

NOTES OF A JOURNEY HOME

THROUGH

JAPAN, AUSTRALASIA AND AMERICA

BY

AN ANGLO-INDIAN GLOBE-TROTTER

LONDON

W. H. ALLEN & CO. Ltd. 13 WATERLOO PLACE

Publishers to the India Office

1892

LONDON:
WOODFALL AND KINDER, PRINTERS,
70 TO 76, LONG ACRE, W.C.

PREFACE.

THESE notes of a Journey Home were not written with any definite intention of having them printed and published, but rather (though not without a vague idea that such might possibly be their fate) with no more distinct object than to keep a journal for the perusal and (I hoped) amusement of relatives and personal friends.

What I have set down is just my own impressions of countries and climates, men and manners, as I have seen them; and I have not devoted myself to transcribing from Cyclopædias and Year Books and Compendia of Useful Knowledge facts and figures which those who yearn for may seek for and find in books of that class. For these reasons, persons who require their mental provender to be set before them elegantly, in a pure and polished literary style, are respectfully warned off, equally with those whose delight is in statistics and historical disquisitions and political perpendings—in the Serious and the Solid. For here is but a careless style, with no more merit in its matter than accuracy and absence of exaggeration, so far as these may be attained by mortal pen, and a frankness of expression such as a man may use in writing to his friends. An Anglo-Indian knowledge (a very different thing from a Globe-trotter's knowledge) of India is assumed as already existing in the reader, and he is accordingly spared the descriptions of things Indian which are apt to figure largely in the book of the returned round-the-worlder. It is a book by an Anglo-Indian for Anglo-Indians; (chiefly, that is; and for as many more as care to read it, of course).

The plates are reproduced from photographs selected from a large number purchased at various places, and of varying merit. Those of Morris (of Dunedin, New Zealand) are—many of them—perfectly beautiful pictures.

I should like to add a remark to the little paragraph on page 285, in which I ask where the vent will take place from the subsidence of Kilauea in March, '91. Is not the answer given by the terrific earthquake in Japan in October, '91? And the earthquake being over, I read in the *Morning Post* of (I think) December 17th, a paragraph stating that the crater of Kilauea is again in full activity.

C. R. SAIL.

CONTENTS.

PART I.

FARTHEST EAST.

CHAPTER I.
	PAGE
THE START—STRAITS—JAVA	3

CHAPTER II.
CHINA	24

CHAPTER III.
JAPAN	53

CHAPTER IV.
MIYANOSHITA—NIKKO—IKAO	72

CHAPTER V.
ISE	107

CHAPTER VI.
KIOTO—THEATRES—END OF FARTHEST EAST	118

PART II.

FARTHEST SOUTH.

CHAPTER VII.
HONGKONG TO SYDNEY 141

CHAPTER VIII.
SYDNEY—MELBOURNE 150

CHAPTER IX.
NEW ZEALAND SOUTH OF CHRISTCHURCH . . . 173

CHAPTER X.
THE OTIRA—THE BULLER—NELSON 189

CHAPTER XI.
THE REGION OF UNCEASING FIRE 206

CHAPTER XII.
THE WANGANUI—AUCKLAND . . . 221

CHAPTER XIII.
AUSTRALASIA 236

PART III.

FARTHEST WEST.

CHAPTER XIV.

	PAGE
HONOLULU—HALEAKALA	255

CHAPTER XV.

KILAUEA 274

CHAPTER XVI.

THE HAWAIIAN KINGDOM 289

CHAPTER XVII.

THE PACIFIC SLOPE 301

CHAPTER XVIII.

THE C.P.R. AND U.S.A. 321

APPENDIX 339

LIST OF PLATES.

SOLITARY COVE, DUSKY SOUND	*Frontispiece*
TELAGA WARNA	*Face page* 21
ON THE CANTON RIVER	,, 32
AUSTRALIAN BLACKS	,, 143
THE WEEPING ROCK	,, 160
AT WAIROA AFTER THE ERUPTION	,, 219
TARANAKI	,, 233
DIAMOND HEAD, HONOLULU	,, 262
HAWAIIAN WOMEN	,, 297
THE BAY OF SAN FRANCISCO	,, 306
NEAR PASADENA	,, 314
ON THE C.P.R.: LEATNCHOIL	,, 325

PART I.

FARTHEST EAST.

FARTHEST EAST, SOUTH AND WEST.

CHAPTER I.

THE START—STRAITS—JAVA.

" FURLOUGH for two years is granted to Mr. C. R. Sail, with effect from the date on which he may avail himself of it."

So said the Gazette ; and gazettes never lie. Two years' furlough : such a holiday as one has never before had in one's life. After some eleven years of service in the East, it is a holiday worth making the most of. Not that those eleven years have been without their pleasant breaks—little snatches of holiday taken as occasion offered—now a couple of months' privilege leave, now a week's casual, or again (it may be), a little " French " leave. At such times one visited the glories of old Delhi, the marble magnificence of Agra, Jeypur with its pink-and-white wide and well-kept streets, or the dirtily holy and wholly dirty Benares ; one sought Elysian heights touched with viceregal splendour, the delights (tempered with dysentery) of Poona in the season, or fled to salubrious cærulean hills, to pick wild strawberries in the "sholas" and flirt with the nymphs that dwell, rosy-cheeked as those in England, among these mountains of Madras. It was then that one wrote verses such as these :—

>Ah! Love shall live with a life eternal,
>   Though Death take all things below, above;
>If he spare nought else of the things supernal,
>   He shall spare at least the sweet spirit Love.
>And our love shall live though to mortal seeing
>   Death bear us away to his loveless shore;
>For our hearts are merged in Love's deathless being
>   For ever and evermore.

And found, when one went back to the plains and to work, that that "ishweet ishpirit" didn't survive one busy season or one hot-weather shikar expedition. What good times they were, those shikar expeditions; when one was one's own general and adjutant-general and commissariat officer and transport officer all in one, and marched off with one's little army of shikaris and beaters, and long line of coolies and bullocks, into the hills, where dwelt, bar a few hillmen scant in number (and in clothing), nothing but the stately sambar, the clumsy-looking but wary blue bull, the tiger and the bison and the bear.

But all these were but little by-blows, as it were, of holiday; and now that one has really got two years to do nothing but amuse oneself in, let us

The Start.

hand over to the next man in, saying, "For this relief much thanks," and bid farewell to the wide plains where the rain comes not and the cotton-plants wither and die for want thereof; to the mighty but muddy river that rolls flooding down till, over-full, it tops its banks and inundates and fertilizes the lowlands, as who should jeer at the parching uplands and say, "No lack of rain where I come from;" to the meagre little metre railway and the muggy and monsoon-bedraggled seaport at the end of it. Let us clear out of the winding river and the narrow shallow bay with its brown and greenish waters, where the screw is so near the bottom that it stirs the sand below and leaves its wake marked with a muddier brown in the muddy waters, out into the open sea where the waves are blue, curling over into snow-white foam-crests, and where it is likely I shall be very ill for a time. We will wander round the world; Ulysses-like, we "cannot rest from travel." What though the good ship *Pataliputra* does only nine knots an hour (for has not the Bison a practical monopoly, and why should it hurry itself?), still there is ample time in two years to go and gain fresh experiences "among new men, strange faces, other minds."

I doubt whether the Anglo-Indian can find so much enjoyment travelling about the Far East as his brother globe-trotter straight from home. To the latter everything is new, and if not everything is pleasing, yet at least this novelty is interesting and in itself a source of pleasure. But to the Anglo-

Indian many features of Eastern travel are stale and unprofitable. He has met daily for years past people clad in outlandish garbs or in almost utter garblessness, so that a further small variation in clothing, or the absence of it, does not strike him as anything remarkable. The vile and variegated odours of oriental towns are so accustomed to him that they pass him by scarce noticed, except to recall to him with a shudder the questions of village sanitation and the due disposal of the defæcations of the dusky millions, and how in many and various ways he has been plagued about them from farthest Burma in the East to the West (Sir R. West) in Bombay. He has seen many races, made himself unintelligible in many languages, admired much fine scenery, marvelled at curious customs, mixed with many strange people, all in the course of his service as ordinary and commonplace incidents thereof; how, then, can he have retained the freshness of the griffin, the tireless eyes of wonder with which the globe-trotting brother from England will gaze on the peoples and places of the East? Perchance also he may become an unmitigated and irretrievable bore (a terrible variety of Sus Indicus), saying at each new people, "They are not a patch on the people in the part of India where I come from," and at each new place, "Reminds me of Parigpur, only not so good."

"Howsoever these things be, a long farewell" —a two-year long farewell—to British India, and off we go. Penang shall not keep us long: it

The Start.

is not a globe-trotter's place; no sights but an "ornery" sort of waterfall in an "ornery" ornamental garden, and a good view from the top of the hill behind. Considering how it rains in Penang, it would be a sight worth seeing if they could show a place where there isn't any water; or better still, a place where water *doesn't* fall. The view is neither better nor worse than any other coast view along the east side of the Bay of Bengal from Maulmain to Singapore. The whole line of coast is beautiful; the best bit, to my mind, is the mouth of the Pakchan, the boundary between Burma and Siam. From Victoria Point the prospect is splendid. A poor place to live at, though; if you bathe in the sea, sharks will shikar you, or in a creek you will be consumed of crocodiles; walk through the grass, and leeches will find you luscious; while monkeys mock you from the rocks, and from the forest gibbons gibber at you. All down the Malay Peninsula nature is too mighty for man: her rain-fed forests overpower him; they crowd him out, so that he lives in scanty numbers on the edge of the sea and the creeks on the lowland and the island; but the inland and the highland know him not: they are virgin, clothed in eternal verdure, untamable. Almost extinct are the Negrito races—black, beast-like, stunted as the pigmies of Darkest Equatorial Africa, who yet survive here and on the Philippines and on the Andamans, "where fragments of forgotten people dwell." The browner, robuster Malay stock has spread itself far and near, over the islands of

Australasia to isolated Madagascar, antipodean New Zealand, eastward to Formosa; but the virgin forest of the Peninsula remained inviolate. She affords a last refuge in the Old World to that singular beast the tapir; in her shady recesses "that murmur at morn" the argus pheasant builds his bower. "Under the shadow of her fair vast head" dwelt safely the nats of wood and hill and water; "solemn, undisturbed, unruffled, like high gods they lived and moved." But, enter the Britisher. Then "cry aloud, for the old world is broken." He has no particular respect for virgins or for high gods or low; he regards nothing as untamable. He strips from her her forest raiment, and plants her with coffee and tea, tapioca, tobacco, and spices; burrows into her, and washes her sands for tin, and smashes her rocks for gold. Here, as ever where "floats a European flag," floods in the Chinaman, and the ceaseless, unwearying industry of the yellow-skin from Farthest East joins the restless energy, the capital and the science of the white-skin from the remote West. Between them they will conquer nature; the argus pheasant will have to build elsewhere his bowers, and the tapir will become as extinct as the dodo. But not without a struggle. The virgin Peninsula is an expensive mistress; she requires much toil and treasure to be poured into her; "with travail and heavy labour" shall her favour be won.

Southward and eastward through summer seas, with here a waterspout and there a shark, and everywhere the flying-fish. I have no opinion of this strange wild-fowl; he is a fraud, and ought to burst like the frog in the fable. The proper function of fishes is to swim and to eat smaller fishes and be eaten by bigger ones; why can't he stick to his business, instead of trying to be a bird? Through the Straits of Malacca in perfect weather; cloudy, rainless days, and a breeze that is soft and balmy; whiling away the hours now with Zola on the social condition of France under the Second Empire, now with Wallace on Darwinism. It is curious how so clever and convincing a writer should close with such an inconclusive and unconvincing argument as is the latter half of his last chapter; nor is his account of Weismann's theory of heredity so complete as to carry to the reader the strong impression it seems to have made on the writer.

Singapore has nothing remarkable except its harbour. It is the Clapham Junction of the East. Steamer lines small and great cross one another here, and little local lines run out in all directions. Men-of-war come to coal, and colliers bring coal for them from England, from India, from Australia. It is never winter here, and is said to be always raining; but that is a slander, for I stayed as long in Singapore as Jonah did in his strange host's stomach, and it rained never a drop. Nor, when the rain does come, is it, as some describe it, a brief cataclysmic downpour, for, on other two days that I waited for a boat in Singapore, the rain was steady, continuous, hours long. To each globe-trotter, I think, a place will present itself differently; and as we arrive alongside the wharf the crowds of curio-mongers that should beset a new arrival are nowhere to be seen. Prickly heat (as usual) spares me; I know it not. The "bloom profuse and (scarlet) arches" are out of season; the trees on the roadside are flowerless, save here and there some intempestive blossoms. Nor is the ricksha in Singapore the favourite and fashionable vehicle that it has been represented to be; it is good for the coloured races, but little patronized by the white. The white man takes a gari—a superior article to that with which the dwellers in Rangoon and Calcutta are content to put up, but not so good as the victoria of Bombay. And all these Indian cities might learn from Singapore and Penang in the matter of hotels: here is comfort and decent service, very pleasant to the "wanderer out of ocean" who remembers sadly past hotels and their badness in Bombay, their equal inferiority in Calcutta, the wretchedness of Rangoon, the misery of Mandalay. John Chinaman has been growing more and more numerous as we go on. India proper hardly knows him; there is a good deal of him in Burma, but almost always without Jane Chinawoman; Mrs. John is generally a Burman, and easily obtained, for does not John reckon as the best of husbands, the Indian second, the European third (chiefly because he is apt to depart in peace, leaving madame disconsolate), and the unindustrious, unthrifty Burman last of all? But in the Straits John comes to stop, and brings his womenkind with him ; and all through the long, monotonous streets, with houses all of nearly one size and pattern and all of a painful blue, the Celestial pigtail is not unaccompanied by the Chinese woman's neat little teapot-handle bob of hair low at the back of the head, bound with a plain band of silver, or here and there of gold. (I did not notice any jade, which all wear in China.)

The museum has a good collection of fishes, and some beasts, but is poor ethnologically. The Botanical Gardens are very fine and large; the gardens of private bungalows are beautiful with a wealth of tropic foliage ; the bungalows themselves are good to look upon, and no doubt to live in. But the residents do not appear altogether happy— what man ever is ?—and the British contingent seems to think some other place would be preferable. What Britisher could live without grumbling? So they "dwell with eternal summer, ill content." The wanderer, too, wearies of Singapore, and spends much of his time there wondering by which line he shall leave—whither wend his way next. Shall it be the Native States ? But they are likely to be inferior versions of Penang and Singapore, with less conveniences, and taking much time to do. And besides, throughout Malaya there is an absence of any "sight" but nature unadorned and man as nature has made him here. Endless change of hill and vale, "the mountain wooded to the peak," with patches of vivid green where *thikke* grass grows thick on the taungyas or hill clearings, the valley dense with flower and foliage, or cleared into fertile field ; but altogether wanting are the works of man, such as have covered India with mighty old-world temples and marvellous tombs, planted on knoll and hill-top in Burma the shining white or gilt pagoda, and built the curious and quaintly-carven kyaung. Or shall it be Bangkok ? But it is a beastly place, and the only interest about Siam is how long it will last, and whether any of it will fall to France, or all to England. Already England has extended her "protection" over the independent Malay states, so that the Malay provinces of Siam (Ranaung and the rest) are wedged in between British India and the Straits Government. By the French in Tonquin and the English in Upper Burma, Siam proper and the Siamese Shan States are shut in on all sides but the sea, that is, Siam is shut in altogether; and how can a state so situated survive ? It is not a question of either France or England wanting her, except to prevent the other having her; it is merely a question of time and inevitable fate. Britain has made three mouthfuls of Burma, and to digest each of the first two she took about one generation. The third may take as much. Tonquin is likely to take France a good deal more. And then Siam will belong to herself no longer ; protected like Zanzibar, or mediatized as Cashmere, or annexed like Ava—in some form she will have to submit.

Sumatra, Java, Borneo Dutch and English, Manila, all offer themselves to the one who would trot somewhat out of the beaten tracks. Of the

Dutch possessions Java is the chief, the central, the seat of Government; let us go to Java, "the Pearl of the East." Cheaper and quicker than any other line, the French mail takes us to Tandjong Priok; we cross the Equator quietly, performing no ceremonies, yet meaning no disrespect, to that august entity. We enter the harbour that cost 40 million gulden, and wonder vaguely how many official and contracting Dutchmen lined their little nests at home with pickings from that noble sum. On by rail to Batavia, and here shall be seen many new things. The town intersected by canals of muddy water whereon boat and wherein bathe publicly (not that that is anything new) a big population of many shades of brown; houses that know not punkhas lest the solid headpiece of the Dutchman take cold from the wind of the waving thereof. European ladies that appear in public—at tiffin, gardening in their gardens, playing croquet on the lawn (croquet! I thought it had long ago passed away in the *evig keit*), or sitting in open street-fronting verandah in the cool of the day—undressed in the costume of the country, a loose-fitting white jacket fastened low on the neck, and a "sarong" or simple petticoat of many colours and marvellous patterns. Fancy an English lady appearing at tiffin, at Watson's or the Great Eastern, attired in choli and sari and slippers; or showing herself out of doors in such garb at 5 P.M., where the public "as it passed by her garden might mark with one eye" her casual costume. Curious also it is to see such ladies as take an evening drive take it hatless and bonnetless, though otherwise dressed as Europeans; and comical are the Malay or Javanese coachmen in glazed bell-hat with gaudy band and cockade, and the footmen behind with short jackets, Eton style, but bright coloured, not black, and jockey-caps of vivid green or what-not. It looks like part of a circus company let out for the job. Meals too are a source of amusement to the mind, though perhaps not of much satisfaction to the appetite. First appears a bowl of rice from which you help yourself into a soup-plate; six, seven, any number of dishes—some distinguishable as chicken, some unrecognizable, messes "undreamt of, unheard of, unwritten, unknown;" and from each of these you shall take here a little and there a little, and if the soup-plate will not hold them all, a second plate is waiting to receive the overflow. To these must be added some half-dozen flavours and condiments: curry-gravy, pickled cucumber, chutney and the like. If you shall not greatly enjoy such a "portion" yourself, you shall at least not be unmoved with admiration at your Dutchman devouring his. Follows beefsteak: at least one fondly hopes it beef, and sadly knows it buffalo. Mutton you shall sigh for in vain, it is not deemed by the Dutchman fit for food. At dinner—in all hotels to which my fate led me—the joint was always cold meat: never a hot joint. Your coffee comes to you in cold decanted extract instead of fresh from the berry. Yet shall your pre-prandial gin and bitters—*free*—be a pleasant and acceptable offering.

But enough of the table; let us go out into the town. It is a big one, 900,000 people some one told me; perhaps he was in the running for the biggest liar in Asia. Wallace gives it barely half a million, suburbs and all. Any way, it is a large widespreading town, traversed by steam tram, and well supplied with light little pony-cars to get about in. The bail-gari has disappeared; pony-carts replace it. The ricksha is altogether absent. There are not so many Chinese to be seen as in Singapore, not by a long way; the Chinese woman is absent, but the China-Malay half-breed is plentiful. So indeed are half-breeds of all kinds. It is curious how the Dutch, who, unlike the English, steadily discourage their subjects from learning their masters' language, are yet so much more native than the English in the matter of clothes (already referred to), of intermarrying (left-handedly, for the most part, but sometimes formally), and in drawing no impassable line between the pure white and the half-breed. Wandering into the museum, you find a really good collection of spears and swords from all the islands of the East; dresses of strange design; strings of shells that serve for the Mosaic figleaf; gods ancient and modern—the ancient are Shiva and Vishnu and Ganesha, and more besides, old friends of the Hindu Pantheon, Buddha, and others unknown— the modern idols of wood, rude, unclothed, disdainful of the figleaf, realistic (in strictly proper Hongkong they are prudishly draped in petticoats of red); models of the dwellings, terrestrial and aquatic, of these children of the sun; drums, gongs, cymbals, and all kinds of music; skulls—and what not else?—a splendid ethnological collection. Add to this a noble library; and you have a museum as worthy of commendation as the "Planten und Dierentuin"—the Botanical and Zoological Gardens—are of unstinted condemnation. They are a fraud and a foolishness. That is no doubt why you pay a rupee —a gulden rather, but it is nearly the same thing—for the gardens while the museum is free. The public buildings—Government House, the Secretariat—are externally plain and simple; so are the clubs—the Concordia, the Harmonie—but, like the king's daughter, the latter are "all glorious within;" their pavement is of white marble, the rooms are spacious and lofty and cool. Their names are sweetly suggestive of unity and peace; but as a matter of fact Dutch and English are not particularly friendly. Perhaps the Englishman does not like some one else being boss while he is around, and thinks regretfully (as well he may) of the days when Java was his, and of the ignorant unwisdom that gave it back to the Dutch; perhaps as in other matters, so in the give and take which renders social intercourse cordial, "the fault of the Dutch is giving too little and asking too much." Certainly to the travelling Englishman nothing can be more hospitable and friendly than the English resident in Batavia, or less so than the Dutchman. The Dutch Government does not care for the stranger within its gates; within three days he must report himself and get a permission to abide on Dutch soil, else shall he be fined 5 gulden a day up to a maximum of 100 gulden. It is true I did not get a permit, and was not amerced; but then I was there but eight days, and doubtless they prefer to wait until the possible maximum is reached, which clearly takes twenty days.

Dutch railway arrangements are perverse and incomprehensible to the uninitiated traveller. You journey by one train and get a certain weight of luggage (30 kilos., I think) free, the rest charged for; by another, and all charged for; by a third, and all free: the luggage remaining the same throughout. Accustomed to the meteoric speed of the Dhond and Manmad, the Oudh and Rohilcund, the Burma State railways, the Anglo-Indian will not grumble unduly at the slowness of the "Staats Spoorweg;" but he will confound the fuel which lands him at his destination as grimy as coal-grit can make him. But "travellers are communicated that a large bath to swim is at theirs disposition in the Hotel" du Chemin de Fer at Buitenzorg (so says an affiche in the dining-room); so that although, unless provided, it is a case of "What, no soap?" one may yet wash and be clean. Buitenzorg, I was told, is the Simla of Netherlands India, and when I saw it I wondered how any one could have invented so foolish a name. The Governor-General lives there, it is true; but there all similarity ends. It is only about 1,000 feet above sea level, and not thirty miles from the sea; the climate is hardly cooler than on the coast. For the mighty slopes and snowclad peaks of the Himalayas, you look on the forest sides and crater tops of Salak and Gedeh, volcanoes dormant or extinct. The scenery has beauty; but it is not that of Simla. Round the Governor-General's palace are botanical gardens, this time worthy of the name; a splendid avenue of fine old banyan-like trees leads up to the house; in the park are herds of spotted deer. At the "Societeit" the band plays; Dutch society parades on the Mall. It is a pleasant drive out to Tjampeac, where you will find an Armenian. Like the Parsee, the Armenian is a race scanty in numbers, but spread everywhere; busy, and successful in business; nothing comes amiss to him, from Minister for Foreigners—Kalawun—to the King of Burma, to shipping in Calcutta, hotel-keeping in Singapore, or farming (the revenues) in Java. You will find an old gentleman—Malay or China Malay—who was in London at the Exhibition of 1851, and never since, speaking hesitating English, and the English-less Chinaman who "hires the mountain" where the birds build the edible nests beloved of Chinese epicures. To see these, the Chinaman will give you a guide, if you are disposed to wade thigh-deep through streams and wet grass where leeches lurk; your "Pistis and Pelekanos" he will accept, and in exchange give you the little brown cigarettes of Java, and he will converse withal in friendly pantomime.

But in this land of volcanoes, we must not leave without seeing one; so on by rail to Bandong through beautiful scenery, now huge hill and forest, now bare round hills like the Ooty downs, now long declivities terraced into paddy-fields. From Bandong to Lembang by three-horse pony-car, and thence on horseback up Tankoebanprahoe, the hill of the Upset Canoe. For long ago, when all this land was wide, wide sea, there came sailing a Prince and Princess, and their "prow" (prahoe the Dutch spell it), unfortunately got upset (tankoeban), and there it remains to this day. So the "mährchen" was told me in German; and I could not, for the weakness of my German, ask for further details. The narrator's wife thought the canoe was a steamer, which the narrator would by no means have. But I think she was right; else how account for the fire and smoke? Up through plantations of much cinchona and some coffee, until we enter the primeval forest. Ferns everywhere, gigantic fern-trees, minute and almost moss-like delicate-fronded ground ferns, tree-ferns innumerable; trees a botanist only knows how many species and genera, each tree a garden with its creepers and mosses and orchideous plants; an excess of vegetation profuse and impenetrable. Over the edge into the crater, and behold the vast vegetation changed to a desolate waste. The odour of sulphur assails one; and fire and brimstone are not sweet to smell. The forest fades away into a few stunted bushes, into absolute barrenness. In the double bowl of the great crater, divided into two by a rough and ragged ridge, curl up unendingly sulphurous clouds, here hot and silent, there bursting out with a roaring as of a great waterfall, or a locomotive letting off steam, and colouring the vent holes of the giants "dungeoned in opaque element" below with bright yellow, and the rocks here and there with red and purple. In the bottom of the crater the rock is like the slag cast out from a smelting furnace; grey blocks of old lava stand out grim and bare round the sides. Altogether it is a sight worth seeing, if you have not seen many or any volcanoes before; and as the mist drives up and fills the crater, it is eerie to sit on the edge and listen to the hissing and roaring of the steam hundreds of feet below, and watch the blasted trunks and branches of old trees show weirdly as the mist half lifts, only to drift over and hide them again.

Returning to Batavia, it is well to leave the railway at Tjandjoer (transliterated in British India, on the approved system, this would be Chanjur) and drive by Sindanglaija and Poentjac to Buitenzorg. At Sindanglaija is a "Gesondheits Etablissement" —a sanitarium, and a climate really cool. Poentjac is the head of the pass, some 5,000 feet high, between Gedeh (about 10,000 feet) and Pangerango (somewhat less). It is a six hours' drive, say forty miles, and a steep and stony ghat; but they do it with only one change of ponies, and charge only 16 gulden— say Rs.16. The scenery is really exquisite. The cloud-capped crater of Gedeh stands out boldly to the south and west; the long sloping sides, seamed with precipitous ravines, are terraced for 5,000 feet or more into endless paddy-land, and the terraces dip over into the hollows and turn every possible

foot of ground into food-producing fields. To water all these miles of rice, every stream that comes down from the mountain is caught and diverted into fertilizing channels, that run perpetually ; under the sunny sky an 'ανηριθμον γελασμα of rippling water. Above the terraces there are grass-grown hill-clearings, and, for some thousands of feet above them, the steep acclivities of the cone with its dark green raiment of eternal forest. To the north and east stretches away an endless panorama of hill after hill, volcanic peaks, dormant or dead; but who shall say when they may not again put forth their might, and wreak ruin on man and his works? The double Shiwa of the Indian, half woman and half man, is a true type of nature; in her, destruction and reproduction are indissolubly combined. Below the pass at Poentjac there slumbers in an old crater the little pool of Telaga Warna; the all but perpendicular sides are dense with that ever exhaustless forest; it is very still and silent save for the splash of a fish leaping in the pool, or the single voice of some strange bird calling in the wood.

To the tourist Java ought to be far more widely known than it is. I have seen only the western corner of it, and but little of that, and I find it extremely beautiful ; nor is the climate—at least to an Anglo-Indian—other than delicious. But go into Central and Eastern Java, and visit the volcanoes and hot springs of Tengir with its Brama and Watangan (Hall of Audience) cones, Papandagang Galunggong, Arjuma, Semero, Grobogan, Talaga

Bodas, Taschem; the temples and ruins of Majapahit, Brambanam, Chandi, Sewa, Borobodo, Gunong Prau; if you are for Shikar, shoot rhinoceri in the jungles; if ethnology be your hobby, study the curious customs of the Malays, their races and their dialects; or if natural science tempt you, you shall find a perfect paradise for the geologist, the botanist, the ornithologist, the "bug-hunter" generally; or, again, there will present itself to you much matter for thought on the manner of government. The country is administered for the benefit of its conquerors, not of its people; but, at the same time, the people prosper and increase and multiply exceedingly. Whether is it better to keep the people ignorant and exploit them, à la Hollandaise, or to "feed them and fill them" with all the learning of the West, making nothing out of them except what comes by way of open trade, as is the British fashion? The Dutch Empire in the East has to pay its own way, and its surpluses go into the Home Exchequer. It must find its own army, for not a regiment from home may be sent to the Indies; and its army it has, Europeans and natives enrolled in the same regiment and battalion, Europeans of all races, and all alike allowed to keep in barracks, and to take with them on expedition, their temporary wives of the women of the country. Besides the regular army, every European in the land (unless medically certified as unfit, and then he has to pay a composition) has of necessity to undergo a military training in the Scutterij every year; and is liable to be called out for duty when the work is too heavy for the regular troops. There is no disputing that Java has done extremely well under the rule of the Dutchmen ; but in other possessions they are content with the coast or but a portion of it, or at most make but feeble and necessarily futile attempts to reduce the tribes of the interior. Most have heard ere this of the eighteen years' war in Atyeh (Achin), no nearer an end than when it began. Floris has got an expedition now attempting to reduce it, with about as much prospect of a speedy issue as in Atyeh. The Bataks in Mid Sumatra, the Dyaks in Dutch Borneo, all the natives of half a hundred islands of Malaysia—what step has been taken to bring them into line, to open up their country, to subdue it and rule it ? I trow none. When the Anglo-Indian surveys the Dutch East Indies and casts a glance at Tonquin, he cannot fail to congratulate himself on his nation's superiority over her nearest neighbours at home in the art of establishing and maintaining peace through all the borders of a subject empire.

CHAPTER II.

CHINA.

IF you wish to be comfortable and well fed, do—but, if you wish to make a quick passage, do not —go by the French mail from Singapore to Hongkong, for she calls at Saigon, which adds nearly two days (quite forty-four hours) to the journey; and the Saigon river is not lovely, nor the town delectable. It is—in August—atrociously hot; the river banks are, except at the mouth, about Cape St. Jacques, flat and swampy; the women are ugly and hideously dressed; there are no scenery and no sights. It is called "Indo-China;" but the "Indo" part of it has all but disappeared, and little but China remains. It is true the ricksha is not present, and only the victoria and the gari appear; but the sampans on the river, with their little josses, and whole family living on board, are thoroughly Chinese; the brilliant-coloured garments of the women of India and Burma have given place to the dreary black of China—paijamas and nightgown and all (of a somewhat different make, however); nor are the women adorned as the Chinese are with jade on hair and ear and wrist, or by anything but simple silver circlet on the neck. The Anamites are believed to be first cousins to our Talaings or Mons in Pegu and Tenasserim : it is said their languages prove this. They are not much like one another to look at. The town of Saigon is laid out in wide streets and tree-planted boulevards, and is not without its cafés and café concerts—a feeble little Paris in petto in the East. The French are very welcome to keep it, and I hope they like it. Let us get on to Hongkong, and admire the town and harbour opening out before us, as we steam through the narrow Sulphur Channel. It is night, and as we round the point, "the lights begin to twinkle from the rocks," climbing high up the steep hill-side : on the broad lake-like harbour they " glitter like a swarm of fire-flies " from sampan and hakau and launch and steamer. And when we land next morning we shall not need to lay aside our admiration through finding that the fair outside is foul within. The Praya is substantial and handsome, the streets, though narrower than in Indian cities, are well laid out, well kept, and wide enough for the wants of the place : the absence of carts and carriages, garis and trams, makes the busy town singularly quiet, for the ricksha runs smoothly and the chair is noiseless. The City Hall (why can't they be content to call it the Town Hall?) is not a bad building, and the Hongkong and Shanghai Bank is palatial ; numberless roads go straight and steep, or staircased, or in slanting zig-zags up the lower slopes of the

Peak, for there is very little level space between the hill-foot and the sea, and up to the Pass runs the Funicular Railway, landing you in ten minutes 1,500 feet above the sea. The Peak—I beg its pardon—Victoria Peak is the glory of Hongkong. Rising abruptly over 1,800 feet, it affords to the dweller in Hongkong a rapid change from (in the town) the climate of Bombay at its worst, to (at the top) that of Poona at its best. It fancies itself greatly, and, not content with the modest hotel that once had to suffice for all wants, it is enlarging the old and building new guest-houses of great size. Hither shall be attracted (an enthusiast told me, and he ought to know, being, as I surmise, a shareholder in the venture) the invalids and seekers of health and repose from all the East—from Japan, from the Treaty Ports, from the Straits, yea, from India and Ceylon; here shall asthma and rheumatism (so prevalent in India!) derive positive benefit from the cold sea-mists, and weakly lungs be restored again. And "thereout," doubtless, shall the shareholders "suck no small advantage." But verily they will have to wait a weary while, if their profits depend on their Peak outshining august Simla and naughty Naini, and more so Mussoorie and all the hill stations north and west and south. Not that the Peak is to be despised; for any one whom stern decrees of fate condemn to exile in Singapore or Hongkong, Macao, or Canton, it is a splendid place, cool and bracing, and with lovely prospects. Abrupt and rugged mountain slopes, gaunt in their bareness—absolutely treeless, save where artificially planted: such a contrast to the forest-hidden hillsides of the Straits and Java;—a far-stretching view over island and bays and harbour and the mountains of the mainland; pleasant walks in a brilliant atmosphere—all these Victoria Peak affords, and only ten minutes up from narrow streets, crowded by rickshas and busy men and coolies and chairs and mosquitoes and heat. The drive or ricksha ride out to "The Happy Valley" takes one through the East End of Hongkong, which is the more respectable and the more European quarter—barracks, naval-yard, &c., lie out this way—and in the Happy Valley there is in the bottom the Racecourse, as picturesque as, and somewhat suggestive of, that at Wellington, with the advantage that there is more room to turn in; while upon the hillsides on the west—the entrance almost facing the Grand Stand —is the last resting-place for those whose race is over —the Cemetery, filled with "the grassy barrows of the happier dead." It is a beautifully kept garden, lovelier than the formal Public Gardens, but the tombstones are sadly many for so young a colony. Neighbouring close is the Parsee Burying Ground; for the Parsee community is numerous, and here are no Towers of Silence—the Fire Worshipper must bury his dead. On the other side the R. C. with its unkind reminder, "*Hodie mihi cras tibi*;" and next it the Mohammedan. In the centre of the town (it calls itself Victoria, though every one calls it Hongkong) the public buildings are poor—Post Office and Supreme Court and Clock Tower. The Club is located in the central street, and looks more like a large office than a club. Naturally it has no grounds or garden, no coolness, no outlook; it is just about as ill situated as a club can be, if a club is meant to be a place of pleasant ease and comfort; but if it is meant to be a convenient place of business, then it is well located, for there is no "'Change," and business seems to be conducted very much in the street, from the Hongkong Bank as far as the Club, or in the porticoes and door-ways of the shops and offices along that portion of Queen's Road, and the Club verandah itself. West of the Club stretches the populous Chinese quarter; above it, on the hillside, are the Police Court and Jail. I found it interesting to go round the Jail; the turn-keys are polite and obliging. About 600 may be taken as the average jail population, and the cramped, confined space which the building occupies is turned to the best account to accommodate the small number of prisoners. With such scanty numbers it is, perhaps, difficult to work a complete system of remunerative labour (they manage it in Japan, however), and I wondered not a little at the excessive proportion of convicts who were earning nothing—labouring at the crank or at shot or stone drill. Under-trials are not kept in a separate ward (which seemed to me wrong), and there is no promotion of well-behaved criminals to become convict warders. The health is good. The daily number of sick is quite a small percentage on the daily strength, and includes sufferers from floggings for refusing the crank, and "general debility"—*i.e.*, opium-smokers. I saw one such—a young man of twenty-six, weight seventy-six pounds, stripped; he was a ghastly scarecrow, a yellow skeleton. Across the harbour is Kawloong, an important place, with a fine dockyard; and behind the Peak is Pokfoolum, a pretty suburb, with a charming road running round Mount Davis, and coming in by the fort at the west end of the town. A board at the approach to the Fort forbids entrance, except on written permission of the O. C.; but the gate being open, I walked in; nor did the Sikh policeman on duty object. He said he recognized me—which was clever of him, never having seen me before. The Fort appears to be wanting in armament. They call the police force Sikh, but it evidently includes a good many others—Pathans, Panjab, Mussulmans, &c. The Chinese police seem to correspond to the civil police in Burma. They do not look smart in their platter-hats and trousers and shambling gait.

Hongkong is a wonderful place for only fifty years of growth. Its roads and its praya and its great Tytam waterworks are things it may well be proud of. But it is not content; it must enlarge itself, and reclaim much space from the sea. Let us hope the Praya Reclamation Scheme will have a more prosperous course than the Back Bay. It was born, as I understand, in just such a time of inflated speculation as was the Bombay fiasco; and, in the inevitable reaction, I fancy it does not present itself to all the colony in quite the rosy colours that its promoters (or would promoter be more correct?) made it wear. At all events, it is started and blessed by Royalty—for is not a memorial stone extant laid by H.R.H. the Duke of Connaught? and perhaps it may be complete in ten or twelve or more years. Meanwhile the colony celebrates its jubilee, and begins to light itself electrically, and yearns for a railway to Canton. And in time no doubt the forts will be duly armed, and the club removed to a better site (it is too shoppy), and the cricketers provided with a ground where they will not need to field hits for two out in the main road among the rickshas and road-menders and coolies, and the huge new and extended old hotels will be making the shareholders' fortunes—or going "phut," like that floating one in the harbour which removed to Canton and started a fresh course there as a "flower boat."

Macao, some three and a half hours' steam from Hongkong, is a very dead-alive little place. Of all the once mighty Portuguese power in the Farther East there remains now but this somnolent little settlement and half the island of Timor, eleven days' steam to the south. (The Dutch have the other half.) There is a governor-general for this Empire, who holds his state at Macao, and subordinate to him a governor in Timor. The place is picturesque enough: a sort of miniature of Hongkong, with the extra seasoning of churches, convents, &c., that is usual where a Roman Catholic power holds sway. There are no sights to go to, unless a statue of St. Francis Xavier across the bay, and the Grotto of Camoens in the middle of the town, may be counted as such. The Grotto is in the gardens attached to some government building—war and admiralty and municipal office it seemed to me to be; the hall adorned with quaint old chairs and oil paintings black with age, in twopenny-halfpenny frames, of kings and governors and ladies of high degree. A memorial bust, with poetical effusions inscribed on headstones all around it, marks the Grotto—interesting probably to a patriotic Portuguese, but not particularly so to the impartial globetrotter. I could not decipher the English sonnet, but the guide-book says that the "pote," Sir John Bowring, begins it thusly :—

> Gem of the orient earth and open sea,
> Macao that in thy lap and on thy breast
> Hast gathered beauties all the loveliest,
> Which the sun smiles on in its majesty.

If this be so, and if it be the poet's province to expound the truth, then friend Bowring is no poet. The "beauties all the loveliest" of Macao are second-rate scenery, half-caste Portugooses, opium-smoking, and licensed gambling. This empire *pour rire* keeps itself afloat financially by the opium and gambling revenue. As to opium, I dare not cast a stone, which leaves me all the freer to condemn the gambling. "Fantan" is the game. From a heap of counters or cash in front of him, the croupier lifts out a handful, and covers them with a metal cup; the gentle sportsmen make their stakes on one or two or three or four. The croupier removes the cup and counts the counters or cash out four at a time; there remain over, of course, sometimes three, sometimes two, or one, or again a full four. Whosoever has staked on the number which remains over receives three times his stake, the rest pay up. Seeing that the odds are three to one against the punter every time he stakes, and that when he wins he is mulcted seven or eight per cent. by the bank, it is clear that the banker has a good time. This splendid game is patronized by the Hongkong sportsmen, who find a Saturday to Monday run to Macao pleasant, and a little fantan exciting. The game is slow, the counting of the counters being done very deliberately; but there is no doubt of the intense interest the heathen Chinee takes in it : observe him as he watches the croupier counting, and as it appears that his last coin, and his watch, and the rest of the portable property about him are all engulfed in the bank.

But to see the Chinaman of the south at home, it is necessary to go to Canton; and the day steamer is the pleasanter to go by, else how shall we see the Canton River, where the captain (a good sort) will point out what was a pirates' lair, and regale you with anecdotes as you pass the forts and the barrier and Whampoa with its dock and torpedo-boats, a

ON THE CANTON RIVER.

pagoda all aslant, like the leaning tower of Pisa, gunboats, fishing-boats with crews in the costume of Adam before the Fall, rice-junks, salt-junks, duck-boats, stern-wheel paddle-boats, where the propelling power is the muscles of many coolis' legs working on a sort of treadmill arrangement in the poop—until you arrive at Canton, where the number and variety of boats passes enumeration. The sampans and slipper-boats are ever active, and yet there are ever scores at rest, tied up in long streets from shore almost to mid-stream. You will notice that the crew lives on the boat, small as it is, and admire how neatly cooking-pots and fireplace are stowed away; you will observe how the crew generally consists of four (sometimes three or only two), and how (almost invariably) it is four males or four females, rarely a crew of mixed sexes. The girls, with a fringe of hair over the forehead, and hair done up in a plain coil behind, are not uncomely, though too short, especially in the leg, and the dress is very ugly; but the older women are not pleasing to look on—fringeless, and with hair done up in the formal teapot fashion proper (I believe) to married women. Jade wristlets and hair-band and earrings all wear, the jade earring being slung not direct on the lobe of the ear, but on the broad band of a metal earring, the thin shaft of which passes through the lobe. The women are far more decent, to European notions, than the cooli women of India, or Burma, or what we shall shortly see in Japan. You never see them bare-breasted, or so much bare-limbed as even a Boulogne fishing-girl. (Even in Burma, though there is nothing indecent in a married woman being bare to the waist, and if she covers at sight of you it is not modesty, but the respect due to you, that impels her; still, for an unmarried girl to expose so much of her person would be highly improper.) The men wear no ornaments, and few clothes. The working women have feet of normal size; tiny feet are for those who need not toil.

But if the river be busy with boats, what of the shore? What shall be said of the

> Marts and the thronged
> Quays, and the noise and the din?

A cacophonous clamour rises from the crowding Celestials. The subjects of the Son of Heaven add the stifling odour of a mass of perspiring men to the legion of powerful perfumes which exhale from reeking refuse and river and tight-packed town, and seize you by the nose and wring it till even the potent trichi fails to protect you. Ah Cum, that guide, philosopher, and friend of all the sightseers who do Canton, has you in his charge, and he parades you, as if you liked them, through smells such as you never dreamed of before; and you shall not escape till you have smelt them every one. Not that he states explicitly that he has brought you to see these; but he takes you, on pretexts of sorts, up and down the long and narrow streets, into all sorts of impossible corners, so that the result is the same : you taste them all before you have done. How interminable they are, these passages and alleys that serve for streets ; barely wide enough for two chairs to pass one another, the garish daylight shut out by overhanging roofs and extended awnings, and all those signboards depending from the shop-fronts, red and black and white, with word-symbols, gilt or black, or white or red, largely worked on them. How strange the noisy silence seems—noisy, for the cry of the cooli and the chair-man, the clatter of bare or clog-wearing feet, the call and the bell of the itinerant vendor, these never rest ; yet silent, for the wind finds no way in, and no wheel of ricksha or gari, no iron-shod fall of horses' feet, sounds on the uneven granite. Yet stay ; here are horses—rough, ill-kept ponies rather—passing in procession, ridden by big Tartars who wear bowl-shaped hats adorned with red crest and "button at the top." They are part of the Viceroy's body-guard; there is the great man's chair borne in the midst of the procession. You cannot see him ; the blinds or curtains are down. But it is enough to see the procession : the lictors, with hats of impossible shape and strange garments ; the soldiers shambling along anyhow, rifles with fixed bayonets on the right shoulder, fans hard at work in the left hand, and their uniform a marvel of sartorial fantasy. These Tartars and their ponies look the only business part of the show ; the rest seems burlesque. The present Viceroy is, I hear, unpopular. He lays on the people burdens grievous to be borne, on pretext of improving the defences, really (it is supposed) to fill his own pocket; and lately he caused a man to be taken out to execution gagged—a most unprecedented and improper proceeding. For usually an accused is compelled by *peine forte et dure* to confess, and without confession is no conviction legal. But in this case, as Ah Cum related, the man had never confessed. A friend of his killed a schoolmaster, of which most heinous crime he was eye-witness; both were arrested and placed on their trial—*i.e.*, under torture. The actual murderer died in jail, so that when orders came from the higher powers that sentence of death must be passed for this murder, there was no one on whom to pass it except the luckless witness. As he would not confess to having done what he had not done, he was taken out to execution gagged, lest he should proclaim his innocence and bring discredit on Justice; whereat the righteous soul of Ah Cum was in no small degree moved, as at a terrible injustice.

I am not going to put down all that Ah Cum took me through—there is a printed guide-book to Canton, and therein whoso wills may read of all the regulation sights. I did not have the good or ill-fortune to see any one being tried (or tortured—it is the same thing in China) in the Court of Justice, or any one's head taken off in the Potter's Ground; wherefore I cannot give you soul-harrowing descriptions of awful agony and exquisite death, such as some have indited, though whether they saw all that they describe as seen is doubtful. Writers certainly do over-colour their accounts most strangely. I read of men in cangues unable to rise from the weight thereof; of others screaming and shouting and banging themselves against the bars like frantic monkeys; of prisoners as half-famished foaming demoniacs; of children jeering and hooting and aping the outlandish white man, or shrieking and hiding at the horrid sight of him; and I say that the eye does not witness these things, nor the ear hear them; that they are only what it enters into the imaginative mind of man to conceive. The cangue-wearers that I saw rose easily, and put out their hands through the prison bars for coin— silently, sadly. The prisoners that crowded round when I went in were plump and cheery: some working at bootmaking, some at nothing, but all in good condition—delighted when I gave one my half-smoked trichi, and only when I threw a handful of small coin amongst them to scramble for did they become over-bold and riotous. Then I beat a hasty retreat amid laughter from me and the "half-famished and foaming" ones, and mild expostulations from the janitor. As to hatred of the "fangkwai," it does not take any active form in the streets. The people certainly are not cordial or friendly, but you cannot fairly go farther than this negative account of their demeanour towards you. The children chin-chin and ask for coppers; mothers point you out to them, or they to their mothers, as you pass. Seeing that there are getting on for a dozen mission chapels and churches scattered about the city, each with its padre (he, it is true, sometimes attired as a Chinaman, pigtail and all), and that the dwellers in Shameen and curio-hunters from Hongkong occasionally visit the native town, the people must be accustomed to seeing white men going about; so that you are after all only one more specimen of an inferior and objectionable race. Why should a Celestial soul worry itself to annoy or insult you?

It is something of a relief to emerge from the city into the Burlington House of Canton—the Examination Halls, with their wide courtyards, where grass and weeds grow green, their long rows of cells, where each examinee is immured solitary for the whole examination,—all tenantless until the next triennial examination comes on; or to make the circuit of the wall to the five-storied pagoda, whence to view the city and the country round. Except in the Tartar quarter, where the public ways are a trifle less narrow, no streets can be seen from above. It is one sea of roofs and awnings, unbroken save where rise the Water-clock Tower, the Roman Catholic cathedral (very fine and large), the square towers of the pawnbrokers—strong-rooms in which they keep pledged property, the slender fire-watchman's stations, and here and there a double-storeyed gateway—that of Eternal Purity or Everlasting Peace, or something equally high-sounding (purity and peace in Canton—what irony!); a pagoda or two; a fort on the nearest knoll outside, a powder magazine down in the hollow; and fertile plains of paddy lying between lines of treeless and rugged hills. All these hills are graveyards : a Chinese grave is always, if possible, on the slope of rising ground, and much care must be exercised in the choice of a site. To my mind the strangest thing in Canton is what Europeans call the City of the Dead, which lies outside the Eastern gate (there are others, I believe, but this is the largest). In the rooms here provided the deceased, duly placed in his enormous coffin, awaits the proper time and place for his burial to be fixed. The coffin seems to be fashioned of two logs slit down the centre, and the four pieces joined together so as to enclose a square, leaving the rounded sides on the outside, so that the section is thus ⊕ ; it lies in an inner room, and in the front room "josspidgin" of sorts is arranged : flowers and figures and fruit and incense-sticks, and a light always burning; in some a table set in front of a chair empty but for a painted board or scroll bearing words—perhaps the deceased's name. Sometimes the due place of burial is never fixed, or the relations cannot find the funds for the funeral, and the coffin remains here neglected; sometimes the "fungshiu" goes wrong, and after burial the thing has to be dug up again and buried elsewhere. When I was at Canton there was a religious tamasha on, which I understood to be on behalf of those who never got buried at all—the drowned, and all who by similar accidents got their bodies lost beyond recovery. Large house-boats were hired after dark, and the interior made resplendent with European oil-lamps, and the exterior with single or double tier of Chinese lanterns round the sides, and a string of them depending from the mast or pole, a crowd of oil-buttis making the front of the house a blaze of light. A joss rigged up inside, priests and acolytes with many changes of vesture genuflect and prostrate before it; the band plays, and away goes the boat, followed by half-a-dozen like it, floating down with the ebbing tide to return again with the flow, and setting afloat (as they do in Burma or in India) numerous little lamps that go shining down the stream like aquatic glowworms. The sight is picturesque, and the eye is pleased by the various lights swaying with the boat's motion on the tide; but the ear is tortured by the Celestial music. What some one calls "the implacable beat of the drum" is not so marked as in India, or even is absent, but the instruments used are of piercing shrillness, and the tunes (?) of a deadly monotony. The steamer's crew furnished out one boat—half-a-dollar's worth of merit per man; the Flower Boats supplied more than one. These Flower Boats are the scene of staid and solemn revelling. Here is a party of Chinamen having a festive dinner; most of them bare to the waist—and no wonder, for it is stifling hot; behind the chair of each sits his *belle amie* for the evening, she not eating nor speaking unless spoken to: face painted, hair plastered, dress of the universal blue. (I am fond of blue, it is my favourite colour, but one gets too much of it here; one does not want to see always blue and nothing but it.) In another boat, a few men lounging on couches, smoking opium, each with his tartlet (if the word may be permitted) sitting by him, silent and demure; in a third they are playing some incomprehensible game with dominoes for cards, smoking the idiotic waterpipe, which holds just one whiff and no more (a waiter stands by constantly reloading), and as usual the fair ones sitting by as prim as prudes and prunes and prisms. A domino player asks me in; I sit down, fanning myself violently with the fan I boned from my boat-girl, for it is abominably close; one of the houris giggles and hides her face behind her fan, another laughs at a joke made by a player, and my host's partner gazes at me solemnly through enormous goggle specs. My host gives me tea, lukewarm and acrid, and accepts a trichi, which he lights at the wrong end and without removing the straw. We discourse in such pidgin English as either can muster; after a decent interval I say I wish to go, and escape into the air. Music and singing are going on in another boat, but nowhere any dancing such as the nautch-girls of India weary you with, and I am told no dancing is done by these girls. Altogether, for a scene of dissipation, anything more decorous, more dreary, it would be difficult to devise. Of course this is the public side; as to what is behind, ask your boat-girl: she knows all about it. But the foreigner may not investigate in person; John reserves the private apartments for himself. So says old Susan, and she knows a good deal, for her age has considerably depassed the septennate.

To other places in Canton I went with Ah Cum the Less—for Ah Cum the Great has a son who is known by that name; to his parents and elders he is Ah Choy; and to his juniors and friends Po Shan (quite a Burmese ring about the last name). This youth has never left Canton, but has acquired a tolerable amount of English—I mean English, not that horrible hybrid known as pidgin English; (Old Susan is fluent and puzzling in the latter). He is, however, by no means perfect. As we went up the muddy waters among the innumerable boats, "This," he said, "is Fa-ti Crack." "Fa-ti Crack?" I queried, getting out my handkerchief. "Yes, Fati Crack," said he, pointing to the water. "Oh, creek—c,r,e,e,k, creek," I explained, and put away the wipe. Ah Choy has a way of exclaiming, "Here we are!" in a tremendously jovial extra-English fashion as we reach our destination, and so he "Here we are's" me to the Fati Gardens. They are called gardens, but you cannot call the art horticulture. It is the culture of the grotesque; trees deliberately and cunningly stunted and dwarfed and made to grow their branches downwards; the graceful bamboo forced into strange serpentine convolutions; plants trained over wires, and clipped and constrained into shapes of baskets and boats and beasts and men. Here is a steamer with masts, paddle-wheels and so on, but the funnel has been forgotten. The lions and fish and dragons and deer are of impossible form, and on these are clay eyes, with tin tongues for the dragons, while on the human figures are clay heads and hands and boots. Those of Europeans are uncomplimentary caricatures, but those of Chinese men and women are almost as unflattering. There are some fine chrysanthemums and poor camellias and other flowers that make a brave show; but there is no attempt at an artistic grouping of colours. The miniature rockeries, with little painted clay men, and pagodas and bridges and boats, and all kinds of things disposed among the ferns and other plants with which they are skilfully clad, are by no means unpleasing. After that are fruit trees and vegetables. The Honam Temple Garden is like unto these. It is evident that the idea of a garden, as we understand it, does not exist here. As we go up the " Crack," with much yelling of boatmen and girls, we come to the Duck Farm. Here are hatched thousands of canards. I asked Ah Choy how they were hatched; and after much thoughtful search for a word he could find none better than "by fire." So I taught him the word incubator, and when he asked how it was spelt, spelt it for him as little Archibaldus Holden spelt his name: i,n, in, and there's your in; c,u, cu, and there's your cu, and there's your incu; b,a, ba, and there's your ba, and there's your cuba, and there's your incuba; and so on. He said he would remember. I hope he may. The ducks hatched here—I saw say a couple of thousand yellow ducklings—are sent out in those duck-boats we met on the river, and then into the country to be fatted for market. But I do not care myself, for reasons, to eat duck in China. There were no eggs incubating, and the only curio they had to show me was a three-legged gosling. He was not doing so well as his two-legged coeval; and, indeed, I do not know how he was arranged internally so as to work at all, for the third leg occupied the whole of that important space under the tail; and it wasn't any good either, for he waddled on the other two.

"Here we are!" said Ah Choy heartily, a little later; and we went into the South Pearl Hall or Merchants' Guildhall. This place pleased me. It is clean and well kept—which alone makes it a curiosity in Canton; and the Shrine of the Queen of Heaven is ornamented, but not over-ornamented, with gilded wooden carving, very handsome. "And what are the vessels on the altar made of?" I asked. "All brrrass," said Ah Choy.

Ah Choy is not a little proud of being able to pronounce an r, and rrrolls it with unconcealed self-gratulation. So I asked him, "What was that you said?" and he answered, "Yes, all brrrass."

"Yes, all blllass," chimed in an unlearned by-stander. And Ah Choy glorified himself exceedingly.

So I asked him where certain big stones came from that lay in the inner room; and he said, "From a Chinese woolwich."

I gazed on him sadly, and said, "Where?" and again he said, "From a Chinese woolwich." Then I

China. 45

jumped on him : "V is not pronounced w, nor is village pronounced woolwich." And I said " Let us go to the Honam Temple."

" Velly well," said the crestfallen one, forgetting his r's in his confusion.

" I wonder," he remarked, questioningly, as old Sue's little girls oared us across the river, " I wonder if I went to England and studied for three years, I could speak English just like Englishman ? "

Unwisely I comforted him. " Knowing so much already, you might do it in half that time."

" Yes," he said, brightening up, "and then I could write an English poem."

Whereat I collapsed. There is quite enough bad poetry in the world, O Ah Choy, without you studying for three years to add to it.

The Honam Temple is in the usual style, but large and clean and spacious. It is not Buddhist, as I understand Buddhism ; which only proves that I don't understand Chinese Buddhism, for it is Buddhist, and I admit that the proof is just. Why don't these priests wear yellow robes, leaving the right shoulder bare, instead of grey-grass coats with ample sleeves? (grass-piper coats Ah Choy calls them, for they are made of fibre). Why do they keep sacred pigs ? (Buddha and pigs seem incongruous) which are never killed and eaten as an orthodox Chinese pig certainly should be (did not the Chinaman discover roast pork ?) but live on till they die of age and fatness, and then are decently buried. Why do they have three Buddhas and a score of images in the temple, and say mass before them? for they say mass; I heard them. (At this time they did wear a small yellow robe over the grey one, covering the left shoulder and not the right; it had an oblong patch of red on the border where it fastened across the chest.) What they sang I do not know, for Ah Choy said it was Buddhist language, and he did not understand that. Nor did I know what language he meant. Anyhow, they burnt incense and sacrificial paper, they intoned and genuflected and lit candles at the altar, and they beat the big drum and the little drum, and the gong, and the sounding-board, and the small bell and the great—not all at once, thank goodness, but each at what was no doubt the proper place in the ritual; and then they marched in Indian file solemnly thrice round the temple, and as they went they sang—

O wai lum o mo mi taw,

with occasionally variation on the "o mo mi." Then, with some intoning, they thrice prostrated themselves, and departed. So did I.

Ah Choy has a "blother," a sweet youth named ITing or ATing or some Ting like that. His English is in a very callow state. He met me as I was starting to go to the White Cloud Mountain, and said "Are you lady?" but I was too much the gentleman to begin teaching him before all the people in the hotel verandah. But at the White

Cloud Temple he was exasperating. He gave no signs of understanding or not understanding what was said to him, and went on his way unheeding me, until I swore. I think he understood that. " Will you lite ? " he asked. So I wrote in beautiful copperplate words that I deemed suitable to his simple mind : " First I like go topside hill, then come back Temple, eat tiffin, then go back Canton." He read and pondered deeply, and exclaimed, " Ah, yes, I know ; " but dubiously. Then again, as with mind made up, " Ah, yes, I know," and started down hill, tiffin and all. I was searching for some way to make him understand, when suddenly he stopped and shouted jubilantly, " Ah, yes, I know ; you want go highest—most high—m,o,s,t, most, h,i,g,h, high." I admitted that that was about it, if he preferred to put it that way. So we went up. I told him that he " no sabe "-d English ; but he reproved me severely : " ' My no sabe ' not glamma-tickle ; ' I do not know ' glamma-tickle." And at the top he told me " You cannot see if you not bring telescope." Bookish youth, who can talk about grammatical and telescope and such long words as these, but can't understand the simplest word said to him. The hills on the way out to and at the White Cloud Mountain (White Cloud is purely fanciful, and so is Mountain, for it is not much of a hill) are one vast cemetery. I never saw such a lot of graves, or hills more completely bare of trees or any verdure—(*as* bare I think the Deccan can show in plenty, amongst its numerous Reserved Forests).

The view from the top is expansive and not wanting in the charm that wide stretches of hill and fields and winding river are wont to own ; and here you overlook a large city and a busy crowd of shipping. I said to the Ting that a point near us was the highest and not the one we were on; but he said, " That more high ; this most high—m,o,r,e, more, m,o,s,t, most." I turned and left the most high, and solaced myself with sandwiches and stout in the Temple. But the Ting pursued me and tried to draw corks without removing the wire, and wrestled with the letter r, and after consulting his pocket vocabulary asked conundrums from the spelling-book. "Which is the most beautiful country?" I said I had seen many countries, and China was the worst; but he didn't understand, and asked another. " What wine is that?" pointing to the stout. I told him it was not wine ; wine is made from grapes. " Grapes " floored him. But he returned to the stout, and murmured softly to himself, " O,u,t—out ; s,t,o,u,t—stout." I gave him some to keep him quiet ; but it only made his tongue wag faster and more unintelligibly. So I wrote him out copy-book sentences, and made him learn them. After tiffin came in an old priest from Honam Temple, polite and friendly like many old Buddhist priests that I have known elsewhere. Like them too, he politely inquired my age, and, still like them, when I told him through the Ting to guess it, guessed it 25 per cent. too high. Soon the object of all the politeness appeared in request for payment for use of the room.

I said I was a poor man—the Ting laughed rudely—and Honam Temple very rich, which was true, for it has houses and land and shops in a way that no Buddhist monastery ought to have. But this temple is poor, said they: which may or may not have been true. The journey back across the plain was unpleasant. For Canton is a large city; and as the night-soil is carefully collected and carried out raw in open pails, to manure the not too fertile soil, you meet a file of open scent-boxes every few hundred yards. And so through " leagues of odour streaming far," and through these noisome alleys, miscalled streets (they pall on you terribly after a day or two), to the comparative freshness and the actual quiet of the little foreign settlement on the concession at Shameen. The dwellers therein are to be pitied; the place is so small, and the surroundings so unpleasant, likewise the mosquitoes are lively.

In Shanghai city there is not the same busy life as in Canton; the streets are as narrow, and poorer and meaner. Here are no large shops which, however dark and dull in their doorways on the alley, are bright within, with light let in from above that shows up well the handsome carving—much of it gilt—and good upholstery and showy wares; here is no profusion of gorgeous signboards; the chairs are rare, and infrequent the burden-bearing cooli. You can walk about in Shanghai city without being rammed by pole-borne goods, and also without being mobbed and jostled by an impolite crowd, as you are sure to be in Canton if you are venturesome enough to foot it through the streets of the southern city. For the natives of Shanghai side are decidedly less hostile to the foreigner than the Cantonese. They are, in comparison, quite friendly. But of sights Shanghai city is empty; it has no curio-shops to speak of, and it has all the dirt and smells that it should not have. Of course there *are* porcelain shops, and jade shops, and silk stores, and wood carvings, and what not; and I doubt not that a wily and experienced curio-hunter could find things that would delight him; but to the inexperienced and guileless there is nought. Of course, too, you may light on strange tortures that the Chinese dignify as trial or as punishment, and you are certain to see some few wearers of the cangue—the thing is too common to deserve much note. But you will, I fancy, soon weary of Shanghai city, nor find great excitement in the temple or the tea-house with its corkscrew bridge meandering across a cesspool (the tea-house stands in the midst thereof), or the garden with its miniature rocks and grottos and tunnels. And the site of Shanghai, how unlovely! A low flat land, cut up by a labyrinth of dirty creeks, the land half-liquid, the water thick with mud; no hill, not a hillock or a mound or ever so slight a rise to relieve the dreary monotony of level endless expanse. After beholding these things the globe-trotter decides that the foreign town or concession is the best part of Shanghai. Here is no lack of busy life. The wharves are crowded with goods and coolis, and the stream with ships; not so extensive, but at least as busy, are the quays of Shanghai as those of Hongkong, that second junction (let us say Willesden, as we have already appropriated Clapham to Singapore) of the Far East. What constant traffic on the Bund! (why the remote Easterns call the sea face the Bund is more than I can make out). How different from the quietude of the Japanese Treaty Ports! Shanghai is proud of having converted a dismal swamp into a handsome town; and it has reason to be. The club is the best of all those that have hospitably opened their doors to me as a visitor, and the town is a pleasure to walk or drive through: it is so well laid out and well kept. Here, as a resident expounded to a group of globe-trotters, are all things municipal managed by a committee freely elected by the ratepayers, and here, he went on, is no meddling officialdom (I said I was off, but he laughed, and I didn't go) to overrule and red-tape and leading-string the committee. A truly independent republic, with consular courts for justice, and all else in its own hands. Here is the British bobby in complete British uniform, and the Chinese policeman in a much better-looking kit than his brother at Hongkong. The racecourse is large (and the ponies small), the community sportive, the climate vile for not so very many months in the year. Altogether the dwellers in Shanghai make their remote existence pass pleasantly enough. But the hotels are very poor. I doubt if in any place money is so freely spent as in this model settlement.

A visit to these outside edges of China—Hongkong, Canton, Macao, Shanghai,—did not raise in me any desire to see more of the country. The Chinaman in British Farther India is to my liking; he is industrious and skilful, and not troublesome. Of course he is a terrible gambler, and apt to fight if his pet sport is "rushed" by the police; and now and again his secret societies bring him into conflict with Western notions of right. But, take him all round, he is a good sort of subject. It is a different matter to see him in his own country. Here his dirt and his cruelty and offensive manners render him unlovely and unloveable. His country is not beautiful, nor is he, nor his women, nor anything that is his, except, it may be said, certain art works, and even these are (to my unæsthetic mind) rather curious and grotesque than beautiful. As a servant, he is not to be mentioned in the same street with a good Indian boy (say a Surati for choice). He brings nothing until told to bring it; he rolls or strolls about in a lazy, indifferent manner, and, when the thing is brought, chucks it down before you in a loutish contemptuous fashion, that make it a difficulty to keep one's hands off him. There is no pleasure in travelling among a sordid unfriendly people, who are lacking in that cheery briskness which makes a tour among the Japanese so pleasant. Let who will go to Pekin, or up the Yangtsze, or the Canton River; I say good-bye to China, with no wish to see more of it now, or any more of it hereafter.

CHAPTER III.

JAPAN.

THERE were four men who sailed from Hongkong to the Land of the Rising Sun. And the name of the first was the Duke. In the beginning he was created alliteratively Marquis of Melbourne, but because of his Dookishness he was raised to the rank of Duke of Melbourne and Sydney. And the second and the third were 'Arry and Alf; men also called them the Bounder and the Other Bounder; likewise they were known as the Bank or the Manager, and as Tapioca or the Huguenot, and by any other name that the brilliance of their own or their companions' wit could devise. The fourth man gave himself the name of Charlie, others that of the Major; a man of not much speech. Perhaps he thought a lot. Howbeit, he did not think much of the Dook's whist. Yet was the Duke a great man, belonging to a great country; wherefore he could not and did not refrain from instructing the Bounders and the Major on the abject inferiority of the countries in which they dwelt and earned their bread—to wit of India and the Straits and China;

he expounded to them the folly of existing in such awful climates as those countries are famed for. "I would not be in them for any pay," he said. "They can manage without you," said the Major. But the pachydermatous dook did not cease to pour out the vials of his wrath on all the climates he had experienced since he left the country of the kangaroo. Yea, also to those three Bounders and to the officers of the ship whereon they sailed he enlarged on the imbecile idiocy of accepting the pay of any master, be it a government, or a company, a corporation, or a firm; why not strike out a line and be your own master in a country fit to live in, as he had done? Whereat the officers and the Bounders marvelled greatly because of his exceeding breadth of vision, and the exquisite delicacy of his tact. Yet was their marvel misplaced; for was he not a B.C.? (and this may be writ large, yet somewhat softened, as Bally Colonial). And they reviled him, and made him a Dook. Now as these four men sailed from Hongkong to the North and to the East, even to the extremest islands of the East, the wind blew and the contrary current ran, and the channel that is called Formosa seemed not lovely in their eyes; so that the Major waxed less and less speechful and more pensive, and the Bounders and the doctor (for was there not a doctor of rubicund visage, ever ready to be stood a drink?) imbibed mournfully their modest potations, and the Dook read guide-books and the books written of globe-trotters; until they came into still, smooth waters, and a gentler air, where sea and sky alike were suffused with delicate gradations of softest grey-blue and dashes of sudden silver, and they steamed swiftly (at least pretty swiftly, say twelve knots) through the delicious haze, past abrupt islets and the death-dealing rock of Pappenburg, into the all but land-locked harbour of Nagasaki. Nagasaki is the southernmost, the hottest, the prettiest, but not the busiest of the open ports of Japan; yes, the prettiest, whatever the lovers of Kobe may say. To call at Nagasaki on your way into Japan is to get a small foretaste of all that you are going to see in that now delectable, now detestable, country. Here are temples of a fashion new to you, yet reminiscent of China—far short of the ornate magnificence that we shall see at Nikko, less severely simple than in Ise; here are the little houses, like toy-houses, with their sliding walls of paper on thin lattice work, the boats with coolis in the universal blue (they do not row, but waggle about a strange oar which they never lift out of the water, the same as the stern oar in a Chinese boat); here too are busy docks and coal wharves (coaling at Nagasaki is a wonderfully clean business), and a jail of European construction. In the streets are many art-dealers of modern Japan, with store of wares made expressly for the unwary globe-trotter; and besides these signs of modern civilization and modern degradation, here, lastly, are the simple unconventionalities of old Japan: the smiling tea-house girl, the nearly-naked cooli, the maid or matron bathing by the wayside in unclad innocence and a common wash-tub. On a bright sunny day Nagasaki is beautiful. It is all up and down, nowhere level, and yet no great height; the hill tops and slopes of all shapes and outlines. It is like a big mountain district looked at through a telescope reversed: the hills of the kingdom of Lilliput. So those four men—having been well mobbed by the rickshamen—verily those of Nagasaki are the most persistent and unescapable of all the men who drag rickshas—and having ridden across to Mugi and back, admired, and passed on well pleased into the Inland Sea. Now the country of Japan has weather, but no climate; and the weather is occasionally good, but most often bad. When the people and their rulers revolutionized the kingdom some twenty or so years ago, and started things all afresh on the most approved modern principles, they forgot to include their weather among their reforms, and it remains unreformed to this day. What d'-you-call-him, who dwells in Yokohama, said, in that formal precise manner of his: "I have lived ten years in Japan, of which nine-and-three-quarters have been wet;" and the local poet delivered himself thus:—

> Dirty days hath September,
> April, June, and November;
> From February unto May,
> The rain it raineth every day;
> All the rest have thirty-one,
> Without one blessed gleam of sun.
> And if any of 'em had two-and-thirty,
> They'd be just as wet and twice as dirty.

In such weather as that there may be a large amount of beauty lying around, but as you can't see it for the fog and the rain, it might just as well not be there. So they passed sightless through the Inland Sea, and hoped there would be more to see inland. And thus they came unto Kobe, and the Dook departed and went his ways, but the other three sailed on to Yokohama. (Howbeit the Dook feared greatly lest he should die of cholera in Osaka; for the folk of that place died daily in hundreds.) There are many people who have heard that Japan is a beautiful and charming country to visit, and they come determined to find it so, so that nothing, be it ever so commonplace or ever so dreary, shall choke them off from enthusing ecstatically—nothing, not even Yokohama or Tokio. These are certainly the least interesting places in Japan, the least beautiful; yet shall you find people who rhapsodize thereon. Here be dithyrambics:—
"When the tide is in, the moat is a joy for ever. Faint grey mists tremble over it in the morning each mist a separate phantasm, and through them the dusky, wide-roofed temples rise, the shaggy arms of the pine suggest themselves, and the water full of beautiful pale half-lights below gives back amongst its deepest shadows a gleam of the gold that is broadening in the sky beyond. In the evening the sky is red, and the tangle of pines black against it. A great ragged crow flaps lazily past the low white imperial walls, which cluster thick in the darkness of the water. And presently the paper

lanterns begin to come out, pendulous drops of light, mysterious swaying globes of black and rose and gold, and the Japanese night is alive, enchanting us," &c., &c.; but for mercy's sake no more. All this rhodomontade on Tokio is proof positive of the poorness of the place as a sight; else why waste words on a moat that is a joy for ever, and yet is so only when the tide is in; on temples that rise through mists which tremble over the moat (are, then, the temples in the moat?); on pine arms suggesting themselves (let us trust they were not unpleasantly suggestive); on water that gives back what it hasn't got; on the extraordinary phenomena of a red sky at night, a crow flying, walls clustering in the water, and pendulous drops of light coming (it would seem) out of that same water? "Imperial walls" sounds well, but the phrase does not alter the fact that the walls are deuced little to look at; and no excess of verbiage or power of word-painting will make Tokio a delightful place. The streets are long enough (ye gods, how long they are!) and most of them amply wide, but they are always muddy; and how can a street look handsome with low little houses of a ground floor and one squat upper story, and no more, and most of them coloured a dull black with tiled roof to match? The effect is dreary and depressing in the extreme. The tram-car is here, but none too well got up, and it does not enliven the scene; the shops—for the most part—show no wares nothing but lattice-work wall and door; all the goods are stored away within. The exceptions are where European style has been copied, even to the signboard, often with ludicrous effect, *e.g.*, "General Wine Keeper; Foreign Beer, Spirits & Co." Why, the streets of Canton are far more cheerful (barring the smells) and interesting to roam through than those of Tokio. The taste of the Japanese is usually applauded; but that of the Emperor—or whoever chose for him—was certainly at fault when he abandoned such a charming place as Kioto, and located himself on the flat unlovely site of his present capital. As for the moat, it is merely a nuisance, winding spirally about the heart of the city, ugly when the tide is in, and most intolerable and not to be endured when it is out. Yet it is strange to see the wild duck placidly resting in protected safety on those city waters. The gentle and patriotic Japanese is apt to speak and write in a strain of oriental hyperbole about the places and things of his country and people; much is well deserved, and much of it he really means, for he has a keen sense of some kinds of beauty, and some kinds of worth; but, surely much is exaggeration. Yet the European writer seems to think it right to take it all as gospel, to give up his own judgment and merely reproduce the Japanese tall talk with his own endorsement that it is all correct; and when the globe-trotter comes round he swallows whole all that his guide-book tells him; and when he writes his book, he tries to go one better. And thus a place that may really have many good points may yet fall terribly flat when you find it far short of the earthly paradise described by the bookmaker. Tokio, for instance, no doubt has much of beauty and interest: when the cherry-trees of Uyeno or the wisteria of Asakusa are in blossom it may be granted that they are lovely, though probably more enchanting to the Japanese than to the European. The shows and shops in Asakusa are lively and cheerful enough at any time that they are open; the Museum at Uyeno has many fine works of art and many relics of old Japan, well housed and well arranged; Shiba has temples that are a good introduction to those at Nikko: indeed the tomb of the Second Shogun is equal to anything at Nikko; the Yoshiwara is the largest in Japan, and a curious sight (some of the inmates are dressed in European clothes of a decidedly dowdy style, and are even less alluring than their fellow houris in their native costume). But granting all these things, Tokio is disappointing. Nor is Yokohama much better. The Bund is nothing great, and is desolate and almost trafficless. The Bluff may be a pleasant place to live on, for those who have to live here, but is not much to look at; and of sights that the guide-books fill their pages with, none is worth seeing. Exception must be made in favour of Kamakura and Enoshima. The Shinto temple, near the station, at the first-named place, is famous in Japanese history, and has a goodly store of relics of famous heroes of the olden time—Yoritomo, the founder of the shrine, and others; but outside the temple little remains to show that all around was once a mighty city, an ancient capital of the Shoguns. It is all gone; and now there is a "Marine Sanitarium" down on the sea-shore—a very modern and European hostelry. And so we ricksha to the great bronze image of Buddha, the Dai-butsu, and read with some admiration the good English of the inscription on a notice-board at the gate: "Stranger, whosoever thou art, and whatsoever be thy creed, when thou enterest this sanctuary, remember that thou treadest upon ground hallowed by the worship of ages. This is the temple of Buddha and the gate of the Eternal, and should therefore be entered with reverence." I fear that clambering about the massive figure, both outside and in, and being photographed upon it, are not conducive to rendering the reverence claimed; but, doubtless, the photographer does not mind so long as the dollars come in. The figure is Indian in style, with long drooping ears, largely pierced, and boss on the forehead; but the robe is not disposed, nor the hands arranged, as they are in Burmese Buddhas. Not far off is a large erect figure of Buddha, not exposed to the open air like the seated bronze one, but carefully enshrined behind the screen in the temple. For ten cents a priest runs a couple of farthing dips in dilapidated lanterns up on a creaking pulley, and makes a show of his God. Your rickshamen soon have you over the hill, round the foot of which Yoshisadu won his way by prayer and by flinging his sword into the sea, so that the tide retreated and gave him dry passage, whereon he marched to meet his adversary the Shogun Hojo, and greatly defeated him; and so you reach the bay of Enoshima. As you come abruptly round the corner on to the beach-road, the prospect is certainly of great beauty. The bay on your left, volcanic Oshima like a cloud in the distance, the island of Enoshima in front of you, and behind it hills that look low and small when you glance to the right front where Fujisan raises its 12,000 feet up into the clear bright air, and catches the warm sunshine on its snow-clad cone. I think the Jap is really justified in bucking boastfully about Fujisan. There are many higher mountains in the world, many ruggeder, more awe-inspiring, more terrific in precipice and moraine and glacier, but I do not believe there is any more perfect picture than Fujisan seen on a clear autumn day from Enoshima, or from Gotemba on the railway, or, better still, from Iwabuchi at the mouth of the Fuji river. The smaller hills stand off respectfully at a distance, and give the Peerless Mountain clear space to raise itself almost from the very brink of the ocean; and it rises with inimitable and exquisite grace. There is but a narrow strip of paddy-land and a few broken peaks of Ashidakayama between the southern foot of Fuji and the sea; and I do not know where else, unless at Teneriffe, you will find a mountain rising with one continuous sweep right from the sea-shore up to over 12,000 feet; where you will see a picture so well composed by nature, or where in the whole world you can match Fujisan for exceeding gracefulness of contour and curve. Enoshima has a cave, that, being here, you have to go and see; but you need not come so far to see just as good. It is a curious little islet (I use intentionally the double diminutive), full of temples and shell-sellers and country-houses; and one is sorry when it is time to get back to the weary insipidity of Yokohama. It must in justice be admitted that Yokohama is, as far as hotel comforts go, the best place to stay in in Japan, or indeed anywhere in the Far East; yet the creature-comforts of an hotel are hardly enough to counterbalance the dulness of the settlement. Nor is there much to be gained by looking about the native town. It is a trite saying that Japan is becoming yearly less Japanese and more European; and, of course, in Yokohama, which was nothing before the foreign settlement located there, the foreign fashion is stronger than in any other place. Here is a racecourse—all in miniature, of course—but all in correct European style; not a detail wanting; not a European there but two blue-jackets and ourselves; everything managed by Japs for Japs. The course is a little short of half a mile; the ponies are not much to look at, ranging from, say, 12-3 to 13-3, shaggy, clumsy, and untrained. Let us watch a half-mile race. Four starters; innumerable false starts; at last, off they go; and our selection—the only pony in the lot that appears to have any care taken of him—romps in an easy winner in the magnificent time of

1 10⅔. Or again, a formal dinner to the Governor. The war paint of the white man is *de rigueur*; the whole procedure, the food and the courses, are strictly European. And so with the Army and the Police and railway servants and officials generally; and most of the men in the street—bar coolis—are in Western attire. All except a few old men up country have given up the ancient national style of hair-dressing in favour of a short-cut mop and a billycock hat. Thank goodness, the women stick to their own costume—I mean the vast majority of the women that the globe-trotter sees in his wanderings—for they look awful in European clothes. Taste deserts them, and they dress like those creatures in the Tokio Yoshiwara, or in garish and ill-assorted colours that remind you of similar fair ones nearer home. Doubtless there are ladies who dress well in European fashion —it is compulsory for them to adopt it at Court. But how should they look well in foreign garb, when not even in their own—devised, no doubt, to show them off as well as possible—are they fairly entitled to be called pretty? They are not pretty. Young girls have a freshness and a rosy complexion that is decidedly pleasing after the yellow of Burmese girls and the darker shades of India, down to the blackness of Madras; but it is merely the prettyness of youth, a *beauté du diable*. I do not believe in the existence of a really beautiful Japanese girl, and I am sure there cannot be a beautiful Japanese woman—I mean a woman of

thirty or more. The *beauté du diable* gone, there remains nothing but plainness. But, pretty though they are not, yet they are charming. Wherein the charm lies I can hardly tell. Not in gracefulness, for their gait is hideous. The skirt of their garment ties in the limbs too closely for them to take an honest stride, even if the said limbs were long enough to take it, which they are not; the feet (generally ugly and shapeless) turn toes inwards, to keep on the useful but ungainly clog or patten; the knees are never straightened, and so they go forward in a totter, a toddle, a shuffle, that who will may admire—I cannot. Then the dress: an enormous bunch of cloth fastened in the middle of the back and extending to the end of it. What gracefulness is there in that? (not to speak of its inconvenient obstructiveness if you wish to slip your arm round her waist. You will find the sleeve more kindly made.) Again, the hair: an obtrusive bob in front, and side-wings, well gummed to keep them in correct curve. Yet again: the shaved eyebrows and blackened teeth of the matrons—how hideous! And yet they are charming. A pleasant cheerfulness, unfailing good spirits and a wish to oblige, readiness to understand your imbecile attempts at the lingo, that *beauté du diable* already spoken of: take them altogether, and you will find them fetch you. After Japan, those Cantonese, whom awhile ago we called not uncomely, appear decidedly dowdy and plain. When I go to a Japanese hotel, I am glad to find, not men servants, as at Tokio, Kioto, and Shidzuoka, but nesans waiting on one, as at Miyanoshita, Nagoya, and all the tea-houses in the country. (Nikko Hotel was in a transition stage—half-and-half.) The "boys" are not good attendants, unless they are boys, not men. The young ones are sharp enough, but the men, though polite and willing, are stupid and slow. Howbeit the tea-house girls round the Treaty Ports of Yokohama and Kobe are spoilt. Contact with the European wanderer has changed too many of them from charming maidens into something that those words would not accurately describe. As to Japanese Europeanization generally, it may be said that they are going ahead too fast—shoving on railways that do not pay (at any rate, the shares of only two lines or sections of lines stand at a premium, for all the Government guarantees), and claiming to be a full-grown civilized power, when it is only some twenty years since the barriers of exclusion were thrown down and Japan emerged from a barbaric feudalism. The European residents in Japan do not apparently yearn to be placed under Japanese law; and why should they? Who will guarantee that the state of affairs which resulted from a revolution shall not be swept away by another, bringing back to power the anti-foreign party? or that —reaction or not—the brand-new codes will be worked up-country in fairness, with no race-prejudice, and above all honestly? Wherefore, the Treaty Revision is something of a burning question, and the "Soshi" (may I call them an association?) bestir themselves against the philo-foreigners.

Talking of burning reminds me that there is a very neat and well-arranged crematorium at Yokohama : in this matter the Japanese is actually ahead of his Western model, and has no wrong-headed objection to burning his dead. I wish the Hindu would burn his as cleanly and decently. In jail affairs, too, there is nothing left for the Mikado's Government to learn. I visited a jail at Tokio—one of three—small, but they think too large a number could not be properly looked after; and extraordinarily insecure and unfenced, but the Japanese criminal is docile and rarely attempts to escape. Its arrangements were just about as good as they could be. Hospitals, sleeping cells, work-sheds, complete and clean and perfectly kept. Here were no prisoners toiling at useless crank and unremunerative shot and stone drill as in Hongkong; all were occupied in hard labour, useful to the jail, pounding rice (with such pounders as the Burmese women use, but here and in China men do that work), cultivating vegetables, doing the service of the jail; or manufacturing simple products for sale for outside use—mats, straw shoes, coarse papers, &c. The diet scale appeared ample; the precautions to prevent the spread of contagious disease are complete. (In passing, one may remark that though the Japanese seem cleaner than the Chinese, yet skin diseases, especially on the shaved heads of children, appear much more common among the former than among the latter.) Flogging is not resorted to as a punishment for breaches of jail discipline ; punitive diet and solitary cells are, as I understand, the only authorized punishment. But one form of solitary cell is certainly a severe one. All light is excluded ; the ventilators are so arranged as to admit air, but not light ; and food is supplied to the convict through a little sliding panel in the door, to which the box containing the food fits exactly ; the food tilted in, the panel is shot to again. In this solitary darkness the wretch remains for the term of his sentence. It is true that he is inspected daily by the doctor, and that the maximum term is five days.

Tokio beats Hongkong again in keeping under-trials apart from convicts ; and it is like it, and all other civilized jails, in keeping the women apart from the men. The women-warders in the female portion of the prison are inexpressibly hideous in their European uniform—more so than the very convicts in their shapeless garments of crushed strawberry or common blue. All were diligently employed in useful labour—the service of the women's prison, and making wadded clothes for winter wear. There was not a good-looking one among them, except one, a geisha, or singing girl, in for ten years for killing a man. It appears that an unwelcome suitor after many rejections threatened to kill her, and she jeered at him and said that rather she would kill him ; whereupon he scornfully asked how, and she made as if to strike him with a knife; in which feigning by some mischance she did actually strike him, so that he died. Assuming this version to be true, ten years is a trifle stiff. The buildings throughout the prison are all on the ground; there is no first floor. As already noticed, the fence is nothing, merely a slight palisade of bamboo. In one place is an office where prisoners are allowed to write letters to friends outside, or, if they cannot write, to dictate their letter to a jail clerk, who will write it for them. And when his term is over, there is a sum of money for the prisoner to receive. An account is kept of his work, and of the sale of it, and when he goes he receives the balance that is due to him on the account (I forget whether the cost of his keep in jail is deducted or not). Outdoor gangs are employed at hard labour outside the jail; I saw them both here, and in Osaka, and at the Ashiwo Copper Mines. Again it was noticeable how slight was the guard kept over these convicts, leg-irons of the thinnest and slightest, and to a gang of thirty men only three police or warders, of whom only one armed; and in some such proportion in the case of each gang that I saw. The gallows is erected in a corner of the jail premises, and executions are strictly private; but they are very rare.

Another very successful European institution in Japan is the Mint at Osaka. It is now managed entirely by Japanese, and turns out " yens " (dollars) that seem to be fast becoming the principal metal currency in the Far East. (China started making coin — seventy-two candareens, I think, made a dollar — but gave it up; I suppose the Mandarins found they could not make enough out of it; for official corruption is great in China, almost as great as in the Spanish Indies or in Spain.) All the fittings of the Osaka Mint are complete, and Japan has made a success of what in Hongkong was a failure. The gentle Jap takes kindly, too, to electric light; it is in all the Japanese hotels and in tea-houses that are rising into hotels, *e.g.*, at Nagoya; Tokio and Osaka are full of it; mines are lighted with it, as at Ashiwo. Your Chinaman has a few imperial telegraphs, but the post office he will have nothing to do with; in Japan the wires and the pillar-boxes are all over the country, the latter black, and each marked "Post." Japanese newspapers are plentiful, and most of them illustrated (who ever heard of a Chinese newspaper other than the *Pekin Gazette?*), books plentiful, and education State inspected and almost universal. There is much in Japan that is redolent of China; but what an entire difference between the peoples! Temples, art, alphabet, language, religion—these all bear marks of the Middle Kingdom; but the globe-trotter thanks the fates that have saved the people from being such as the Celestials are in temperament, manners, customs, dress, and personal appearance. Where do they come from, these Japanese? From what stock have they sprung? Are they Malay, as some assert? (including, says Froude in his *Oceana*, Sir George Grey). Verily, they are evolved into something most unlike Malay, such at least as the Malay appears in the Straits and Java. They are probably, like ourselves, a very mixed lot. " Saxon and Norman and Dane are we," with a little Roman and Kelt and Scandinavian thrown in, and we boast ourselves to be the best all-round nation in the West. So some strange untraceable fusion of races has, no doubt, produced the modern Japanese, who are by far and beyond question the most go-ahead people in the East.

CHAPTER IV.

MIYANOSHITA—NIKKO—IKAO.

Now, after they arrived in Yokohama, the three Bounders spent a night and a day in acquiring experience of the town, and the Major took upon himself to engage a guide. For the Major had large plans of much travelling in the interior, and was full of ardour to climb hills, and march marches, and see out-of-the-way places and people. To this intent he had become learned in guide-books, and in the phrases that are taught to the guileless in the vocabularies, and had bought a dictionary and studied laboriously therein. Yet was he not complete without a guide—one who should be courier and interpreter and cook, and should see the unwary foreigner safely through strange places, and guard his pocket from the unscrupulous curio-monger. Wherefore he engaged a guide, and the name of the guide was Matsuda. Now the Tapioca Bounder did not greatly yearn after mountain-climbing, or dote on footing it, or wandering around away from the cities of men; he allowed that he could walk when he had to and was paid for it, and that that was enough; he wasn't going to waste his time on unremunerative peripatetication; his soul inclined to fix itself in comfortable quarters, and there abide in slothful ease. Howbeit they two—Alf and Charlie—in solemn conclave, under the presidentship of the guide, decided to see it through together; the Major curtailing, and the Huguenot extending, his plans of travel. Unto them also joined himself the Bank Bounder, for such period as the times and seasons of his leave permitted. And with him came yet a fourth, ycleped Jim, or, distinctively, the Bank Manager, for that the fame of his coming, albeit he was not the manager, sufficed to secure the best rooms in advance, and that his possession of some local knowledge and colloquial lingo made him the guide, philosopher and friend of the three Bounders who were strangers in the land. And for a time the guide Matsuda took a back seat.

I wonder why the globe-trotter when in remote corners of the earth goes to the theatre. What went he out for to see? Surely not very indifferent companies playing plays that he can see infinitely better mounted and played at home? Yet to such a sight did these Bounders go; and next day betook themselves to the railway which deposited them at Kodzu. It has already been said that Japan is now delectable and now detestable; also that it has weather, but no climate. It showed off, this day, its weather in the detestable side of its character. It rained steadily continuously, and not gently. Some little time before it had been doing the same, yet more vigorously; result—broken bridges, inundations, breached railways. From Kodzu the tram runs to Yumoto, single line, with loops at crossing-stations. With exact Japanese foresight and care, the tram-car proceeding from, and that returning to, Kodzu passed the loop and met in the midst of the single line. How the passengers sang songs of praise as they changed from one car to the other in the pouring rain! The four Bounders and the guide, having taken a car to themselves, looked on in pity, and the pleasure derived from others' pain. But then came they unto the broken bridge, and had to get out. And behold! the bridge that had been broken was mended; not wholly repaired, yet so far sound that the baggage-bearing coolis crossed thereby. Wherefore they also walked thereon, even unto the farther end of the bridge —almost. But ere they were yet well over, came one with much gesticulation and many words in unintelligible language of the country; one in authority (peradventure a P. W. D. Overseer), who stayed them, and would by no means let them pass. And they waxed wroth, saying, "Lo! coolis have crossed; are not we better than many coolis?" Yet that one in authority hardened his heart, and would not let them go. And his heart, being hardened, was glad, for that he had held sway over four miserable Englishmen, so that they turned back and crossed the river on a very wet and cranky raft. And the Major wondered sadly at seeing this thing; to wit, himself obeying such a person as a

Miyanoshita.

P. W. D. Overseer. And Alf and 'Arry and Jim beset the guide and said, "What manner of country is this wherein when the bridge is made whole, the cooli may walk thereon and not we?" And they baited him exceedingly. So they went on until the Japanese tram-car ran off the Japanese rails, and the Japanese near pony bit the Japanese off pony, so that they fought together; and all four praised the country and its bandobast, and all that was in it, and grieved sorely the guide Matsuda. And thus they came to a place, miles short of Yumoto, where the road and the tram line were all washed away; and they got into rickshas and began the ascent of the ghat. And all the while the rain fell, and the wind blew, and the rickshas jolted through mud and ruts and over stones and rocks; and things were gay all round. "I believe we are travelling for pleasure," said the Major, as a temporary gleam of sun let them out to walk. "That is what they call it," Jim made answer, as they all fled back to the rickshas to avoid the renewed downpour. In time they reached Miyanoshita, and the Fujiya Hotel received them hospitably, and they took their rooms in the Japanese quarters. And all next day, until long past noon, it rained and rained and rained. Yet were they not cast down, but made merry and disported themselves after their kind.

The Bank Manager had been there before; he knew his way about. The Major loafed around radiant in a lungi of crimson Burmese silk, so that the nesans admired him greatly; and he studied earnestly the language of the Japanese. The Bank Bounder stuck to English, but forgot that the walls of Japanese rooms are of paper, and, as he discoursed after the manner of youth, was recalled, by a most significant cough from his unknown next-door neighbour, to a sense of the fact that his conversation, whatever O Kuni San might think of it, was hardly such as should be proclaimed from the house-tops. But Tapioca, discontented with the baths provided in the quarters where he abode, made voyages of discovery, and was found in remote places where the Japanese bathe after the manner of their country, and what that is has been set forth in many books. In the late afternoon fair weather took them out of doors, and they collected some of the curios of Japan. Here are one or two of them. In Naraya Hotel garden : " No tree and any flower is permitted to take off in this garden. No fish is permitted to catch in this ponds." On a notice board :—" To let, with picture—sque view of Fuji in the up and the island Enoshima in the down when the weather is most beautifully." And in the evening, lo, the Dook ! Escaped safely from choleraic Osaka and the dangers of the rapids near Kioto, he arrived ; and being in great form, he first condemned the country and its weather utterly, and relegated to the category of fools all who did not flee from it instantly as he would do ; and then instructed the bank men on the way bank business should be conducted, clearly demonstrating to his own satisfaction, and no one else's, that they were mere pawnbrokers, and that no banks were of much account outside Australia ; and the silver question he deemed capable of instant solution on lines of his own. And they all with one accord acclaimed him Dook.

On the following morning weather fair but doubtful ; yet, as afternoon it still held up, they went out to walk. Now, Jim could walk, and Charlie fancied he could, and Alf and 'Arry allowed they would too. Jim thought he knew the way of Doriosan ; howbeit he led them into waste places where no way was, and Alf and 'Arry followed him sadly back until they struck the road (it wasn't the road's fault though, so why should they strike it ?). But Charlie made a way for himself through much grass and rock up the steep hillside, and smiled on them serenely as they came panting up the ridge. From the top the view landwards was poor ; it consisted chiefly of clouds ; but Miyanoshita and Kinga just under them, and on the other side Odawara and the sea, were good to look upon. And the clouds came up and caught them as they descended, and Tapioca turned tenderfoot and 'Arry was very weary, so that they declared with conviction that they preferred scenery admired from below, and that views from mountain tops were frauds. But Hamlet (for is not Hamlet the barman and dispenser of drinks ?) ministered unto them, and the girls waited on them, and their souls revived. Howbeit next day, after the usual morning rain, they refused to walk to Hell, and were carried thither in chairs. For the meaning of Ojingoku is Big Hell. It is a place where the whole sloping mountain-side is broken up with jets of sulphur and full of sulphurous water, and the air is heavy with the vapour of sulphur. Less imposing and more ugly than Tankoebanprahoe, it is not a delicious place; and you have to take heed where you walk, or you will stick inextricably in burning mud. Charlie and Jim had a fine walk back by another track, and found a charming little waterfall perfectly embowered in trees. Hamlet ever prophesied fine weather, and next morning it seemed his prophecies were to be realized. A splendid morning, "just the day for a walk to the top of Otomitonge pass to have a view of Fuji, which we haven't yet seen;" and off we went. Now Hamlet is a good sort of man, but he doesn't know everything; and it has long been laid down as an axiom that you should not prophesy unless you know. The weather was very fine at starting—and hot; off went coats, which were loaded on to the luckless cooli; off went the Major's puttis, leaving his legs as bare as his arms, as though he were back in the old jungles on a shikar daur; Matsuda, the guide, almost fainted by the way. But clouds came rolling up behind them, and travelled much faster than they, and covered the top of the pass and the hills around, and filled up the valleys, so that they went not up into the high places, but walked steadily on through the downpour, past dairy farms (Californian cattle and good milk), through bridgeless nullas waist deep (the Japanese are a fine race, and Matsuda is a fine Jap, but fording rapid torrents on a stony bed is not his forte), through tall wet grass and trickling rivulets that should have been paths, until they came to the little tea-house at the end of the lake of Hakone. But it rained on, and as the boatmen waggled their oars to take them to Hakone, they put up many Japanese brollies against the wind and rain, and lay out under blankets, and drank much whisky and smoked endless tobacco. Just one break in the clouds to show how pretty the lake could look if it chose, and then rain on ; until at last the Mikado's summer palace and the cryptomeria avenue on the Tokaido and the Hafuya tea-house. Here were three wrathful warriors, arrived first yet refused the upper and best rooms reserved for the Bank Manager! And Jim and 'Arry and the rest took them without a blush.

Have you ever been shaved by a Japanese barber with a Japanese razor? If not, don't ; it is not good enough. The Major thought it due to his personal appearance to take the scrub off his chin ; but he shuddered when he saw that razor! Yet he could not back out with credit ; and after near a quarter of an hour's agony, he emerged with face flayed and all but as hairy as before. And the barber so exasperatingly polite that you couldn't swear at him! Pictures are extant of Fuji seen from Hakone Lake ; it may be presumed, therefore, that such a thing may occur as clear weather at Hakone. But the Bounders fled next morning, and it did not clear until they were well over the hill and into Ashinoyu —a pretty walk and not severe ; Ashinoyu, a place consisting of three or four hotels and sulphur-bathing-houses, and nought else. Thence to Miyanoshita it is one long steep descent ; and here the Major came to grief. A slip on the slippery red mud, a fall, and a hurt knee ; and lo! the Major with his shikar clothes and puttis brought in from Kowakidani ignominiously in a chair! But the nesans soon stripped him and tubbed him, and tiffin re-established him. "We have had enough of this," they all agreed ; "we will go hence to Nikko," said they. " For one day's rain here, you will get two at Nikko," said Jim ; but he also prophesied without knowing, and was all wrong. So the three strangers left him and went to Yokohama. (This time they were allowed to tram in peace across the broken bridge.) Now there is in these days a railway to Nikko ; but *more Japanico* the embankments have been built here and there a foot or two below the flood level of the Tonagawa and other big streams from the hills, so that naturally a mile or two of bank and a bridge or two, not to mention culverts, were carried away ; and the breach was not yet mended. Thus the problem was to get through to Nikko in the day with the least possible amount of extra-matutinal rising at the start and of delay on the road. And they thought they had solved it. Leave Yokohama by afternoon train and sleep in Tokio (the two railway stations in Tokio are miles apart ; why don't they run the lines into one central station ?) ; start by the 8.50 A.M., and so catch the 1.23 on the far side of the breach, and that gets you in to Nikko that evening. It went very nicely at first; the rain that made Yokohama and Tokio so cheerful ceased; Kuki was safely reached, and the train there left for ricksha; the ride to Kurihashi was longish but good going most of the way, and for the rest the mud was not so *very* thick. But at Kurihashi the plan broke down; for lo! there was no 1.23 train at all, nor any train for four mortal hours, and that would be too late to make the connection for Nikko; no chance of getting there to-night. "Can't we ricksha it, or ride it?" "No, impossible." "Well," said the Bank Manager, "Cookey has curried our hashey this time," and the Major turned green with envy, for he considered the perpetration of bad puns to be his own special private monopoly. Four hours come to an end somehow, even at a little roadside station on a hot autumn afternoon in Japan; and nightfall saw the three in Utsunomiya. Here, for the first time, they experienced a tea-house; that is, a tea-house pure and simple. The Japanese quarters at Miyanoshita are grades removed from tea-house style: bedstead and furniture and fittings are European, nor do you have to take off your shoes to go in; only the baths are of true Japanese heat— but it is natural hot mineral water; and the attendants are bright, clean, pretty girls (would, O Yamaguchi, that the girls in other your establishments were as clean). At Hakone, you have bedsteads and a few chairs and tables, but the Europe kit is limited; you must remove your shoes on entering, and bring food with you if you would dine well. But at Utsunomiya, you sleep on quilts on the floor, with vast mosquito curtains of dark colour hung round you. You will not dine at all unless on Japanese food (the Three had seen too much of Eastern dishes to hanker much after that); of course your boots must go at the outer door; and your rooms overlook the Jap bath-room—a busy place, well patronized in the evening by naked men and women. The Major insisted on having a bath, and for long it seemed as if he could do it only by laying aside, with his clothes, the European standard of modesty, and adopting the Japanese; but at last he secured a little pantry of a room to himself. Then food: being unprepared for more than tiffin away from an hotel, and all the tiffin being eaten in those four weary hours at Kurihashi, how were they to feed? But the great Matsuda found a "restaurant," into which foreigners were admitted by the back door, and at which might be had a regulation dinner of several courses. So forth the three sallied with a British manufacturer in like sad plight (only worse, for he had no guide), and on the way to dinner and at dinner experienced the only rudeness that was shown them in Japan. For vulgar little boys heaved pebbles at them in the street, and pelted in more through the open windows until put to flight by the maître d'hôtel. And the dinner was by no means bad, considering. Early to bed and early to rise was the order, and off by the first train to Nikko, where their wrath died down as they found themselves arrived, and after all not so much behind time. Quite early enough, at any rate, to do the temples and shrines that morning.

I am given to understand that the Japanese lay down that no man is entitled to speak of beauty as if he knew what the word meant until he has seen Nikko. That is a bit of Japanese bluff. The eyes that have seen many things out of Japan remember many things more beautiful; but they will still recognize much that is marvellously fine. First the splendid contrast between the temples and their surroundings. Enshrined in groves of tall dark stately cryptomerias, through which, on a bright sunny day, enters but a softened and subdued light, and covered by dull-coloured copper roofs of vast expanse, stand temples resplendent with an excess of ornamentation in carved wood and lacquer and painting and gilding and bronze and gold. The cryptomerias are solemn and impressive, and but for the ugliness of their interminable copper roofs, the temples amongst them, seen from a little distance, look well, extremely well. But on entering almost any temple and examining it round, the eye becomes wearied by the excess of decoration. After walking through a dozen or so of such temples, the weariness becomes almost a nausea; and whatever religious feeling may perchance have been inspired by those sacred groves and shrines, on which untold treasure has been lavished, shrinks away to infinitesimal proportions when Matsuda relates how it is all for the glory of " Mr. Iyeyasu " and " Mr. Iyemitsu "—as he persists in calling the first and third Shoguns—and for the crippling of the power of the Daimios, so that their wealth might be expended on these holy works, and not on strengthening themselves and becoming dangerous rivals of the Shogun. So all this religous art, this gorgeous magnificence, is but the tangible embodiment of a plant—a political dodge! Matsuda was in form this day, and discoursed fluently on the temples and their builders. The Major, fancying he took interest in the comparative study of religions, tried to get enlightenment from Matsuda on Japanese Buddhism and Shintoism and pure Shintoism. But Matsuda was much too emancipated to have any ideas on such subjects. "I have been to France, and to England; and in France was Roman Catholic, and Protestant in England." "And what are you now?" "Oh, now I am Buddhist." "Nothing to do with Shinto?" "Oh, yes, I follow Shinto too. But I do not believe in any of these things. Do you, sir?" The Major gave it up. He could not understand why a Buddhist temple should have been removed bodily from the enclosure where Shinto temples stood. "That is to restore pure Shinto," explained Matsuda. "Then why are not all Buddhist symbols and images removed from the Shinto temple?" And to this there seemed to be no answer. It is almost exasperating, in going through these temples, to find no rest from noticeable bits of art. There is no relief, no respite; the whole place is crowded with elaborate or minute

Nikko.   85

work, wrought of the richest materials with exquisite skill and labour, lasting over, it may be, many years. Now and again the eye is startled by something absolutely hideous : a horrible pattern in green and blue and white and red painted on wood, a pattern that would disgrace the wall-paper of a common lodging-house ; or in the midst of "the splendour and the blaze and symmetry," some common piece of plain wood, unfinished, unvarnished. These things jar on one, as do the misshapen monsters that are meant for animals. In bud and flower and foliage and decorative designs, the Japanese artist of old time is as perfect as a human workman can be ; but his humans are usually grotesque, and his animals impossible. That in the temples themselves there should be no contrast, no cessation of superabundant display, seems the more strange because of the perhaps intentional contrast between the groves and the temples in them, and the certainly designed simplicity of the tomb of Iyeyasu, which is led up to by shrines and gateways of most rich and elaborate ornamentation. After passing through all this overdone decoration, it is extremely effective to find the tomb of plain bronze, with plain well-shaped figures of tortoise and crane, surrounded by the dark-green cryptomerias. At one place there is a much dented lantern—one of those innumerable stone or metal posts, with four-windowed chamber on the top to place lamps in— and Matsuda, the sceptic, explained that here dared no man, or woman either, pass at night because of the "goods" that appeared in the lantern. Many had vainly struck at them with swords and hit but the lantern, and the dents and scratches are there to attest the truth of the tale. "But what kind of goods?" asked 'Arry and Alf. " I don't know what you call in English, bakemono," said Matsuda. "Ah, ghosts," said that learned Japanese scholar the Major. The Bounders refused to go up the pagoda of many stories, or to have their names put up (in Japanese) for future fame among the donators for the up-keep of the temples, whose patronymics and gifts are placarded on huge hoardings at the gateway of the holy ground. They paid their twenty cents for an old lady in a shrine to perform a religious dance—a slow and not ungraceful business of fan-flirting and hand-flipping and woven paces; and went home agreeing (when they did agree their unanimity was wonderful) that they were glad to have seen the Temples of Nikko, but did not want to see them again. They did not find the garden of Dainichido particularly interesting, nor the long line of Buddhas by the side of the stream, which no man can count up accurately. These Buddhas are in stone, and on an apparently inaccessible rock overhanging the stream is a rough scratching of the sacred figure. Nikko being no longer interesting, ensued therefore a long discussion as to the next move. "I don't want to sit in this verandah all day looking at that ugly old mountain," said the Major. " But that is a beautiful mountain," expostulated Matsuda. "All *gentlemen* from Europe and America say it is beautiful. You have not such fine mountains in your country, sir." And Alf and 'Arry joined in and helped to pull the leg of the patriotic Matsuda. And after they had discussed fully, the Major gave up his notion of going beyond Yumoto and up Shirane San and round by remote routes to Ikao and Kusatsu, and 'Arry and Alf consented to leave hotels and take to tea-houses for a bit, and they drank one another's healths and were happy. Happy as schoolboys, larking about the corridors "in a way that I grieve," and that must have scandalized respectable stayers in that hotel. And now, for a stretch of days Japan showed itself delectable, for the weather thought fit to be perfect, and they saw all the fine inland scenery (and it was the finest of all they saw in Japan, excepting only Fujisan) just as well as it could be seen. There are three ways of getting to Chiusenji— on foot, in chair or kango, on horseback; for the road is too steep for rickshas. The Three decided on horses, and started a goodly cavalcade of five : their three noble selves, the guide, and the baggage pony. First they rode to the waterfall of Urami. It was a day of waterfalls, and the Major shot upon Matsuda the former witticism about wishing to see, just as a change, water that fell up, not down. "You may see that in heaven, sir; not here," said the guide. Under the Urami waterfall, between the water and the rock, you may scramble, if you are sufficiently energetic—the name Urami implies something of the kind. It lies off the road, and the track thereto is decent enough, but that therefrom is vile. To ride a Burmese pony along the knife-edges of paddy-field bunds "when the weather is most beautifully" wet, or through the paddy-fields themselves when the mud is so thick that you have to get off or get stuck altogether ("we used to call it patent log rolling," said the Major, "being dragged through hanging on by the pony's tail as the patent log is towed by the ship"); or to upset, pony and all, in the quicksands of a Burmese chaung—these are pleasures of a kind; but they pall before the pleasure of that ride from Urami to the road. The track is narrow and winding and steep, and the mud and the ruts would be incredible if they were not solid—or rather half solid half liquid—facts. But the Japanese pony, though no beauty to look at, is no fool, and those four ponies came through this slough without a mistake, stepping over each rut and into the mudholes between the ruts, surefooted and safe. Once back on the road, the going was good enough until they came to a place where the road was washed away altogether. Farther on the mountain-side looked as if a great part of it had been washed away too. Altogether there was rather too much washing. The ghat up to Chiusenji is a very picturesque one. Matsuda pointed out Hanya and Hoda waterfalls, but he reserved the best for the top—the Kengon Fall is really good. It is also a good example of Japanese

Chiusenji.

bluff, for they call it 750 feet (and a Japanese foot is fourteen inches), whereas it has been found by measurement to be only 350 (English) feet. Teahouse and tiffin were welcome in Chiusenji, and delicious the trout you see caught from the lake and cooked in a trice. It is a very curious little village, Chiusenji, all temples and tea-houses. The long street is full of pilgrims' houses, now empty and shut up; only in a few tea-houses, whose verandahs charmingly overhang the lake, are a few people to be found. But at the due season the whole place is crammed full of the pious pilgrim, so that no room may be had. For Nantaisan, that rises to 8,250 feet right over Chiusenji, and half a score of mountain-tops around, are to be visited by devout worshippers of the gods, to the profit of the priests and hotel-keepers. But tiffin over, on went the Three (and the guide) on the untiring tats, past more waterfalls—the Dragon's Head which are rapids rather than waterfalls, a turmoil of white water hurrying over black and broken rocks; and across the Senjogahara (moor of the battle-field), a swamp surrounded by mighty mountains. The Major was always quoting the guide-book, much to Matsuda's discomfort. "That book is old and not all true. The gentleman did not see himself, and what they told him he wrote." So when the Major and his book insisted that the place was Akamunagahara, or "the moor of the red swamp," Matsuda insisted that it was not, and named the hills around in a way that completely upset the Major's guide-book topography. Just before you get into Yumoto there is a very pretty waterfall—a rush of water down a long incline, a sheet of broken silver. They call it Yunotaki, "the hot waterfall," because the water is not hot. But if the water of this fall and of the lovely little Yumoto lake be not hot, that of the Yumoto sulphur springs is hot as Hades. The village consists only of the houses and baths, and lives on its springs and in the steam and smell of them. Of course the Three had to take a sulphur bath, and found accommodation to perform that feat *more Europeano* and not in public like the many Japs, men and women, whom they saw bathing. This public bathing is referred to by most bookwriters as terribly shocking to decency. Yet I do not remember to have read in any book diatribes on the immodesty of the men and women of India and Burma, who bathe just as publicly and innocently at the village well or the ghat on the river; and I do not understand, therefore, why holy hands of horror should be raised and the head of reprobation should be wagged at the Japanese for performing his ablutions promiscuously *coram publico*. The ride back to Yumoto found Alf and 'Arry rather sore. The paces of a Japanese tat are not easy, the saddles were old and misshapen; and though there may be nothing like leather, it is not pleasant to wear it off. 'Charlie, having appropriated the best saddle, would not admit any rubbing; and all were glad when their thirty miles' journey was over; thirty miles according to Japanese reckoning—two and a half miles to a "ri," but a "ri" is, like a kos

Nantaisan.

or a daing, by no means a constant quantity. Any way, not a bad day's work for the ponies, and a thoroughly enjoyable one for the men. Now Chiusenji is about 4,000 feet high, and Alf considered that at last he had got what he had come for—some real cold—and Charlie grumbled at the same; and they nearly asphyxiated themselves with a pan of charcoal under the dinner-table within closed walls (you can't say doors or windows, for there are none; you pull the sliding wall along its groove and it does just as well). Why, in a country where the cold is pretty severe in winter, don't they have decent fire-places in the rooms? The Major insisted on going to the top of Nantaisan—a good two hours' pull up 4,000 and odd feet. Tapioca absolutely refused; the Bank Manager allowed that he would on the whole prefer to see the Major do it to doing it himself. Matsuda said, "Yes, sir, if you want me, I must go, but I should like not to." He also said, "You should start at two, so as to see the sunrise from the top;" but the Major said he had seen the sun rise a good many times, and was likely to see it a good many more, and didn't yearn to see it here. So at the dark and chilly hour of four, up got the Major, leaving the other two Bounders snoring, and was led by a cooli-guide up Nantaisan. You pay the priest 25 cents. and he gives you a written receipt and two little cakes of rice and sugar. Now the road up Nantaisan is fashioned in this manner: take a steep hill-side rising in one continuous unbroken gradient, with never a slacking off or an easy; straight up this, with never a zig nor a zag, cut steps two feet high (or more at discretion), and face each step with a plain piece of jungle wood, round and rough; turn on a young typhoon with rain *ad libitum*, so as to wash out most of the earth from behind the wood, and knock as many as possible of the wooden pieces themselves out of position; over all add a plentiful dew to make everything nice and slippery; and there you are. The Major found it a pretty stiff pull and decidedly warm work even in the cool of the morning. But up and up through the twilight, now through forests of those "green-robed senators of mighty woods, tall oaks," and then through firs and conifers (" Not that I saw any coneys," the Major explained to his pals, describing his journey), past the three stations where a little hut and grateful water awaits the weary wayfarer, at the last of which, lo! a States man (which is being interpreted a man from the United States) descending, and enthusing ecstatically to the perspiring Major on the "glow and glory" of the sunrise which he had just seen. And so in two hours and ten minutes the summit, with ice thereon, and a bleak and cutting wind from the cruel north; but a bright clear sky above and a brilliant atmosphere and far-spreading landscape of hill and lake and river and fertile plain. There is Nikko with its groves and temples straight below you, with the river winding by it and on until a larger stream receives it, the Daiyagawa, and they flow united, by fertile fields away into that golden haze on the horizon where, beyond the peaks of Tsukuba San, lies the invisible ocean. You stand on the rim of an old old crater; the side farthest from you is all broken down and the hollow of the huge bowl is filled with forest, whose foliage is many-tinted "with autumn laying here and there a fiery finger on the leaves." One side of the crater-edge hides from you Yumoto and that moor of uncertain name that you crossed yesterday; but the blue lake of Chiusenji, and beside it a tiny lakelet hiding cosily amongst the embracing mountains, shine bright in the morning air. Beyond the lakes, among the hills that hide the gorges of Ashiwo, the mist and smoke of many charcoal-burning fires and of the busy copper-mines hang heavy, yet slowly drift away; and far away past these and many another tumbled range—Akangi San and the mountains of Koshiu—appears the perfect cone of Fujisan. All round you, close at hand they seem, are the volcanic verdure-clad peaks of Omanago and Komanago and Niho San and Taro San, and behind them the bare rocky tops of great Shirane San. Truly a prospect worthy of some labour to behold it. But the cooli, after he had satisfied the Major's questioning curiosity, preferred digging up the coppers and bronzes (sens and rins) scattered by the pious on the holy ground on the summit; for all pilgrims to this place or to any other holy place or temple throw there small coin, which the priests usually fail not to gather. But here were certainly many going to waste. By the time his cooli had collected two handfuls the Major concluded to quit ; and returned to find 'Arry and Alf going out on the lake. That afternoon their noble steeds bore them back to Nikko—except that the Major would walk much of the way and got the Bank Manager to walk with him ; and they arrived weary but well-pleased at the comfortable hostelry, and the nesans came around the Major and waited on him. "You see I speak the language; that is why they flock about me," he explained to the other two. But they mocked him and his language. It was here that the Three came upon another three of whom Alf and Charlie saw much in their after travels, that is to say the Nebraska Sportsman and the Merciful Broker, and one who, since he was the eldest and came from Philadelphia, may be called Old Phil. And they talked much of Yokohama and counted the days since they left there, and discoursed on the beauties of Japan.

The copper-mines of Ashiwo are a day's journey from Nikko. It is a long two hours up to the top of the ghat; along a road skilfully graded and zig-zagged, and good enough going for the tats. Most of the roads in Japan are well made ; there is not a place on the ordinary tourists' round that has not a fairly engineered road to it. There is no heavy traffic on them ; for carts of ordinary type are non-existent ; such fearful road-ruiners as the unregenerated cart of India, or still worse of Burma, are unknown ; and the roads have to bear nothing more destructive to them than coolis and pack ponies and rickshas and handbarrows, or, rarely, two-wheeled frames dragged by a bullock, or a pony, or a man. But occasionally the heavy rain plays havoc with them. The way up to the top of the ghat is pleasant, for the hill-sides are forest-clad, and the forests of Japan are not that excessive, impenetrable, overpowering forest of Java and the Straits, but good, clear, open woods of trees, and light, thin undergrowth; a happy medium between tropical too-muchness and the bareness of Chinese hills. And there is many a charming backward glimpse of Nikko and Toyama, and the plains beyond. A halt for tiffin at a rather mean little tea-house at the top (and how neatly the Japanese do up your tiffin for you: all ready carved is the succulent murgi, and light sweet roti, and other good things, and packed up in such tidy little white sweet boxes of wood), and then down into a very different country. Those copper-mines down there want fuel; and the forest is gone or going, leaving the hill-side bare and ugly, while the charcoal-burners' fires fill the air with smoke. The scenery is as ruined as that of many a place is in what was once lovely at home, and is now the Black Country. The people too are changed. No cheerful smiles and happy cries of "Ohayo" from the children in the road-side cottages ; no pleasant greeting from coolis passing on the road ; but a sullen silence, and grimy faces, and unfriendly looks. The Major waxed exceeding wroth with the drivers of those drays, taking fuel and stores to the mines or copper therefrom, for that they did not make way for him and his fellow-voyagers; "Lucky for them they are not in my country, but their own; else would I have belaboured them soundly."

"Yes, of course," said Tapioca; "the bloated official whacks whom he pleases, but if a poor planter touches a cooli——"

"Oh, shut up," said the Bank.

And they talked of other things and jogged along (the tats probably thought they were trotting, but the riders had different opinions on that head, and something else on a portion of their physical frames remote from the head) right away to the copper-mines. Here the Three went over the whole place, the which it booteth not to describe, for it is not in any way different from an English mining show, except that it is in Japan and run entirely by Japanese. Note, however, that the natural water-power available is being ably utilized and turned into electric light, to light all the workings which run miles into the mountain. There are over 20,000 people employed here one way and another; and there is a jail with an outdoor gang of the usual very mild and orderly Japanese ruffian. A small but comfortable, snug tea-house was full up when it had taken in our Three; and they watched others arrive and ask for room in vain. There was no rowdyism in the village, as certain travellers had led them to expect there might be in a mining village. Nor in this or in any other tea-house did they find sheet or quilt populous with lively and voracious reasons against sleep; Keating's Powder was not in the least in request. All next day's journey was down the gorge of the same stream from Ashiwo right on to Omama : a very pretty ride, without stupendous or magnificent scenery, but always pleasing and picturesque. Here is a road-side temple standing, as usual, in a grove of cryptomerias, and as ever, with a torii as gateway thereto. The torii is as indispensable as the pair of chinthes (lions) that guard the approach to a Burmese pagoda. Now we pass through villages all mulberry-trees and silkworms, with girls winding the silk from the cocoon in every house-front. In places the valley widens out in level hill-encircled plain ; elsewhere it narrows, leaving the stream scarce room to force itself through among rocks and boulders. One boulder there is that is fabled to have come from far-off Ise, though no fable seems required to account for its being where it is. There is a rice-pounder turned by a little stream falling into a wooden tray ; the tray being full, round it goes, revolving a bar which lifts and lets fall the pounder, while a second tray comes into position to receive the water. The people are agricultural and cheerful again. The Major recovered his spirits and walked along, setting the ponies a four-miles-an-hour pace which they could not keep up with ; and when he raised it to five, the little Japanese syces with much laughter found themselves also obliged to jog into a gentle trot. And yet as they neared Omama a ricksha man insulted the Major by shouting at him, " Sha, sha!" Omama is one long wide street.

Many of these Japanese townlets are nothing but a string of houses on either side of a wide, well-kept street, with no side streets, reaching along for a mile or two. And the width and the well-madeness and cleanness of the streets—with what admiring envy the Anglo-Indian eye beholds them! If only the mild Hindu would house himself as tidily, and keep his gam as nicely! Even the smallest villages in Japan that our travellers passed through, here and elsewhere, are clean and sweet-smelling; the houses, even where poor and mean, are not dirty; and their build is generally more picturesque than the mud-built flat-roofed ghar, or the wattle-and-daub hut. I think the paucity of cattle conduces greatly to this cleanness, together with the absence in Japanese cultivators of that prejudice against the use of night-soil as manure, which is so strong in India. You very rarely see cattle or ponies employed in cultivation, and but rarely in transport; no herds of "bails" driving out in the morning to eat the hillsides bare, and coming back in the evening to cover all the "basti" with dust and dirt. Man supplies all that is required; *manual* labour and *manure* are what the fields get here. And so, of course, each field is cut up into multitudinous little patches, and cultivated to the highest degree of which it is capable. I do not think the soil is generally of very high fertility. Every scrap of that rich manure is carefully collected and given to it, and the laborious individual toil on each little patch gives it the best possible chance; yet the crops are nothing remarkable. The Major had seen in the valley of the Irrawaddy and elsewhere many paddy-fields with heavier crops, and Tapioca thought these Japanese paddy plants nought beside those of the Straits. The cotton plant is small, the vegetables good. There is not so much irrigation nor so extensive terracing of the hill-sides as in Java; nor are the landscapes so near the perfection of scenic beauty as in that favoured isle. But the Three, as they rode and strode into Omama, felt well pleased with themselves and Japan, and filled themselves with beer. Very good it is, the beer they make in Japan, far better than the medicated Pilsener and lager with which the East is flooded now-a-days. The Ebisu brand is good, but Kirin is better. The Major drained a bottle of this, and subsided into pensiveness and bad puns. Matsuda made himself agreeable to the buxom daughter of mine host, whose kimono did, like words and nature, "half-conceal and half-reveal" (rather more than half the latter perhaps) what goes to make a well-shaped bust. "You're a scorcher," the Bank informed her; "Yu ra sa kaw cha," mimicked the fair one. The tea-house at Omama was about the least comfortable of all they had yet experienced. The Bank had found the lot of them rather trying; but here the rooms were small and back-yarded; the bath-room was a terrible hot corner close to the kitchen, and pretty nearly as public as a Japanese washing-room; and the attendants less attentive than elsewhere. However, it was the last night that the Three were together; for next day the rail (of course, being Japanese, the trains were running at every hour except those mentioned in the official time-tables) bore off the Bank to Tokio, while the other two, leaving the rail at Mayebashi, betook themselves to Ikao. Sad was the parting; no more would the Bank hear Tapioca sing his affecting song,—

> I can't forget my mother dear,
> I'll tell you why, becos
> She was so good and kind to me,
> She was, she was, she wos,—

with which he had so often beguiled the hours; no more would he revel in the Major's puns; for from Tokio he would go straight to Kioto, while the others went there through Ise ("we can Ise-ly manage it," said the Major). One horse-tram runs from Mayebashi to the Tonegawa, which river has to be ferried across, and then rickshas carry you up to Ikao. Another village of hot mineral springs; conduits carry the steaming element all through the houses and streets. It is very picturesque, the main street of Ikao; so steep that the ground-floor of one quaint house is level with the first-floor of the next; the street itself is staircased with stone, the steam rising thickly from the channel in the midst thereof. Crowds of those pleasant Japanese gather in balconies and at shop-doors to gaze in a friendly way at you as you loaf along from shop to shop. And the view from the hotel verandah: what a splendid expanse of hill and valley and far-off mountain! The one thing wanting in it is a touch of water, some rivulet or lakelet or stream; but there is none visible. Alf and Charlie, as they sat and smoked in the delicious atmosphere, thought it about the best Japanese hotel they had come to; and when drink was wanted, what was easier than to comply with the inscription on the electric bell knobs:—"When business request push this point once." Late that night Old Phil and his friends also arrived; and next morning, in lovely weather, all five set off across the hills to Haruna: a splendid walk, with varied conversation — the Englishman with phrases and pronunciations not understood of the 'Mercans, and occasional Hobson-Jobsons from the India and Straits men, and the Eastern and the Western States men each with locutions peculiar to his own country not to be comprehended by others. And the Nebraska Sportsman sang of how he gathered shells; and the Major told tiger stories, so that even Matsuda related his experiences of tiger-shooting (it appeared he had once been with a man in French Cochin China, and gone out with him under protest and in a great funk to kill a tiger); and the Merciful Broker studied Japanese, and tried to teach English to the Japanese boy that he had picked up, and is going to take with him to England. So they went past the Haruna Fuji, with a view of the grand old real Fuji in the distance and the Haruna Lake, a lovely mountain tarn, and down the steep and rocky gorge, full of forest, to the Temple of

Haruna. Here too may be seen pilgrims. See those two, each wearing, slung round his neck so as to be placed in the middle of his breast, a full-coloured mask, with most elongated proboscis like a tapir's, of the "tengui" or mountain sprite, at whose shrine they have been to worship. These shall they keep with them for a season, and then return to the shrine with other masks like unto them.

It has been remarked that the old original Buddhists in India loved to locate their temples and monasteries in picturesque spots, lovely in themselves, but near some great route, as at Ellora, Ajunta, and Karli. So too the modern Buddhist in Japan has an eye to natural beauty of scenery in selecting a site for his god. The wild character of the narrow Haruna gorge, with its broken rocks forming here a natural bridge, there a pinnacle of many angles, its pretty woods, and its mighty cryptomerias enshrining and solemnizing the temple, form a first-rate example of this principle. So it is at Miyongi San to which the two Bounders and Old Phil betook themselves next day, while the Nebraska Sportsman, and the Merciful Broker and the Boy went off along the Nagasendo, there to meet with much rain and hardgoing and torrents, with their boat upsetting therein, until they should arrive at Kioto. So they said *au revoir* to one another at Idzuka; and if ever you should go to that place, do not drink of the beer sold there called stota (a colourable imitation of "stock" or "stout"):

it is what the schoolboy said "the delights of our ancestors were — unmitigated filth."* The Japanese are a good deal like the Burmese, happy, cheery, pleasant, but happy-go-lucky, unsteady, wanting in balance, liable to lose their heads. One man here at Idzuka lost his, and his life, poor fellow. He was trespassing on the bridge as our travellers' train ran on to it ; he could easily have saved himself by jumping into one of the little refuges on the piers of the bridge; but no, he must needs throw himself over on to the stones of the dry river-bed below — and throw so badly the twenty or twenty-five feet of drop as to break his head. So he died. But our sportsmen reached Isobe, and disembarked from the train, and while waiting for rickshas experienced for the second time that day a most poisonous drink. The stota was bad ; but here was worse. At all tea-houses they give you cuplets of tea, not particularly pleasant to an unaccustomed palate, but capable of winning your approval after much practice : Old Phil must have drunk oceans of it in the course of his Japanese tour, besides eating mountains of wafers and cake-lets of rice and sugar, such as they often give you with your tea. But here at Isobe a charming little maid from school proffered a small glass of "sakura no yu," pretty to look at, but abominable to taste. Fancy taking cherry-blossoms, preserving them in salt, and then making with them and hot water a

* Traditional construing of "Delicta majorum immeritus lues."

decoction to give to a thirsty Christian to drink. The Christians there present tasted and spat, and would have no more of it.

The paternal Japanese Government looks after cholera epidemics as carefully as it does after other things. That fell disease was in a village on the usual route to Miyongi, and no one who lived in or entered into that village might come out of it without purification with carbolic and the like. So the Three made to Miyongi by another road, and saw the preventive stations on the way to that cholera village, with their watchmen and their bottles ready to waylay the suspected wayfarer. Miyongi San is not a long ricksha ride. Here, by the way, it may be remarked that it is certainly a curious thing that the Japanese, who seem to copy readily almost everything European, do not go in for tongas or garis to get about in. Their roads are good enough, both on the flat and up hill; the former good enough for any kind of vehicle, and the latter for tongas, except that all would want widening somewhat; yet still they stick to the comparatively slow and unaccommodating ricksha. It is true there don't seem to be many ponies in the country; but a demand would soon bring out the supply. It is true also that of all possible ricksha men the Jap is the best; fast, willing, cheery, untiring. And a ricksha is by no means uncomfortable even for a long journey. The Major rejoiced in them, and even Tapioca, though he growled at first, grew to like them. It is not, they say, a Japanese vehicle by origin, but the invention of an American; the very name is only half Japanese, the other half being Chinese.

From the tea-house at Miyongi the view is pastoral and pleasing; homely rather than magnificent. But behind the village towers a mighty mass of rock covered with evergreen forest, and away behind this, some couple of hours' walk distant, is a huge jumble of broken hill and pinnacle and arch, what the guide-book calls "nature in chaotic confusion." After a long hour's walk up hill and down again and up a long steep climb on a decidedly warm morning, Old Phil said he had had enough chaos (pronouncing the ch as in church) and would take the rest next time. He seated himself to admire the prospect—one worthy of all admiration—while Charlie and Alf went on to see the First Natural Gateway and the Beard-scraping Rock and the rest. Of course there is a priest's house below the rock and a god on the top thereof; the beard-scraping comes in but rarely, for few Japs have any beard at all, and on those that have one it is not a thing worth talking about. It is a fanciful name enough, for there is, as a matter of fact, quite room enough to scramble up between the two rocks without rubbing your chin on either of them; it is your shins you have to look out for. At the First Gateway—a great natural arch of rock—behold Old Phil strolling on and defying them to guess its height correctly. But he was far farthest out himself, putting it at 200 feet, while it is in fact not more than seventy or seventy-five. And so back to the only evil-smelling tea-house that they had the misfortune to meet in Japan, where the Major disported hinself with trying to play the guitar on a samisen and learning from the nesan the correct way to sit down respectfully in Japan. Get down on your knees, turn your heels well out, your toes well in, and sit right back into the cup formed by your two feet so placed; lay your hands, palms downwards, just in front of your knees, bend your head till your forehead touches your hands, and there you are. Tapioca went about crowing like a cock; it is supposed that he intended to convey to the nesan that he wished for some chicken to eat. And then ricksha and rail back to Tokio.

CHAPTER V.

ISE.

NANGOYA is some twelve hours by rail from Yokohama and the route is full of beautiful scenery, when you can see it; but when it is all seen awry through driving rain and heavy hanging clouds, the enjoyment of it is reduced to a vanishing point. English as the Japanese railways are in many respects, with their name-boards and notice-boards and tickets all printed and painted in that language, they have not yet achieved the proud product of civilization known as a railway refreshment bar. Consequently you take your tiffin with you and eat it in the train. When the carriage is full of a miscellaneous assortment of people this is attended with some difficulty, as Tapioca found when his bird fell into his whisky and water, and tobacco-ash got mixed with the salt. The Major looked forward with some misgiving to a night at Nangoya; he had read of the tea-house there as typical of the extreme noise and discomfort of a Japanese guest-house, and that in the book of a traveller whose journey must have been no farther back than 1886 or 1887. Incessant clatter of arrivals, of bathers, of moving those sliding walls; the watchman tootling his trumpet in your room to show he's all there—and so and so on. Evidently things have very much changed since then. It is not a tea-house at all; it is the "Hotel du Progres"—electric-lighted, furnished with beds and tables and chairs, rooms for Europeans remote from the Japanese side, decent food and liquor, quiet, comfortable, and not yet (thank goodness) improved to the extent of banishing the girls from waiting on you. "Kirei no musume," too, one of them is, as the Major murmured softly. But we must be off early in the morning, and ricksha to Miya and there take steamer to cross over into Ise. A beautiful morning; the Two in good spirits and disposed to make light of the scanty accommodation on the little cockle-shell of a boat. But lo! at the first port of call (Yokkaichi) a clouding sky and a freshening breeze; and an hour or two after, a mighty wind and thick rain—dirty weather that would be too much for a much bigger and better found boat than this. Nothing for it but to put back and anchor under a lee shore. Tapioca toyed with his tiffin and passed; the Major ate his and made a mighty and successful struggle to keep it; Matsuda collapsed utterly and would not be comforted. And into the little den of a saloon, berthless, lavatoriless, bathless, behold they thrust a small crowd of gentle Japs who were all most obtrusively sick. Verily a cheery and blissful way of spending an afternoon on a pleasure tour. In the middle of the night—for they went to sleep at dinner-time, there being no dinner—the Major woke famishing, and, foraging round, found and devoured the tiffin that should have been Matsuda's; so that when that disabled philosopher arose in the morning in the calm weather and sought for some breakfast—he found none. The morning was clear and fine, and the travellers landed without further adventure at Kamiyashiro; but the misery of that night in the Bay of Owari will remain a mournful memory in their minds for many a year. The ricksha run from the port to Furu-ichi is soon done, and there they find the largest, best built and least Europeanized of tea-houses that they had seen. Only here did they observe the nesan sit respectfully down to receive orders as is in accordance with Japanese propriety; and here were no electric lights, and very little furniture, but many splendid costly silken quilts for your bed. Charming waitresses too. What would the Mamlatdar or old Daji Patil have thought, or that old scoundrel the Wun, had they seen the Sarkar, the Asoya Min, kneeling—clad in little but a consciousness of his own virtue—to have his hair combed by a laughing Japanese tea-house girl? Furu-ichi is in a way the most revered spot in Japan. For here the gods descended to earth and gave to the Land of the Rising Sun its birth as a kingdom and a nation, and therewith its first Mikado. The scenery is pleasing in a quiet way: nothing largely picturesque, nothing grandiose; homely, happy, serene. The tomb of the First Mikado is here, and shrines and temples stand about it, all, as ever, made solemn and holy with groves of sad-hued stately cryptomerias. And what a contrast between the

Shoguns' tombs and temples and these of the Mikado. Those costly, elaborate, crowded with excess of ornamentation exquisite in itself, but overpowering, sickening, in its riotous superabundance; these plain, simple, absolutely undecorated save for gilt or brass chrysanthemum at the end of the great logs that lie crosswise on the top of the roof. The immemorial custom of the place renders expensive work and ornament impossible, for it is a rule, unalterable as the laws of the Medes and Persians, to pull down everything each twenty-fifth year and rebuild it with the beautiful white wood of the Japanese cypress (*hinoki*) in exactly the same form as it was before. The year of grace 1890 happened to be the twenty-fifth year; and the Two, when they had crossed the bridge over which no wheeled vehicle but the Mikado's may go, and passed under the torii, where even he must alight and walk, found everything fresh from the carpenters' hands. The building and the palisades are strong and substantial, of plain smooth wood; the roofs are straight, not curved and turned up at the ends as in the Sinico-Japanese buildings at Nikko and elsewhere; and at right angles to the ridge of the roof are laid across big logs projecting far over the roof on either side—with what object it is impossible to say, unless it be to keep the roof on. (All over the country, especially in the mountain gorges and passes, you see the frail roofs of the châlets and cottages loaded with stones, lest a typhoon bear them bodily away.)

Ise.

For a payment you may have performed for you the religious service known as kangura. The form of religion here is pure Shinto, and when you have paid your dollars, you are admitted into a matted room empty of all images and very sparingly adorned. Fine chiks with red and purple tassels to the cords of them hang round the walls; at the farthest end is an altar—a perfectly plain wooden table, with nothing on it. (One globe-trotter describes in his book a large and appreciative audience gathering to share in the show provided by his dollars. There is nothing of the kind. The curtain—a nearly plain blue cloth—which you raised on entering, is let down behind you, and none but those in your party enter with you.) Enter first a simply dressed attendant, who, after reverence to the altar, waves over you green branches and twigs, brushing away, it may be hoped, all worldly wickedness from you. Then comes in the band—five men who take their seats, three on one side, and two on the other, near the altar, but below it. Then four young girls in strange attire: long cream-coloured jacket, with red and purple tassels hanging thereon as on the chik cords, voluminous scarlet trousers, dragging a foot or more behind them, so that it is a marvel how they walk without tripping, and hair done in a fashion of their own, adorned with multi-coloured gew-gaws of sorts. These sit two on either side below the musicians. Enter two more girls in like attire, bearing plain wooden trays with offerings; these they present kneeling to the two girls on the right (or it may be left) side, who bear them with many reverences to the altar, and lay the offerings thereon. The trays are of the same white sweet wood as the temples and tombs, and are shaped something like a caricature of the silk hat of civilization. The operation is repeated, the girls on each side bearing alternately the gifts to the altar, until all are laid on it. Then the two who brought in the offerings dance in front of the altar between the musicians a strange figure, very curious and picturesque in the half light and the old-world and impossible costumes, the musicians all the while playing melancholy but not wholly unmusical and tuneless strains on their instruments, and one or two of them singing in somewhat nasal and ear-piercing accents. The dance over, the two girls kneel below the other two girls on one side, and the priest who shall read prayers comes in, and (after reverence, of course,) kneels where the girls have just been dancing. He wears quiet-coloured robes, and the head-dress of ancient Japan. After prostration and silence, he unfolds a large scroll, and with an affected but sonorous twang gives forth words which (Matsuda says) imply that strangers have come from a far country, and paid their offerings to the god, and that the priest humbly prays his godship to do well for them in the future. Then exit the priest; the offerings—eatables of sorts and *sake*—are removed with the same ceremonial as was used in placing them, and given to the stranger whose coin paid for them; out go girls and orchestra, and the service is over. Before the show began, Matsuda begged his two charges not to laugh at it; but they felt no inclination to: there was nothing ridiculous in it; it was strange, interesting, not unimpressive. A dance of a far different nature awaited them in the evening. Tapioca was not inclined to go to it; after rickshaing over muddy roads and along the bunds and kazins of paddy-fields all the afternoon to Asamayama (not the mighty mountain of fire beyond Ikao, but a bit of a hill near the sea), and Futamingaura with its sacred but not specially noteworthy rocks and rocky islets, and getting not a little damp in the process, for the afternoon turned to rain, he did not feel inclined to leave comfortable quarters to march through mud and slush to see any kind of an Eastern dance. "They are all rot," he said; "they are not dances, only attitudinizing, and mortal slow at that; when you've seen one, you've seen all, and I saw quite enough at Nagasaki." But Matsuda kept urging that this dance was danced only in Ise, and no gentleman should visit Ise and not see it— else why come to Ise? and it was very, very fine. The Major, too, said that he was going to see all there was to be seen, and forth he dragged the unwilling one to a house not far off. After a bit of a wait, they are ushered into an oblong room, and take their seats (or their lying-downs, for there are no seats) in the centre of one long side. And the orchestra having come in and taken its seat in the middle of the room, behold on the opposite side and the two short sides the floor rises and forms a stage, and the lamps float up behind the red hangings, and a railing of carved wood rises round the stage, and more lamps come out from the sides. Alf began to cheer up; all this stage management must mean something good. Then the dancing girls appear—a score or two dozen of them, coming half from either corner right and left of the spectators, and walking along the stage that filled the three sides of the room until they filled it. There, standing each in her place, each performed a kind of flip-flap with her hands, and a mild little kick with one foot. "You must note them now," said Matsuda; "you will not see them again." The Two noted that they were all precious ugly, but the costumes were unusual and effective. After about five minutes they departed, each half set by the door opposite to that by which they had entered; and "that is all," said the guide. Alf most magnanimously refrained from the "I told you so" style of argument, and Charlie went silently and savagely to bed. A dance? Bosh. It is, let me whisper in a male ear, merely a method of showing off the inmates of the house a little more effectively than the usual style of sitting in rows behind the bars of the houses in the Yoshiwara.

It was fortunate that Charlie took kindly, and Alf was reconciled, to ricksha-riding, for they had a dose

Ise.

of it next day. "There is a train at Tsunge at 5.15 P.M. by which Kioto is reached at 8 ; shall I telegraph for dinner ?" asked Matsuda ; and he did, and the 21 ris (supposed to be 52½ miles) had to be ricksha'd somehow by 5 P.M. A perfect day luckily ; not too bright, but clear ; and a charming rural district to go through, fertile, prosperous, populous, and pretty. Through Matsuzaka (6 ri) to Tsu (5 ri more), a big town, where halt for tiffin and change of ricksha men (the leader has to be changed more frequently than the wheeler when you are going tandem fashion), and Mukumoto (4 ri on), where halt for a rest: 15 ri in six hours ; 4 hours more to do the last 6 ri—surely ample time. But the country changes. No longer roads level and good-going, with villages and hamlets all along them ; the children toddling merrily from or to school ; here a gentle sportsman of Japan bicycling along, there another with a marvellous fowling-piece of remote antiquity going out for to shoot; again, a long string of wrestlers marching to the next place where they will give an exhibition of their art. To the next stage, Seki (2 ri), the road is a good deal up and down hill, and rather hard going, and beyond Seki it is a regular ghat road, one a good deal knocked out of shape too by the railway that is being made through the hills on from Tsunge to Yokkaichi, where the station is already built. A good bit of engineering is required, some longish tunnelling and big bridging. Half way between Kitazaiki (2 ri), the last stage, and Tsunge, the top of the ghat is reached, and then what a splendid down-hill run with home in sight! Down we rattle and up to Tsunge station at 4.45—half-an-hour before the train starts. Well done; this is really good. Imagine the dismay when it appeared that there was no 5.15 train at all, and none till 7.30; imagine, if you can, the choice blessings that Alf and Charlie showered on Japanese railway bandobast, and the miserable state to which they reduce Matsuda. All that excellent going wasted because the railway department would not publish correct time-tables; and no dinner to be had but the remains of the tiffin. Crossing a river in the morning, the bridge over which had been (as usual) washed away, Matsuda had had a bad time, for Alf wanted to know how it was that bridges and railways so often got washed away in Japan. Matsuda said no bridge could be built to stand the current of this river in flood. " Of course not, if it's built on a wrong principle as this is," said Alf. Matsuda made out that the principle was all right, but the material, namely wood, not strong enough. "Then make one of iron, on a right principle;" but no, it is cheaper to make a cheap one of wood, which is sure to be washed away periodically, and to rebuild it of wood when required, than to make a costly fabric which the floods are equally sure to carry away. " But make it so that the floods can't breach it." " It can't be done," said Matsuda. " Of course not by Japanese; but get the English on it." "No man can do it," said the patriotic guide. In that argument he had at least some show to make ; but in this about the railway times he was defenceless, and had to surrender his country at discretion to the maledictions of the foreigners. But all evils end sooner or later ; and weary and sad, our travellers reached the Yaami Hotel after midnight, too sleepy for supper or for anything but bed.

CHAPTER VI.

KIOTO—THEATRES—END OF FARTHEST EAST.

KIOTO is as pleasant a place to stay in as there is in Japan. The Yaami Hotel stands on a rising ground overlooking the city, and it is a pretty outlook across the town to the hills beyond. They do you well enough in the Yaami. Just below it is a little temple whence the girls look up laughingly at you as they walk round and round it, dropping at each circuit something into the box by the door. Kioto is *par excellence* the place of the curio-monger, the maker of lacquer, of cloisonné, of porcelain. Here may be bought silks old and new and embroideries, and cheap things and dear; the long laborious process of lacquering and cloisonné work and vase-making may be watched and seen in their various stages, and much amusement and interest may be drawn therefrom. Here, too, is bronze work, some good, some indifferent. The ways of curio-buyers are various and their tastes diverse. Old Phil was always fetched by bright colours—the brighter the better, and the more of them with glaring juxta-positions of the very brightest, the more enamoured he became of the piece. Alf liked many and small things of modest price, while Charlie must needs prefer a few things of high price. The Merciful Broker was a perfect godsend to the seller; he seemed greatly to enjoy paying all that was asked for an article, or for choice even a little more, and never bothered about bargaining or beating him down. There is a lot of very poor work done now-a-days, and there is also still a lot of very good work, so that you have to know what you are about if you would avoid being let in. It is doubtful whether you had not better let it alone and buy at Liberty's in London; there you will be certain of buying what you want and getting your money's worth. For all that there is a certain fascination in buying curios yourself on the spot, so as to be able to say hereafter, "Oh yes, I picked up that little thing at Ikeda's in Kioto;" and the Major was unable to resist it, and got rather more than he wanted. The porcelain is, much of it, made from clay brought from Satsuma, in the southern island; there are various pieces of old Satsuma ware to be seen in the shops. But it takes a connoisseur to know all about these things, and none of the five who met in Kioto pretended to be a chinamaniac, or a specially cultured and æsthetic person. What is the good, anyhow, of being an expert and buying things that are understood and appreciated only by experts? The persons who really know all about it are very few; the great mass of your friends and relations will not know a decent copy from a rare original; so why pay a fancy price for the real thing, when you can get for an "ornery" sort of price what will please yourself and them just as much to look at? So let us seek out what pleases our eyes, and let us assure ourselves as best we may that it is good quality of its kind, and buy it and be therewith content. Do you like these cups and small bowls—said to be Satsuma—each with innumerable (the vendor says 3,000) butterflies painted on its surface—each minute insect painted fully, carefully, correctly? No, I don't. It is wonderful, laborious, most skilful, but I prefer something of which I can appreciate the beauty without the aid of magnifying-glass and miscroscope. Try, then, these tea sets, coffee sets, napkin rings, of Western shape. Thanks; but I prefer something distinctively Japanese in style as well as in material and make. Here are damoscene plates and salvers —metal inlaid on metal, such as Indian art-workers also turn out; but of finer thread, finer pattern, finer finish. (And mind not to pay double the price for them as Alf and Charlie did, while Old Phil got them at somewhere near the real cost.) For cloisonné work you must pay for finish. You may get it at any price; but place a cheap bit beside a carefully selected expensive piece, and note the difference. So too with lacquer; it is not all lacquer that will lie at the bottom of the sea for eighteen months and come up uninjured as did certain pieces in the Uyeno Museum, or that will last for centuries unimpaired as in the temples and shrines of Nikko. Swords may be bought cheap and in any quantity, for now that the old Two-sworded Class (Samurai) is not allowed to wear a sword, all the brands and dirks in the country are useless and find their way to the shops. Yet even now for a blade by Muramasa or other famous maker a goodly store of dollars must be laid down.

But there are other things to see and to do in Kioto besides inspect curios, modern and antique. First there is a big bell—not so big as the broken-down old monster near the ruined, weed-grown pagoda at Mingun, but having the advantage of being duly slung and sound and full-sounding, with its temple near it, extensive, ample, holy. The Chion Temple is many-roomed, and the sliding walls are much painted with valuable works of famous artists. But at Hongwanji there are rooms and paintings even more elaborate and renowned. This temple was once a castle miles away from Kioto, but was removed bodily and rebuilt in its present site and dedicated to religious use long ago. In the largest hall—looking low from its extreme length and width, and filled with designs of distinctly Chinese type—Matsuda states that the young Princes of Wales stayed when in Kioto; though it is not easy to guess why any one should wish to live in a place so ill-lighted, so gloomy in its seclusion and low-roofed amplitude. Here is a garden—the usual cramped little space, with corkscrew paths amidst contorted trees, and bamboo bridges meandering erratically across stagnant and unwholesome-looking ponds. In front of the main building is a very fine old "Icho" tree, fabled to spout forth water and extinguish any fire that should dare to lay flame on the temple. The other Hongwanji is rebuilding—a mighty big temple it will be too, costing goodness knows how many millions of yen. And in a corner you find a huge pile of ropes of human hair offered by the devout as their contribution to aid the building; and a little printed placard (in English) informs you all about the number and length and weight of these curious coils. I forget what was the amount of the weight of these "awful tresses that still keep the savour and shade" of their human origin, but it was something very large. English greets you again as you enter the Temple of the Thousand (or is it 1,001 ?) Kwannon, and begs you from a wooden board over the door " Don't give a step with your shoes." But here the great shoe question is got over by dragging linen bags over your boots. (Elsewhere in Japanese house and tea-house and temple, there is nothing for it but to unboot; and a very cleanly and commendable custom it seems to me to be.) There is no beauty in the 1,000 Kwannon—long rows of gilt wooden figures, upright, each with some slight difference from the others, but all alike to a mere general glance; many-handed, haloed, impossible; 500 on either side of a group of the monstrous frowning gods familiar to us in China, hideous, vengeful, grotesque. And many more temples are there if you care to see them, and are not wearied to death of pilgrimage to sacred shrines. One really begins to doubt whether religion was devised for any other purpose than to provide at vast cost endless sights

Kioto.

for the sight-seer. The Daibutsu is coarse, common, and ought to be burnt, as it has been more than once.

Notwithstanding the English that greets you on temples and in shop signs (such as Glog and Soap-Seller; Biscuits, Bread and Spongy Cakes,—unconscious veracity in that adjective), Kioto is essentially Japanese. The whole aspect of the place is un-Europeanized, clean, quaint, and therefore pleasing. And besides this and its art wares, it has dancing and singing girls, better, it boasts, than all other in the Mikado's dominions. The Major rather hankered after seeing them; but Tapioca, after his experience of the Ise ones utterly refused; and the Major was too crushed by his defeat on that occasion to insist on this. But other amusements there are—streetsful of them: Aunt Sally sort of arrangements, three shies a penny (5 for 2 sen, I think it is); horse-riding, hire a horse and ride him at a gentle jog round a little railed-in space, at so many sen a round; the sight of this amused Tapioca greatly; then fencing shows, reciters, wild beasts, shows of beasts supposed to be curious, but extremely tame; catchpenny menageries; and last, but not least, theatres. In the men's theatre—that is the one in which the parts are taken all by men—the play was a farcical comedy, and the dialect was (so Matsuda declared) so local, so bucolic, that not even he could make out what it was all about. In the women's theatre (all parts played by women: no men admitted on any pretext), the play was a romantic drama, and Matsuda proved a capable interpreter. The acting was very far from bad, the bodily action small, and somewhat conventional; but the facial expression varied, pointed, appropriate, and not more exaggerated than stage requirements called for. The plot was simple enough. An Old Lady, widow of a Daimio, has a son—one-eyed and mis-shaped, but a man of wealth and influence. A neighbouring Daimio desires to get him into his power, and annex his feudal domain. Enter to Old Lady a retainer of neighbouring Daimio bearing gifts of food, begging their acceptance. Old Lady thinks she'd rather not; retainer presses; long and animated discussion; Old Lady justly suspecting poison in the food (Timeo Danoas is an old tale of world-wide truth), kicks the gifts ignominiously over. Exit incensed retainer. Enter (after interval) neighbouring Daimio, bringing other gifts; at first all politeness, then arguments, threats, brandishing of swords; Old Lady immovable. End of act. Next act: Old Lady has been carried off to neighbouring Daimio's house; One-eyed Son returns from journey, arrives seeking for her, summoned by letter sent to him by a person in the house; retainers forbid him entrance, put him off; plot to shoot him; man hides behind tree; One-Eyed Son smells rat, produces box which he breaks open with sword, pistol within goes off, and shoots man in tree; alarms, excursions; explanations by sender of letter; duel between One-eyed Son and another; Old Lady, rushing out to stop the

fray, receives sword points in breast; death of Old
Lady; finale. The scenery was simple enough;
but the girls were well made up; and the scene-
shifting system is curious, the stage revolving,
until the scene set behind comes round to the front.
So is the long raised way up to the stage, by which
some characters (those coming from a journey or
from a distance) enter at the back of the pit, and
make their way right through the audience to the
stage, acting as they go. Extremely conventional,
some of the stage business. The superbly attired
Daimio and Lady must have attendants to arrange
their dresses; and these appear in common every-
day cooli-dress and shrink about the stage—invisible in imagination, but only too visible in reality
—or bring in samisen or other property required in
the piece. When the One-eyed Son shot the man
behind the tree, there was a very distinct interval
between the blow which fired his shot and the report thereof; and when the report did come it
came from *behind the tree*. And so when the man
fell dead, in came a cooli with a bit of red cloth,
which he extended while the defunct got up and
walked away under its cover. On the whole, it
was decidedly interesting; the dresses handsome,
and in complete accordance with the fashion of old
Japan; and the whole performance far in advance
of anything theatrical to be seen in India or Burma,
I mean of the indigenous theatre; the English
theatre has, of course, been copied in India, so that
you may see a Bengali pantomime in Calcutta,

or the *Comedy of Errors* in Marathi at Poona. Acting there is in the Burmese Zatpwe, good acting too, in its way, clever and racy of the soil; but the accessories and style are barbarous as compared with Japan: satyric dances to the drama of Sophocles. The Major being fond of things theatrical, went to see a performance of the forty-seven Ronins at a theatre in Yokohama. The general story of these Ronins is well enough known to any one who has read Mitford's *Tales of Old Japan;* and any one caring about things Japanese who has not read that excellent book, had better read it soon. But the play introduced many incidents not detailed in the story; and here as in Kioto the acting had very considerable merit, and the stage business was as conventional as could be. One Ronin who has intended to take part in the killing of the enemy is too late, and, as in honour bound, kills himself, and commits hara kiri on the stage; but there is no attempt to show any blood-letting, and his dying is not quite so elaborate as Irving's. The fighting is even more stagey than in a Shakespearian play, and the head of the foe, when it is cut off (behind the scenes) and exposed in front, is the woodenest head you ever saw. So too you cannot imagine more palpable cloth than the pond into which one combatant knocks another, or a more obvious lift than the one by which the upset one—dry as an Indian April day—returns to the upper air and combat of the stage. A good deal of killing goes on in the course of the piece; and the musicians, at the side, not in front of the stage, sing their comments and advice Greek-choruswise during the progress of the action. The music, though not charming to English ears, is at least not ear-splitting, outrageous ; rather shrill and apt to the minor key.

There are many charming excursions to be made from Kioto : to Nara, an old capital, to Osaka, to Lake Biwa, to the Katsura rapids. For the latter you ricksha out across the thickly cultivated plain (what Matsuda says is indigo is certainly a very different plant from the Indian ; but indigo there certainly is, else where are all these innumerable blue kimonos and jackets and breeches dyed ?) until you come to the range of hills which seem to enclose Kioto round on every side ; and then the way lies up a little hill-pass, with the usual excellent road. At a tea-house on the way, notice a pine dwarfed and trained out laterally till its branches extend for yards on either side the trunk, forming a hedge ; and observe the bamboo growing in plantations in single stems, not in clumps as you are used to seeing them. The Japanese is as fond as the Burman of young bamboo shoots as food. Arrived at the head of the rapids, a capacious boat of the lightest imaginable draught receives travellers and 'shas and coolis and all, and the current carries you rapidly along. If you haven't done much of that sort of thing before, it is pleasantly exciting ; for when the stretch of rapid is steep and long continued, and a trifle mixed as to which is practicable water and which rock, your boat gets an impetus that whirls it along, bumping on the waves so that the thin bottom bulges and bends with the beating of them, at such a pace that you admire hugely the skill with which the four boatmen keep it off the abrupt or rounded boulders safe into the comparatively placid pool that lies between each rapid. There is one bit of very picturesque scenery, where a small stream forces its way through a wall of rock into the main stream; and as you come quietly down the last stretch into Arashi, the wooded hill-sides are lovely with the many-changing tints of autumn. Here come in May time crowds of Japanese to picnic opposite the cherry-trees, and feast their eyes on the blossoms hereof—the fruit they do not grow; and here the globe-trotter feeds more materially on delicious fish from the stream, and is waited on by girls that in the national style squat humbly on the floor, watching you while you feed, until, in despair of getting them to laugh or lark, you ungallantly ask them to go.

The Major and his friend rejoiced at meeting in Kioto again the Nebraska Sportsman and his party, not forgetting Kinzu the boy; and heard all about their adventures on the Nagasendo; and then decided to return by easy stages by rail to Yokohama. This gave them a day at Nangoya and time to examine its castle—a very large one of the old Japanese feudal times, strong withal, and spacious. Here is quartered a large garrison, and you see many a French-uniformed little Jap with his rifle and bayonet doing sentry-go. I wonder what sort of stuff they would make in action with European troops. The Major was inclined to think they would make but a poor show. The Jap is too like the Burman; individually capable of great personal bravery, facing death courageously; and collectively utterly incapable of sustaining organized formation under the tension of a protracted struggle or the discouragement of a first reverse. The cavalry are, beyond question, useless except as ornament, and not much at that. The Jap, in this respect unlike the Burman, can't ride worth a dam (the equivalent, I believe, of one-tenth of a farthing), and the 3,000 or so of cavalry that the army contains would be wiped out in no time by a troop or two of—say the H.C.C. A parade did not come off at any time that our travellers could arrange to see it; but if they had a fair sample of the drill and set-up of the men in the example they saw one day in Tokio, why, then the infantry are worth no more than the cavalry. Seven men with bugles came along—six buglers and a bugle-major, it would appear; they loafed along two and two, slouchingly, all out of step, uniforms not only shabby but ill put on—no smartness anywhere about them; and all the while they performed a sort of independent firing on their bugles, each man giving in his own time his own version of what calls he pleased; melancholy and grotesque cacophonies, caricatures of the stirring notes of reveille and last post and the rest of them. "Thus with a grating and uncertain sound" did "they bleat and bleat and bleat." The glory of the castle of Nangoya is the pair of golden dolphins—or fish of some hitherto undiscovered species—that adorn the topmost roof-ridge; they are of great size, but at that height look small, and are said to be worth 180,000 yen. Nangoya boasts too of its art-ware—cheap porcelains and lacquered cloisonnés. And if you should ever travel that way by rail, you will find, after passing glimpses of Lake Biwa, and before you reach Nangoya, a bit of mountain scenery which in the glorious sunlight of an autumn afternoon (the afternoon light is the best for all landscapes) will give a feast for your eyes that you ought not to miss. So, too, between Nangoya and Shidzuoka there are some pleasing views; while from Shidzuoka almost to Kodzu you have—if only it be fine weather—ever-changing and charming prospects of magnificent old Fuji. And so the Two returned to Yokohama and spent there many days idling and buying photos, and growling horribly (at least as far as concerns the Major) at the bitter biting north-east winds that swept in from the sea; making excursions now to Enoshima, now around the environs (there are many tea-houses with manners adapted, as they suppose, to please the foreigner), again to Tokio to see the jail. Matsuda was generally better dressed than the Major, who rather affected shikar cloth and puttis, except in towns, and then it was white drill or brown holland or flannels and jharan; but on the visit to the jail he surpassed himself, and was certainly the biggest swell of the party. I must say I do not know where else three strangers could go up to a jail and say, "We are So-and-so, and wish to see the jail," and would thereupon be at once admitted and shown all over it by an extremely polite, intelligent, and information-giving official. Yet this can you do in Tokio. Matsuda gave the Major several steps in promotion so as to rank him with at least a Chief Commissioner, and made the Huguenot out this great officer's bosom friend and trusted counsellor. With much bowing (it is a thing to see, else you cannot believe it, the amount of bowing that a Jap meeting friends puts in in the course of a single interview), permission is given by the European-clothed superintendent, and a European-uniformed policeman or warder under his orders shows them all over the whole establishment. At the end, the superintendent again, with tea and cakes and polite inquiries (through the interpreter). The Japanese are almost too polite; it is a little overpowering at times. Yet sometimes they are impolite enough. A fat old priest in a railway compartment was occupying with his bundles and kit and portly person room enough for two men and a boy; enter a crowd, enough to fill every seat, amongst them one lady; yet never an inch of his excessive share of seat space did the old boy yield. Nevertheless, when he got out he raised his hat and bowed to every one in the compartment.

And so at last curios are packed and despatched, and Matsuda paid and certificated and bidden farewell to; and the *Tokio Maru* carries them to

Kobe, there to wait until that most excellent ship the *Kobe Maru* shall take them to Shanghai. A short voyage, with far better views of the coast than from the P. and O. boat, for the latter kept much farther out to sea; the *Tokio Maru* runs in close under the land, and the coast scenery is worth seeing. And much pleasant talk with an artistic fellow-traveller on travelling and yachting and sketching, and the atmosphere of Japan, which, it appears, is somewhat hard and not tender, more like Italian than any other atmosphere; and about Balzac, and the Hermetic Philosophy, and Sir Edwin Arnold, and the truthless stories about him and his new book; and many other things in heaven and earth and elsewhere. Kobe is a pleasant place in which to loiter in the late autumn. Sheltered from the north-east by the hills behind it, it is far milder than Yokohama; it is prettier, both in natural scenery and in its settlement, which is managed by a municipality; and the residents are good fellows, friendly and hospitable. Globe-trotters go to see the Waterfall, which residents most carefully shun; and they get pestered outrageously by most civilized tea-house girls. There are various excursions to be made—to the Moon Temple, to Arami, to Mino Glen and Waterfall, to the islands of the Inland Sea; and Osaka may be done from here. It is a big town, full of canals and bridges and electric light and missionaries. The citadel is famous for its size and the enormous measurements and weight of the stones of its walls. There is no castle left in it; only barrack-rooms and store-rooms and the commandant's and officers' quarters. On the topmost platform is an old gun, and over it a notice-board states that "No person but those who are capacitated to manage the cannon can touch it." Shop sign-boards are erratic as usual : " Seller in foreign articles ; " " Book selling for all useful edition." And then at daybreak away for Shanghai on the most comfortable of all boats, the *Kobe Maru:* deck cabins larger and better fitted than any yet experienced, large saloon and good table, and a skipper of the right sort. The weather was kind this time, and all revelled in perfect calm and clear bright air as they passed through the beauties of the Inland Sea and out through the Straits of Simonoseki. Much whist with the captain in the chart-room, and much comparing of notes between departing parties of globetrotters. Was Japan overrated? Yes, on the whole it was; more than that, thought the Australian signor, it was wholly a fraud, and, once seen, never to be seen again. But the general verdict was that it was not so bad, but by no means the Elysium that romantic and imaginative pendrivers have made it out. And the Japanese, what of them? Certainly the most capable people in the East; what other tribe or family or nation could have adopted, and made their own in a brief twenty years, all the learning, the science, the practical energy of the West? And their morality?

"We had better not discuss that," said the skipper; and proceeded to relate experiences extending right down to the Loochoo Islands. All that can be fairly said is that the standard of morality is different ; for any deviation from that standard is just as much (or as little) fatal to the transgressor as any deviation from the European standard is to the Western sinner. Some think it an awful thing that the daughter of " poor but honest parents " should sell herself for money down ; but, awful or not, is it not just as common in the West as in the East, with the sole difference that there is more hypocrisy about it in the West? There is just as much morality in the one as in the other, and just as many immoral or unmoral persons. The matter of decency and modesty in the way of clothing is such a purely conventional question that it is not worth discussing. But it is certainly to be wished that when the high-placed Jap learns English, and adopts European clothes and fashion of feeding, he would not omit to learn the Western conventionalities of good breeding. The *Kobe Maru* belongs to the Nippon Yusen Kaisha—a Japanese company with a State guarantee—and of course Jap gentlemen travelling by her have a fair claim to good seats at table. Yet it is not pleasant to hear the admiral, seated on the captain's right hand, afflicted with a bad cold and clearing his nose and throat most noisily without the aid of handkerchief or other extraneous assistance. Nor is unrestrained and resonant eructation at meals pleasing to the Western ear. However, they all leave at Nagasaki, and we get in exchange a detachment of Shanghai people who have run over (as they often do) just for the change. Nagasaki is thought by some travellers to be the prettiest harbour in the world; not the finest, but the most charming in its natural scenery. Alf was content to view its beauties from on board; but the skipper said the road out to Ava was a pretty one. "Ava," thought the Major, "what is the name of that ruined capital doing out here? Ava, a place of miles of crumbling walls waiting to be pulled down and made into roadways, of scattered little hamlets, ruined pagodas, great tamarind trees, sylvan and park-like scenery where was once a famous city." So he went to see what the Japanese Ava was, and had a pleasant ricksha drive to the top of the pass, with a fine view of Shimibarat and sea and inlet and rocky promontory; Ava a little fishing village under the corner of the hill. It is pretty all about Nagasaki; and here through the town comes a bevy of pretty young geisha girls, all dressed in their best, with faces painted, and bearing each a wand of artificial flowers. Ah, well, it is time to go! The anchor is weighed, and as we steam westwards down the long entrance of the harbour the moon, past her full, rises from behind the hills, and we bid farewell, "with lips but half regretful," to Japan and all its discomforts and its joys. Good-bye to all of you— "O Mat San, O Hana San," and the rest, " Sayonara, iroonna," farewell. Past the lighthouse, out of the clear blue waters of Japan into the muddy green and brown of China seas. On to Shanghai, where behold Old Phil, tired of travelling and bent on returning to his own country; with whom the Two wandered about for several days, to the Bubbling Well, to the Garden Tea-house—how different from a Japanese tea-house!—admiring the Chinese ladies of the whole world and the half with their tiny feet, their long finger-nails cased in golden sheaths, their garments of unimaginably crude blue and pink, painted faces, gummed tea-potty hair; to the smoking and opium rooms—crowded, stuffy, unlovely to the Western nose; but orderly, quiet, respectable. O ye Anti-opium Leaguers, when you have made clean the inside of that vast City of London, and made decent (for example) the gin palaces and the Haymarket at midnight, then, and not before, will it be seemly for you to set about making moral the outside world. And not even then will you have just cause to inveigh against all use of opium. Come and live awhile in the East, and understand, if you can, that the drug can be used, and is used, by vast numbers moderately and rightly; that only its over-use is bad; and that even its over-use is not more of a calamity to the individual, and far less of a nuisance to the community, than the over-use of alcohol. Good-bye to Old Phil; on by P. and O. to Hongkong. The P. and O. in the Far East is a fraud; it is not in it, for accommodation or comfort, with the Japanese mail, or the French mail, or, for all I know, with the German mail either. For meanness and uncleanness of her cabins, for poverty of table and for unnecessary liveliness in a choppy sea, it would be hard to beat the English mail steamer which bore

Tapioca and the Major through the Lymoon Pass into Hongkong again ; where they met once more the Nebraska Sportsman and the Merciful Broker, and at home in his own palace the Bank Bounder ; and after a day or two of feast and song and dance (and drink—in moderation), the Major said sadly farewell to those good friends, and waited many days for a ship wherein to sail across the sea to Sydney.

PART II.

FARTHEST SOUTH

CHAPTER VII.

HONGKONG TO SYDNEY.

THE Eastern and Australian Steam Navigation Company boasts of being the pioneer of steam navigation between Farthest East and Farthest South, and loves not the rival company, run by a firm whom it calls The Jackals of the East. But if it wishes to gain the sympathy of the travelling public, it must get better boats. It is, I believe, doing so, for the *Tannadice* is sold; but the sister ship, the *Catterthun*, may be safely recommended as not the boat in which to make a more than three weeks' voyage. The saloon will not seat more than twelve, the cabins are very small, the rats are bold and hungry. It is not pleasant to be chewed about the nails and the quicks thereof while you sleep. Nor is it pleasant to have a chief steward who is an ass, and puts on the table, at least thrice, meat so lofty as to shriek aloud. For all this, it was not such a bad time, that twenty-four day spell from Hongkong to Sydney. The north-east Monsoon in China seas (I hate the China seas—they are dirty, and so is the weather in them) was disastrous to most of the passengers on board; but that was past in two days; and then came a fortnight of perfect weather as we passed down the lee of the Philippines, land nearly always in sight, through the Sulu Sea and on to Port Darwin. I love the tropics. It is only near the Equator that an equable temperature of a pleasant warmth is always to be had; there, to me, the air seems softer, the verdure greener, the aspect of sea and land more lovely than in colder climes. And I love seeing the savages of tropic lands. There is not half the interest and amusement to be got in going from city to city of civilized men, as in "wandering far away on from island unto island at the gateways of the day" among strange peoples, brown, and yellow, and black, lank-haired, frizzly-wigged, and shaved, clothed or half-clothed, or unabashedly nude. With what regret I see and land not, for want of time, and pass by Luzon and Mindaro, Panay and Mindanoa. We pass so close by Samboangan, the little port and fort on Mindanoa, that almost one can 'call to the men on the shore." A beautiful land, and curious peoples dwelling therein. Then after the isles of Spain come the Further Indies of the Dutch, below the Equator, which, for the third time, I cross unsaluted. There is Amboyna, ill-famed in history, but the loveliest garden in the East, and Serhattan, and more; and at last Bathurst Island and the northern coast of Australia. By no means lovely, these last: low-lying, level, parched, and brown. These are not the tropics that I love; nor does my soul go forth affectionately to

AUSTRALIAN BLACKS.

the black man that I see here. He is indeed black, and ugly withal. With which Dravidian race in India is it that ethnologists have sought to link him? Was it the Gond? I have certainly seen in India hillmen as black and as unprepossessing. And probably the black man of Australia would have done as decently well as the wild man of Indian woods had he been as decently dealt with. Indeed, stories are extant, and I believe true, of their kindly entreating the white men who first strayed among them; but the desire of the white men for their land, and their own objection to vacating, soon brought that to an end. And now, except as regards the few friendlies or tame blacks, it seems to be a case of shooting them at sight—if oral yarns of northern whites may be taken without the proverbial grain. It is only in the North that the wild black survives; and there he is few, relatively to the whole population of the continent, but still not so very few relatively to the white population of the northern portions only.

Port Darwin is emphatically not picturesque. It is a big land-encircled bay, with lots of room for many ships; but the land is monotonous, unrelieved by any striking feature. And the way to it is through ticklish passages, wherein course rapid currents amongst deadly rocks. You cannot pass the Vernons except in daylight. Palmerston is the dreariest place, bar none, that I have ever seen. Are not those mangrove swamps lining the shores of the bay? A little pier runs out from the end of the little railway on which there is a *bi-weekly* train to and from Pine Creek (or some such name). Not a ship in harbour except our own, and a couple of Government launches ; no boats, no bustling to and fro of busy men. On the cliff above, wide tracks are cleared for streets, but the streets are not built yet, only a few scattered shanties looking solitary and sad in their isolation amid the waste and unoccupied lots that surround them. Even China Street has no activity, no life. The Post Office, a little wood shanty. " Dear God, the very houses seem asleep." And the wide deserted roads stretch away into the heat-quivering distance ; a few blacks, all but nude, loaf around or squat under stunted trees ; a Japanese, or quasi-Japanese, girl or two, shows at the door of her house of call. Yet there are Europeans here and some business ; for lo ! an enormous accession of passengers, more than the limited *Catterthun* can accommodate. What with strikes and breakdowns they have not had a ship here for five weeks, and many are anxious to leave ; and no wonder. Palmerston seems to me to have no chance of becoming anything but an abomination of desolation, unless three things take place. First, that foreign labour may be freely brought in, as it may not at present ; one Chinaman for every 500 tons is all that is allowed, and a motion to alter this to one in fifty was promptly thrown out by the people's representatives. Probably the thing will not be allowed by the wiseacres of Adelaide, and the territory will only get what it requires when it is separated from South Australia. Second, that the Transcontinental Railway be made from Port Darwin to Adelaide, with branches to Melbourne and Sydney. This would greatly shorten the voyage home ; and would give Palmerston an enormous lift, if it succeeded. But, thirdly, it must be good enough to beat the competition of the new route, all through British territory, and by British steamers, from Sydney to Vancouver, and on by the Canadian Pacific. Granted all these and Palmerston may yet wake into life ; but now it is a weariness that we are glad to bid farewell to. And so, full up as we can hold, we go on to Thursday Island, to Cooktown (where some land, but not I), and Cairns (where none land), and Townsville (where all go ashore). We are rather a motley collection. There is the Australian Bank Manager returning from his tour in Europe ; truly a bootyful boy, whose mind has been much enlarged by his travels. We were talking of Russia, and I asked him what he thought of the Eikons in the churches. "You mean the Iconoclasts?" I explained that I meant not destroyers of images, but the pictures of saints in Greek churches, the Eikons. "Oh yes," he cried, gladly ; "I know ; the Iconoclasts—*they're called Eikons for short.*" He was dubbed the Great Unwashed ; a little joke of ours, the point of which I had better leave you to guess. Then there was the Adelaide lawyer, also returning from a year's tour on the other side (the right expression, I believe, in the Far South for anything north of the Equator, the south being this side), really a good fellow. Then there was Little Nibs, and Long or Lean Nibs (that's me), and Big Nibs, and Bigmore Nibs, and the grass-widow and her cavalier servente, and several of the beauties of Palmerston (oh, so beautiful!), and one lady, and a baby or two (how we loved the squalling one!) and some children. Then the officers: the skipper, an Old Father Christmasy looking greybeard, but somewhat "shirty" withal—never mind his name, let us keep it Darke—and a good old Salt for a chief; and a third, who, though a New man, was the right sort. The Doctor was great at the piano, and our choruses were fine. And the Doctor on board was always called Turner, because that was not his name. And others there were that made up a full complement of passengers; and it was pleasant dining out on deck at sunset, and sleeping thereon at midnight.

Thursday Island is a pretty poor sort of a place. I suppose it is even smaller than Palmerston; but then it makes no pretensions to being large, and so does not strike one as being quite such an abortion of a town as does the capital of the Northern Territory. Still, it is mean enough: little shanties scattered about higgledy-piggledy, unfenced and untidy; one short row of small shops. It is not a town, but a shabby village of odds and ends. White men and Malays and Japanese (did not Tommy Jap, of Thursday Island, win the 20,000 dollar prize in the lottery?), Chinamen, blackmen of Australia, curly-wigged blackmen—impossible for me to say whether African pure or American negro, or perhaps dark Papuans,—all these are to be seen. Mauritius is said to live on two canes : sugarcane and hurricane. Thursday Island lives, I should imagine, on pearls and peddling. The pearl fisheries are being carried on at greater distances than formerly from the island ; the peddling is for the pretty numerous ships that call there. Hence on we are protected by the Great Barrier Reef from all tempest and rolling seas from the east, and we run pretty close to the mainland on the west. The sea is full of sharp-pointed rocks ; there is a sailing vessel run on to a reef (maybe she was well insured) ; just over there the *Quetta* was wrecked. It is pretty enough too, in a modest way : the group of islands, of which Thursday is one ; the narrow Albany Passage with its little homestead on the mainland ; Whitsunday Passage and various little bits along the coast. Townsville (what a name !) is the first reasonable attempt at a town that we have come to yet—unless Cooktown be granted the compliment ; really a fine street of good shops. And a jail—such a funny little place, with such a funny old jailor (friendly and sociable withal)—which some of us, led by Big Nibs, himself a jailor, must needs go over. Quite nice hotels, with bright, active, white waitresses—most pleasing to the eye after a long course of various black and brown and yellow boys. And a terrible lot of " How d' ye do ? Glad to make your acquaintance ; come and have a drink."

Moreton Bay, reached on a Sunday, and anchored

in without going up to Brisbane, rendered a visit to the capital of Queensland impossible, except for such as elected to leave the ship and land here ; and a couple of days more (outside the Reef with roughish weather that defeated the Bootyful Boy and others once again) brings us to Sydney and the end of our twenty-four days' voyage. On the whole, with all its drawbacks, it has been a pleasant time. I put away my Dilke and his Problems—the greater part of which might have been written, so far as I can see, without visiting the country at all, and merely from an encyclopedic study of newspapers and Blue-books,—away for the present with *Oceana*, not without wonder as to what it is that our sensitive cousins find offensive in the book ; good-bye to our whist and cribbage and casino parties, and the musical (and somewhat metaphysical) Doctor, and our old Salt, and Newman, and all the rest. But easy all; do not be in too great a hurry. The colony of New South Wales, though not reckoned Protectionist in fiscal matters, takes immense pains to protect itself from all sanitary dangers from without ; as do all the colonies. At every port, from Port Darwin on, we have been boarded first and before all by the health officer. It is quite insufficient for our Doctor to show a clean bill of health for the ship ; at each port—not merely the port first reached in each colony, but at each and every port—crew first and then passengers must all be passed before the local medicine man, that he may assure himself by a momentary inspection of each person that the horrible infections of the East—cholera, small-pox, or any other—have not been brought down to imperil the healths of the local residents. And here at Sydney, though we have been passed all clear by seven successive health officers, plus our own doctor, yet must we by regulation go into Quarantine Bay for two hours, and lie idle, and wonder at the wisdom of those who make sanitary rules. It is lucky we are all free from taint; had any one been suspect, all would be detained for three weeks; and vastly improved as the Quarantine quarters are since the old days when they were such as Mr. Coffyn describes in *Miss Milne and I*, still another three weeks seclusion—and in sight of town—would have pleased us exceedingly ill. Having guarded themselves against danger from without, I suppose the colonial cities will in course of time proceed to guard against danger from within. Unless they do, they will become very fine beds for zymotic disease to home and grow in. At present their sanitary arrangements need improving. Up country, of course, such matters have not passed beyond the early rustic or barbarian method of treatment.

CHAPTER VIII.

SYDNEY.—MELBOURNE.

"AND what do you think of our beautiful harbour?" A "new chum" just arrived in Sydney ought to carry about a placard hung conspicuously on his person, inscribed with some set reply to this set question which he is certain to be asked several scores of times. Such an absurd question too; for the questioner more than suggests the answer by the fixed and invariable epithet contained in the question, and feels mightily insulted if he receive not the suggested answer. My placard should run something like this: "In answer to numerous inquiries, I beg to state that after a cursory inspection of your beautiful harbour, I can frankly say that I have never seen anything like it." This is safe; it ought to satisfy the questioner by its seeming adoption of his immutable adjective, while at the same time it does not give one away by an expression of unbounded admiration which one does not really feel. For, to tell the honest truth, Sydney Harbour is not wholly beautiful. It is no doubt very fine and large; lots of water and plenty of room for big ships and many of them. But that is not what I understand by beautiful. Surely, to be beautiful, a place must possess some special nobleness or grace of form and colour,—some harmonious arrangement of tone and contour that will render it more pleasing to the eye and to the æsthetic sense than the common work-a-day aspects of scenes that are not called beautiful. I confess that I do not find any such distinctive feature in Sydney Harbour as a whole. After passing the Heads, which are beyond question fine, bold, rocky headlands, a splendid gateway into so safe and spacious an anchorage, I see nothing but low, unpretentious, undistinguished undulations, of no picturesque outline, covered with poor thin scrub of no attractive colour, or with the unlovely buildings of a modern town. There is no point of vantage from which you can command the whole—or anywhere near the whole—of the arms and branches of the harbour, the winding and extent of which constitute, I understand, one of its chief claims to pre-eminence. "Beautiful harbour?" For a general view of a fine harbour, good to look upon for scenic effect, there are half-a-dozen places that I have seen that I prefer to Sydney, and doubtless there are as many more that I have not seen which are as beautiful and yet make no fuss about it. Bombay, Hongkong, Hobart, Auckland, San Francisco, and, on a smaller but most perfect scale, Nagasaki—all these I deem "beautiful," each as a whole, in a way that Sydney is not. Sydney should drop the "beautiful" and substitute an adjective more suggestive of utility. But it is not in the least likely that she ever will; or that her people will cease from questioning the new-comer as to his opinion of her beauty.

The one sight in Sydney which her people have elected to praise being thus found wanting, one begins to fear that places which they praise not may be even less pleasing to the much-enduring globe-trotter. But in this he will be agreeably disappointed. There can be no question that the Botanical Gardens deserve most, or it may be even all, the encomiums lavished on them by innumerable wanderers, small and great. Farm Cove is, I think, the name of a particularly charming corner on an arm of the harbour that may safely claim the title of beautiful. And I know that there are other bits in her numerous parks and gardens and domains which may not less deserve the coveted distinction; but I can only say that I did not see them. What I did notice in the parks and gardens was the large number of loafers; men lying listlessly about on the grass all day, doing nothing, or smoking, which is only a pleasanter way of doing nothing. Working men, most of them, or at least men able to work. Why are they here, idle? Is it that they are the wrecks and relics of the great strikes? or has the great question of the unemployed reached already so large a growth in this the oldest city of the South? or is it only that this is holiday-time, Christmas and the New Year, and these men holiday-makers wiser than their fellows, in that they take it easy instead of rushing from place to place? My belief (worth very little) is that a qualified affirmative answer to the first and second of the above queries will give the true reason, and that the matter of the third query has but little to do with the subject. Anyway, there were the loafers, such as I observed nowhere else in my wanderings in Australasia.

On Sydney as a town there is nothing very much to be said. It is, of course, the only town in New South Wales, and, according to Sydney people, by far the finest town in all the colonies. If you wish to grieve the soul of a Sydneyite, to make him weep tears of blood and wish to lie down and die, prove to him how much finer a town than Sydney is Melbourne. You can, I think, bring forward lots of facts to support your thesis; you will prove it as far as any such futile sort of statement can be proved; but you will, of course, entirely fail to convince him; he will remain of his own opinion still. Odious as comparisons are said to be, and futile as I have just suggested that I think them, it is almost inevitable to compare Sydney and Melbourne. The people themselves force it on you. The intercolonial jealousy on each side will not admit any superiority on the other side; yet it is always afraid that after all it may lie over there; and so each city, with true colonial self-consciousness, is always seeking to persuade herself and the stranger within her gates (there are no gates, but that is a detail) that she is the finest and best. The pre-eminence, if it be worth deciding, lies between Sydney and Melbourne; for Adelaide (which I did not see, I am glad to say) cannot be said to be in the running, and no other place rises above the size of a decent town. As already hinted, I give the palm to Melbourne. (I hope Melbourne will feel duly grateful, and much good may it do her.) Her streets are wider and better laid out. This is natural enough, seeing that she was laid out designedly on a fixed plan, while Sydney grew along tracks as they sprang up. Perhaps some people will prefer the comparative sinuosity of Sydney to the, as it were, machine-made regularity of Melbourne with its chess-board parallels and right angles. Sydney avers that wide streets are all very well in fair weather, but narrower ones are better in the days of hot winds and dust-storms; and she is welcome to make the most of the contention. Hot winds and dust-storms are poison anywhere, and a few feet of street-width won't make much odds to them. Then as to paving: a loyal Sydney man assured me that whatever else might be said, Sydney was certainly the best paved city in the world. A large order! I should say bosh; but I hate arguing, even if the question be worth it, and this wasn't.

Again; in public buildings, a matter on which, in my monumental ignorance of all rules of the science, and all denominations of the styles, of architecture, I am eminently qualified to give an opinion, I should suppose that Melbourne is not on the whole behind her more northerly sister; albeit I must own to great admiration of the latter's Centennial Town Hall and its noble organ, and cannot name any building in the former that I like so well.

Finally, in street locomotion Melbourne romps in. Her hansom cabs are as good and not so costly to hire as the Sydney article (1s. per quarter hour, the Sydney rate, appears a trifle tall to one accustomed to pay 10 annas for the first hour and 6 annas for each subsequent hour), and the trams of the Victorian capital come in an easy first. The system is a very large one, and works with admirable smoothness and regularity. I have not seen anything like it, so far; and honestly believe that it cannot be better done. Cable tramways, worked as they are in Melbourne, are certainly the thing. Everybody uses them. The bustle and energy of life are much more apparent in Melbourne than in Sydney; there is more go, more strenuous activity. In "beauty," perhaps, Melbourne may fear the comparison which folk will make, and which I am getting a bit weary of discussing. Her Botanical Gardens are really beautiful—as good as Sydney's, except for Farm Cove; but her harbour and her seaside resorts (St. Kilda and the rest) are not; nor do I think any pretty bits are to be found about them. (Mind, the opinion that Sydney Harbour is not beautiful as a whole is my own opinion only, and not shared in by all others—I mean others besides Sydney people. Some find pleasure in sailing or steaming up the various arms and inlets, and affirm that they are beautiful. I am not concerned to deny it. I make no question that many little bits are to be found, pretty in themselves and delightful to picnic about in in fair weather and good company.

But I firmly maintain that they do not make up the harbour ; that go where you will, you cannot obtain a general *coup d'œil* of the whole harbour or of any large part of it ; that besides the pretty little bits there is a vast deal which is simply unpicturesque ; and that therefore the harbour as a whole cannot be called pre-eminently beautiful.) For a business life, Melbourne is better than Sydney ; the air is full of push and stir of active commercialism. Sydney is better than Melbourne for a life of leisure ; there are more of the amenities of existence, a tranquiller and softer-mannered influence prevails.

With which final statement of opinion, let us pass on, and give Sydney its due as a very pleasant place to stay in. I found time pass so quickly there that I had none to spare in which to make any of the excursions recommended to the sight-seeing globe-trotter ; up the Paramatta, up the Hawkesbury, to Botany Bay, &c. I did one afternoon find my way across to Manly, past the Middle Head, whence the big guns at practice boomed away over our little steamer, at a movable target far out between North and South Heads ; and there I enjoyed " a pleasant walk, a pleasant talk, along the briny beach ;" and that, with a trip to the Blue Mountains, was all that I saw of New South Wales outside Sydney. In Sydney the days passed only too quickly. Charming weather, fine and warm in the day (not too hot, that came afterwards, as we read in the papers), not too cold at night. Business to attend to, batches of home letters to read and answer, friends, fellow-passengers from Hongkong, to meet, smouch round with, say farewell to; old friends from home to hunt up. Here I find E——, whose services medical wisdom refused to India, rubbing along in the same Bohemian sort of way as in those old "coaching" days when we sat at the unfrocked Professor's feet and learnt the lore that should floor examiners, spiced with the full-flavoured stories that the learned man loved to lighten his lectures with. How the Professor would turn in the grave to which, alas! he is gone, if he found his teachings so far forgotten as E—— has forgotten them; for E—— declares himself unblushingly an out-and-out Protectionist. But he has gone down; certainly he has gone down; for he desires to enter the Legislative Assembly, or whatever New South Wales calls its version of the House of Commons. And I think no man could go much lower than that. I suppose, though, that for £300 a year I too might turn into a Protectionist if I had nothing better on. Here too I find G——, reminiscent of days even farther back than those coaching times—of the little midland village in the old country, with the "beautiful" river (for I swear the Severn *is* beautiful) running near it, where we boated and bathed the holidays through,—of all the friends and relatives still living there, and of some that are no longer living. I should vastly have liked to stay longer in Sydney; her people are kindly and good to meet, and life can be lived in her very enjoyably. But it can't be done; for there is so much to "do" in the time that can be spared before we get back home.

In my trip to the Blue Mountains I had Little Nibs for a companion. American, young, travelling on his father's dollars, to improve himself, I suppose; needed it, too. Arriving at Katoomba at night, and starting forth for a drive next morning, we were not at all favourably impressed with the scenery. The gum-tree excludes all other trees, and here on the top it grows scraggy and poor in the poor and gritty soil. And the outlines of the ridges and ranges of hills seen from above are monotonous and uninteresting. It is only when you get to the edge and look over that you find the picturesque, and only when you go over down into the gully that you see the beautiful. The name Blue Mountains is justly given; the hills look blue at all times, " in daylight, moonlight, sunshine, rain" (as the Demon Detective advertisement says, or something like it); the tone varies, of course, but it always remains blue. The principal views that you get to from Katoomba are Govett's Leap, the Wentworth Falls, Leura Falls, Katoomba Falls, Nellie's Glen. Their characteristics are all much the same. As waterfalls they make but a poor show, from the deficiency of water; but there is a beauty in delicate streams falling from high ledges of barren rock into deep recesses of blue-green forest. "Slow-dropping veils of thinnest lawn," "wreaths of dangling water-smoke" and all that, you know. Everywhere that you get to the edge of the range and look down, you see, a thousand feet or so below you, the valley sloping up, seamed through the middle with a hidden watercourse, and both hither and farther side all clothed with endless stretches of gum-tree, unbroken, undefiled with the clearings and burnings that we shall see elsewhere making the bush hideous. The vast blue forest comes steadily up until suddenly there springs from it a great wall of bare rock, here perpendicular, there overhanging; again, worn into deep clefts and chasms or into such strange peaks as the Three Sisters or the Orphan Rock. This natural battlement of Silurian rock runs all round the crest of every range, and on the top is mostly a comparatively flat land, here widening to a plateau, there narrowing to a neck. From a place they call the Narrow Neck you look down such a valley on each side of you widening out into the distance. I did not see Leura Falls. I meant to, and knowing not the wiles of the land-boomer, I took off from the made road where large notices in blue and white announced "Leura Estate, carriage-road to the Leura Falls." There *was* a roughish cart-road for a bit, and a bridge over the railway; and then the "carriage-road," and the Leura Mall, and this street and that street came into view. Each was just a cutting through the bush, surrounded by bush and ending in bush, leading nowhere. We wandered along trying to find a way, until rain came on and drove us home. The township of Leura has yet to be born, for hundred-foot cuttings through the jungle do not make a town; and long may it go unborn and keep that boomer out of his hope of profits, for I love not him and his flaring notices in blue and white. We drove to Govett's Leap and Wentworth Falls, and rode to Katoomba Falls and Nellie's Glen, in the order given, and found each better than the one before, so that the first feeling of disappointment had clean vanished by the time we had done. Govett's Leap (why so called I have no notion) has nothing beyond the general characteristics that I have already tried to indicate; at each of the others there is some special additional feature. At Wentworth it is paths that wind along the upper part of the battlements, now under overhanging cliffs that you stoop hatless to get past, there running out on to a prominent projecting point of rock. Here too is the Weeping Rock, one worn so nearly level on its edge that the water runs off it all round the rim almost as evenly and regularly as from those artificial cisterns that we saw in the temples in Japan. At Katoomba it is a fern gully, a narrow cleft down which you scramble amongst ferns, between massive walls of rock, to the foot of the Upper Fall, and those Three Sisters and Orphan Rock already mentioned.

Nellie's Glen is a grander and longer fern gully, and down it runs the bridle track by which we rode to Jenolan. For we rode that thirty miles or so, and a splendid fine ride it is. Little Nibs is, I reckon, more used to trading by sea in a sailing ship and to the amusements of towns than to riding Walers along bush tracks steep and rough. With

toes well out and knees inches from the saddle, back rounded like a bow, trousers up to his knees, he didn't look like a rider, and the larrikins called after him, "Go it, young 'un; hold on!" He got pretty sore at the end (not the top end, the other), and tired withal. We rode the distance in seven hours, including half-an-hour for sandwiches and pegs at Cox's river, which is not bad time considering the track. It is a long descent from Nellie's Glen to Cox's—quite three hours; past grazing paddocks and through miles of gum-tree; the battlemented ridges seen from below look grand. Then there is a range to cross up, and down again to Little River, and then a long steep pull up Black Range with Table Hill in view. A long piece of level through everlasting gum-trees brings us on to the coach road from Mount Victoria, and then there is a final descent of some miles of corkscrew convict-made road to Jenolan. The site of the caves is very picturesque. A great bar of rock stretches across the valley, completely blocking it. But water has eaten its way through, and you ride under a wide and lofty natural archway to the accommodation house just beyond. Penned in by steep hill-sides all round you, you seem quite cut off from the world. That great barrier of rock is eaten out into numberless hollows, the famed Fish River Caves. (Fish River is miles away from them, and now they are called Jenolan after a Mr. J. E. Nolan, though what he had to do with them I can't say.)

It was such splendid weather out-of-doors that it

seemed a shame to spend the day burrowing under ground; but that was what we had come for, and it had to be done. Enthusiasts may do the whole of the explored caves if they will; we thought that three would be enough—the Right and Left Imperial and the Lucas. The former have electric light laid on all through them, and the guide (a very intelligent and good fellow) carries magnesium wire to light up the show places with. Various opinions of the caves are recorded in the Visitors' Book at the inn. One unctuous idiot thanks God that he has been privileged to be the first to hold Divine Service in one of them, and spells image with two ms. Another gentle sportsman, hot from the newspaper office, bursts forth into pages of fervent strophe and exuberant antistrophe, touched with the true penny-a-line afflatus : " Carved by an angel's hand," and so on. (I don't know what authority he has for supposing that an angel's hand can carve any better than an ordinary mortal's. If it can, I wish we had had one with us at the race luncheon at Randwick on Boxing-Day; for there was a tough old rooster there that three of us tried to carve, and couldn't!) A phlegmatic Britisher opines that the caves are not bad, but nothing to rave about; at whom patriotic walers hurl anathema and M.L.A.'s and M.L.C.'s solemnly record their high and mighty approval of what God has been pleased to make here, and Mr. Wilson is so good as to show them. Mr. Wilson is mine host of the inn, Government guardian of the caves, one of their chief explorers, and principal guide (there are two guides under him, Jack and Voss). He is as deaf as a post, only more so ; say deaf as a poster. He is also a man of humour, as humour is understood in Australia. Ask him to tell you the story of Elijah, or to explain in the caves how stalagmites and stalactites are formed by drip, drip, dripping, and you will find out what passes for humour here. When he exercises his " wit " on you, you are at a disadvantage, for he can't hear your withering rejoinder. It drove Little Nibs nearly frantic. But his inn is a comfortable enough one—we shall experience worse before we have done with Australia. Any one not a teetotaler, though, must take his liquor with him ; for he will get none here.

To see the caves parties are taken round at fixed hours, morning and afternoon, clad in their roughest kit, or in clothes hired on the spot for two shillings a day. And beautiful, beyond question, are the sights that they see. It is useless to give a list of the names of the numberless grottos and nooks full of strange shapes and varied colours ; the names are fanciful, and for the most part meaningless. It is almost equally useless to try to give by description an idea of the beauty of those shapes and colours. For ages and ages water has percolated through the rock, and trickled slowly, or dropped yet more slowly, from roof to floor, here falling direct, there finding way down the rounded or sloping cavern-roof or side. Everywhere it has carried with it the colour of the formation it has come through and borne with it to deposit in stalactite and stalagmite. So long has this gone on, that many a time the two have joined and form one solid column; many a stalactite hangs long and tapering, with but a puny answer to it on the floor below; many a one, as the water willed it, has been far-distanced in growth by its aspiring stalagmite. And snow-white, and cream-coloured, and orange, and red, and pearly, are the hues of them; some dull and unresponsive to the bright magnesium light, other sparkling as though sown with diamonds. In one cave mass upon mass of "natural sculpture in cathedral cavern," awes you with its majestic immensity; in another, tiny, delicate formations of bright and glittering crystal charm you with their exquisite loveliness. And then those "mysteries," as they call them, fantastic, unexplainable threads and buds that, scorning gravity, run out at all angles—upwards, crossways, aslant, and form a wilful fairy work of infinite gracefulness. Here are curtains of pure white, with a dull red border, that looks as though blown by the wind, and translucent, yet as hard as rock; here is a tall Lot's wife, though not of salt; a crystal city with walls and battlements and bastioned forts and towers; vast organ-pipes and cathedral columns; diamonds of the Queen and gems of the West. Though all the morning and all the afternoon you pass on "from stately nave to nave, from vault to vault," and find every minute some new combination of form and colour to strike the imagination or delight the fancy; each one you will declare the best you have yet seen (it is the regular thing to do), and at the end you will hardly remember which was which, so as to name it correctly. Descend by a steep and somewhat swinging ladder to the underground river, and view the cold and silent streamlet that has been nature's instrument in fashioning these marvels. Do not descend by somebody's short cut (I forget his name) from the upper caves to the lower, or you will break your bones as he did. In the Lucas cave you can do a bit of a scramble by ways where no steps are cut, and no hand-rail set up; and you will find a formation that will give you a better impression than anything in the Imperial of the incalculable length of time that these caves and their contents have taken in the making. For here are wide caverns in which by that slow, persistent drip, drip, drip of silica or lime-charged water—five years of which makes no perceptible, no measurable increase in the growth of stalactite or stalagmite—by it were formed many a column, thick as a man, and taller than any child of man (giants excepted); and after they had formed and grown, the floor, ceaselessly undermined by the streamlet working beneath it, fell in and broke off these pillars that joined floor and roof, and dragged down curtains, and made a mighty mess of things generally. Yet, still the drip, drip, drip, went on, and has gone on for again so long a time, that many a pillar is reunited, and many a curtain joined again to its supports. You can trace the fracture and the new growth easily with the eye. Yet not all have been mended. The Broken Column, as they call it, is left disjointed, standing in the midst of a vast cavern amongst a wild jumble of monstrous boulders. I don't suppose all this gives much idea of what the caves are like; but at least it may indicate the impression they made on me. Photos also fail to reproduce the effect of these splendid forms as they stand out in the bright, white light from "far within each aisle and deep recess." The only way to understand them is to see them; or something like them, only I don't know where anything like them is to be found. They are unique, or "one of the most unique sights," as some enthusiastic visitor put it with a bold, if unconscious, disregard for the meaning of words. New Zealand has something of the kind at Waitomo, in the North Island; but they are not very easy of access, nor made convenient to go about in. Anyway, at Jenolan I expected to see something worthy of admiration; and I was not disappointed. And so after a well-spent couple of days, climbing about the hill-sides in the evening, and watching the rock-wallabies running about (they are many and not over-shy, knowing well that they may not be shot around the caves), we coach up the steep zigzag of 1,500 feet rise, and on by a bush track to Oberon. On again next morning to Tarana, and so by rail back to Sydney to eat our Christmas dinner at the Grosvenor Hotel. I do not particularly recommend this route; it is a good deal longer than that by Mount Victoria, and there is not much of interest to see on the way. It is largely bush, all gum-tree and nought else, and partly clearing—pasturage for sheep. The "townships," as they call them (not a township as understood in Burma, by any means), are small; a few scattered plank shanties, dotted about in the wide, rolling sheep-runs. Oberon consists of three churches, two "hotels," a couple of "stores," and a dozen or so of houses, plus a school and a bank. Of the hotels one is a tolerable inn, the other appears intolerable; and besides the "houses" in the "town," poky little wooden huts: I wonder people are content to live in such narrow quarters. There are, of course, a good many out-stations. Katoomba is like unto Oberon; and if these be fair samples of New South Wales up-country places to live in, I am thankful that the state of life to which it has pleased God to call me does not lie here. It is curious to note, though, how every township, however small, has its school and its bank. Government goes in for education, compulsory and free, and does it thoroughly—gives the taxpayers their money's worth. If the school be too thinly attended to employ a teacher all his (or her) time, two or more are put under the same individual's charge, and the teacher goes round and round them regularly. Anywhere near mines, the bank is naturally required for bullion business; and away from mines it is equally necessary, because of the universal custom of paying wages at regular periods, and even quite small sums at any time, by cheques rather than in cash. Tiny little places the Bank premises are; and the managers, I suppose, are such cheerful specimens as our Bootyful Boy. This cheque system is, I imagine, largely responsible for the process known as "lambing down," which I understand to be by no means overdrawn or over-coloured in the accounts that one reads of it. Do you know what the process is? Briefly this. A shepherd or stockrider, or the like, receives his season's, or half-year's, or year's wages in one cheque, and gets leave from the station. He arrives at an "hotel," and, of course, "shouts" for every one round; "shouting" goes on till he is gloriously drunk on stuff (it may be) that would poison an ostrich; cheque handed over to mine host; a little management of the poison that he and his "shoutings" consume, aided by bottles empty of liquor that they did not consume, leads to the cheque being worked out in a greater or less number of days, and our friend is duly "lambed down," to return to work penniless, to get over his "head" and earn another cheque.

From Jenolan to Oberon and Tarana there is nothing of scenery except brook and sheep-run, and now and again a pleasing view of the hills. From Tarana by rail you pass Lithgow and Bowenfels, where there is mining and the "townships" are bigger, but the houses quite as small and mean as before; up the little zigzag (two reversing-stations instead of one as on the Bhor and Thal Ghats); on by Mount Victoria and Katoomba—hill-stations for the Sydney folk ; down the great zigzag (like the little, only larger) ; across the Emu Plains, and through the suburbs of Sydney, populous, but narrowly-housed as usual, into Redfern Terminus—a ramshackle sort of place that a city like Sydney should be ashamed of. (Melbourne, with its Spencer Street, is no better ; if anything, a trifle worse. They needn't build a Victoria Terminus—the Bombay, not the London one—but they might have something better than paltry sheds.) I asked Little Nibs if he would come with me to hear the *Messiah* in the Town Hall on Christmas night ; Madame Patey would be good to hear, if nothing else were. He came ; and his first remark was, " Why, it's sacred ! " The chorus was very fair, but I cannot say that the colonial soloists greatly charmed me. The tenor was tolerably good, but the soprano and bass I did not care for at all. After this, Little Nibs deserted me. I will give you a tip. If you wish to part company with such as he, lend him a little money ; you will see neither it nor him again.

Less than two days of somewhat boisterous weather in the floating palace of the French mail, and I am in Melbourne. It is a city of varying climate ; one day delightful as in Sydney, the next hot-winded and dusty as the Indian plains in April, again chill with drizzling rain. Every man here is as good as his neighbour, and a trifle better too ; politeness and attentiveness are, by men in shops, by men that work or wait, most carefully avoided and eschewed. What crowds of busy men at the "Squatter's" Hotel, as Scott's is called, at tiffin-time, and indeed everywhere else all day long! The Dook of Melbourne and Sydney had grounds for boasting himself a citizen of no mean city; but it is a mighty poor thing in climates that Melbourne has to put up with. No lack of amusement for the idle. A Wild West show on the Buffalo Bill lines, with the addition of Dr. Carver's fancy-shooting; intercolonial cricket match, with Giffen piling up a mighty score; races, theatres, and what not. The "cornstalks" are good at many things, but horse-racing seems to be the favourite of all pastimes. The number of meetings and the "added moneys" and the entries leave our Indian turf far behind. Good courses they are too, and good racing, both at Randwick (Sydney) and Flemington (Melbourne). The theatres are also many degrees removed from what we endure in the shape of drama in India. Not that I think the melodramatic stage is good. At Sydney we sat it out, but laughed inevitably at the most touching pathos or most stirring tirades; at Melbourne we could not even sit it out. But in comedy and comic opera they do the thing well; quite as well as in any but an exceptionally good London theatre. In both capitals the pieces I saw were well mounted, well managed, well acted, and (in case of light opera) well sung. The theatres are commodious and comfortable, and the highest price (bar private boxes) 5s.

In Melbourne my time was even shorter than in Sydney, and I made no attempt to see anything of the country outside town except in a run to Ballarat, not a long journey by rail. All lines in Victoria, and almost all in all Australasia, are State railways : a system that I have long been of opinion is the best. But the opinion of some local men that I have met by no means agrees with mine; they were inclined to growl at Government management almost as much as those mighty organs of public opinion, the Rangoon papers, objurgate the direction of the Burma State Railway. They are certainly liberal with their free passes in Victoria; the courteous Secretary for Railways made me a present of one, and naval and military officers may claim them (I understand) as of right. I wish they were not so Sabbatarian, though, in their time-tables; no trains run on Sunday, except a few local suburban ones : a fact that impedes you not a little when your time is short and you wish to make the most of it.

Ballarat is quite a town—any number of gold-mines round it; lake and well-kept gardens, wide, straight streets, some moderately fine public buildings—these are its adornments. Of course I went down a gold-mine—the "Sir Henry Loch"—the managing director most kindly and courteous, and the manager on the spot only too intent on making us understand all about it. He began at the very beginning—how a reef was formed, how the gold got placed in it, how you scientifically found it out; then how you worked it and how you financed it. Donning miners' kit, we descended to the lowest working but one—some 1,180 feet, the lowest being

1,290; and returning to the upper air were shown over the stamping and crushing part of the operation, with which I was already acquainted, as it was identical with that obtaining where I saw gold-mining in India. And then back with "The Norfolk Regiment" (my companion on this trip) to Melbourne; and good-bye to him and to his brother, and to the little Doctor, and to all friends made in this the Second Act of my world-encircling globe-trot, to make new friends and acquaintances in the Third—a tour through New Zealand.

CHAPTER IX.

NEW ZEALAND SOUTH OF CHRISTCHURCH.

NEW ZEALAND is fond of boasting herself as a "Wonderland" (*vide* advertisements *passim*), and she has a fair claim to be called beautiful. And with grand variety of beauty too : Alpine snow-scenes and glaciers, vast stretches of pathless forest, fjords of majestic magnificence, harbours of quiet and peaceful loveliness, terrible volcanoes and lakes of boiling mud, geysers and wondrous terraces. But the first aspect to one approaching from Melbourne is not delightful. We have passed Hobart, with its strange rocky headlands away at the mouth of the bay (more fantastic but less imposing than Sydney Heads), and its broad and beautiful harbour backed by the massive bulk of big Mount Wellington. It is a pretty place, Hobart; more English-looking is the town than the Australian cities ; and one regrets not seeing more of Tasmania, notwithstanding the hot wind that is blowing the dust about so boisterously (most unusual weather in Hobart, of course all the local-knowledge people say). We have, in our crowded ship, endured the cold wind that blows ever about the southern seas, and arrived at the Bluff—a bleak and barren spot, where the township (or whatever they call it in New Zealand) consists of the same old mean wood shanties, scattered fenceless and higgledy-piggledy all over the place. A brief railway run takes us to Invercargill, as cold as the Bluff, though it is midsummer, with no beauty of situation, no adornment of art. It has laid out its streets as wide as though it meant to be a second Melbourne—far wider than in most other New Zealand towns; but the shops and the traffic on those streets are as yet meagre, and the tramway is a most modest one-horse affair. But the journey to Queenstown on Lake Wakatipu (usually pronounced Wawkatip) is a pleasant one. By rail to Kingston; at first across wide sheep-grazing plains, past mutton-freezing factories, with distant hills ringing in the horizon. We gradually work up into a gorge through these hills, and slowly ascend between the big bare sides of them—bare of all trees and all but bare of herbage, bare even of that on many of the winter-worn tops—until we surmount the barrier that shuts in the lake, and descend to the little quay at Kingston. Hence a steamer takes us half way up the lake to Queenstown, and much we admire the scenery as we go. The hills rise very steep, clad in bracken or some such fern, for 2,000, 3,000, 4,000 feet—nay more—above the lake, their summits weather-worn into countless ridges, serrated, dentated, peaked, bayoneted, hiding here and there in the chasms beds of shining snow, dropping from cliff and cleft the streamlet that falls and falls till it reaches the lake. The Remarkables, as the name-givers of this region have in clumsy fashion thought fit to christen a great double-coned mass of barren rock, reminded a friend of mine strongly of what he had seen in the Engadine; and the view of Ben Lomond and Bowen Peak as you approach Queenstown struck both him and me as superb. The usual tourist thing to do is to get to the top of Ben Lomond, 5,747 feet above the sea, 4,677 above the lake; so of course I made a start for it next morning. Easy going, though pretty warm, up to the saddle (one and three-quarter hours); then thick cloud and heavy rain and an ignominious retreat, wet through, to Eichardt's Hotel. The tourist is also bound to go at least to the head of the lake. If he has time, he should stay there some days; many a splendid walk to lake and mountain and glacier is to be done from Glenorchy or Kinloch. Years hence, when the track is made, or now, if he likes camping-out, carrying his own kit, with certainty of at least one day in two being wet, he may foot it across hill and bush to Milford Sound; let him not stray by the way, lest he be lost and no more found, as a certain Professor was, and others besides. The steamer makes the trip to the head of the lake and back in the day; and a very beautiful trip it is. We started with band playing and children cheering, for we had on board a school treat which we deposited at Bob's Cove—a pretty little nook near the second bend of the lake.

For Wawkatip (why should I not spell it phonetically if I prefer?) is shaped much like this, where 1, 2, 3 stand for Kingston, Queenstown, and Glenorchy respectively; and it is not until you get round the second corner that you come in view of the snow-mountains and the virgin heights of Earnshaw. Seen on a beautiful bright day, as I saw it, the view is bad to beat. Earnshaw is 9,200 feet high; a second crest is 9,160, and a splendid arête connects the two. I say "virgin" heights; but one Harry Burley, a guide, asserts that he has reached the top. Some believe him, some do not. If he has, he is the only man that has. Earnshaw's snow and glaciers fill the right background; the centre holds a number of peaks of varied shape, snow-clad, known as the Cosmos Peaks, though each has its own proper name, and Cosmos applies strictly to only one; the left is shut in by the Humboldt mountains and the hills above Kinloch. All the foreground is blue lake-water, with fern-clad hills, bare-topped, to right and left. Mount Alfred in the middle distance looks black with thick birch forest, and all the left bank is covered with the same—but here, alas! black with the ruin of fire. There is much more of lake scenery about in Southland and Otago: Wanaka, with its curious island, in which is a lake of higher level than the main lake; Hawea, Te Anau, Manapouri (curiously Indian this last name), and others. But time failed to see any of these; I could only attack Ben Lomond again before I left for other scenes. This time the weather behaved splendidly. It is not much short of three hours for an "ornery" walker like me from hotel to summit; and you must carry what lunch you want with you. But at the top the view is extremely fine. To the south and west, right under you, you have Lake Wawkatip with its mountain walls, it blue and beautiful, they with even their grim greyness softened into some touch of graciousness by the glorious sunlight ; to the east the outlet towards Frankton, the cultivated lands of Shotover, and far-off ranges dying into the dim haze of the distance. But all the north, from east to west, is filled with unbroken ranges of snow-mountains; there is far-off Mount Aspiring trying to reach, and all but winning, a height of 10,000 feet—a most regular cone of unblemished snow ; and all across, glacier and snow-peak and mountains of unknown names right up to Earnslaw and Cosmos. Don't omit to stroll to the Waterworks when you are at Queenstown ; it is a charming little glen, and man's handiwork has damaged it very little. Sunset at Queenstown was not any great show, that I saw ; but the sun and clouds favoured us with a beautiful effect on the Remarkables as we steamed away, returning Bluff-wards. Great masses of morning mist rolled up, covering all the upper half of the hill ; they broke and left an oval chasm in which the double cone was perfectly enframed on a background of soft blue sky ; on the cones and on the skyward side of the cloud shone clear sunlight, making the edges of the frame too burning bright, almost, to look on, while all the rest of cloud and mountain remained grey and sunless.

The only means at present available for visiting the West Coast Sounds is to join one of the three excursions made thither by the Union Company's s.s. *Tarawera* in the months of January and February. The probabilities of your having fine weather increase in direct ratio with the lateness of the trip, but exigencies of time compelled me to go by the first. The ship is given up wholly to this excursion business, so long as it lasts; and the Company's advertisements assert that it assumes the form of an extended picnic. Not a picnic at all in the proper sense of the term; but as to its extension there is no doubt—the ten days devoted to it might be cut down by half, or to a week at most. Of course, among a troop of over one hundred excursionists, parties form themselves, that hang together, holding more or less aloof from the rest; and equally of course, among the rest there are sure to be a certain number that you would be likely to keep aloof from in any place. The plan of the trip is to make one of the Sounds and there remain all day, sending off the excursionists in boats to fish or botanize, or scramble about on shore and picnic amongst the sandflies. We were a very pleasant party on No. 4 boat. There was Our Enthusiast, up early and late, not to miss any possible "bit" of scenery, and rapturizing over it all under the most adverse circumstances of weather and temperature; and as a counterpoise Our General, or opposite pole, who enthused not at all, and showered cynicisms, tempered with much genial laughter, on the whole arrangement. He was abetted therein by Our Ceylon Benedict, one of the best of fellows, in whose train came wife and sister and brother-in-law. Then there was Our Warrior Bold, and his wife the Authoress—(I have not read any of her books and do not know whether they are Hentyresting)—dear good people—he tottery of step, poor martyr to gout; and Our Humorist and his wife, let us say Mrs. H. Lastly, a youth, a scion of a noble house, and Our Stanley (so designated from his fondness for forcing his way through pathless jungles), or Indian Exotic (being particularly touchy to the cold). Perhaps I need hardly say that I mention myself last. Well, this was the boat that, after we had reached Preservation Inlet and duly proceeded up to the end of the fjord and returned to Cuttle Cove and anchored there all night, proceeded to the shore in spite of the half gale of wind that blew and the squalls of rain that at times descended upon them.

The day's proceedings were very much the same at each place of halt: to go ashore with lunch or afternoon tea, or both, and spend the afternoon or the day in rambling about in the forest or catching fish in the sea. Here, then, is the journal. First and Second days as already stated. Third day : To Dusky Sound and Wet Jacket Arm by 11 A.M. Fourth day: Doubtful and Smith Sounds, Hall's Arm, Thompson's Sound, George Sound; anchored at 2 P.M. Fifth day: At George Sound. Sixth day : Milford Sound by 8 A.M.

Seventh day : At Milford. Eighth day : Left Milford at 3 P.M. Remaining two days getting back viâ Bluff to Dunedin. Now of all these days there was only one wholly fine day—the third. Yet we enjoyed ourselves for all the wet. There is no denying that the scenery is fine ; and it is so kind as to get better and better as you go on. Cuttle Cove is pretty when you see it first, but, after you have been through the rest up to the climax of Milford Sound, it is quite a poor thing to look back upon. All the little adventures that befall you—how one boat catches a shark, another a thirty-eight pound fish of ugly shape and uglier name, how one gets bogged and another deprived by a carelessly dropped match of the inexpensive gingham, what splendours of ferns have been found here, the fine waterfall or lovely lake successfully scrambled to there, how the sandflies have lunched on you—all these form the amusement of the day ; and at night concert or dance or entertainment (for me the social rubber) make the time pass as gaily as may be. Our cynics declared the whole thing to be too much of the " 'Arry hout for a 'oliday " style of thing. And to my mind it would certainly be far pleasanter if one could do the Sounds with a small nice party of one's own friends rather than in the company of a mixed crowd, to most of whom you are no more interesting, I presume, than they, I am sure, are to you. How can one delight in the society of the Honourable ?—(the 'Orrible Our Humorist aptly called him)—a life peer of some Australian colony, and oh, so colonial! To see him and Our Hereditary Legislator play "bull" together was a sight "to shake the midriff of despair with laughter." Then the young man got up regardless of expense, "Calico" he was named; and the detachment of undisguised cads, and of cads disguised (as far as dress goes) as decent fellows—their room had been better than their company. Therefore our "push" (this I understand is Australian for a party of people) left the ship, wet or fine, at each anchoring-place; preferring forest solitudes and a wetting to the deck of the *Tarawera*. The bush is different from anything I have ever seen. It is always wet here; for though its rainfall is not so heavy as at (say) Akyab, I think the rain is more constant; the intervals of pallid sunshine are so brief that nothing has time to get dry. Then there are no men nor any quadruped in these jungles; "no birds are flying overhead—there are no birds to fly," or at least very few; so that the Vegetable Kingdom has it all to itself, and evidently has had for many a long age past. Accordingly the soil is hidden beneath mass upon mass of decaying vegetation, clothed over with a wonderful wealth of moss and fern. You tread on a mossy knoll, and sink knee-deep into the rotting trunk of a fallen tree. You simply cannot walk on the ground, you walk or scramble on dead wood in all stages of decay, on wide banks of moss of varied kinds, lovely to look upon, through thickets of splendid ferns. The *Todea superba*, most exquisitely frilled, shaped like the Prince of Wales's feathers; the Kidney fern, most curious and delicate of tree-ferns (I mean ferns that grow on trees): here it is in seed—note the spores sticking out round the edge like a line of spikes; fern-trees (I mean ferns that grow to the size of a tree) many and large and handsome. There are few flowers; here the crimson blossom of the rata, there the thick-clustering small white flowers of the manuka. And never a thorn nor a briar; the "bush lawyer" is absent; nor do creepers annoy you, except here and there a "supple Jack," a kind of cane. And the whole of this wild land is covered with bush; no break nor clearing. Except only that one hermit lives in Dusky Sound, and that there are two huts in Milford City, there is no settlement, no station, no human soul in all the long deep-indented coast-line. I have not seen the fjords of Norway, with which, as I read, these challenge comparison; but in their utter solitude and silence—undisturbed for who shall say how many ages?—I imagine these Sounds of the Farthest South must offer strong contrast with their cousins of the Remote North.

The scenery is, beyond all cavil, imposingly grand. The constant rain that preceded our entry into Milford Sound had set all the mighty mountain walls that flank it, on this side and on that, streaming with water; and the clouds still lowering and clinging to the mountains as we came in the countless waterfalls seemed to be pouring down straight out of heaven. During the day these clouds lifted and fell again

New Zealand South of Christchurch. 183

and drifted round, forming in the recess behind Mitre Peak a chasm of awful blackness, breaking to let the sunshine through on to the snows of the Darran mountains, and curling waywardly across the glaciers of Pembroke. Then before sunset it was fine and cloudless, and we could see the magnificent scene in undimmed glory. It is curious to find oneself in an ocean lakelet, the narrow channel by which we came in shut out of sight by a bend in its course, and, around one, mountains that raise their huge sides sheer out of the many-fathomed water for literally thousands of feet, ere they slope up to the name-giving cone of the Mitre, or the rounded crest of the Lion, behind which gleam the eternal snow and glaciers of Mount Pembroke. The air is so clear that (in guide-book phrase) it annihilates distance; those glaciers that it would take hours of steady climbing to reach, seemed to Our M.L.A. but a hundred yards away. Close to our anchorage the Bowen Falls pour a volume of water from a height of 540 feet; not sheer down, for, about fifty feet from the top of the fall, the water strikes on a point of rock which shoots it up and out in a splendidly graceful curve of snow-white spray. The Sutherland Falls, about half a day's arduous journey from Milford, are claimed to be 1,904 feet in height; but this not in one unbroken leap, there are three successive falls of some 600 odd feet each. The rain prevented even the most enthusiastic tripper from getting any farther on the way than Lake Ada—a beautiful piece of water shut in by the Devil's Armchair and other big bulks of mountain.

Altogether the Sounds are worth seeing, if only they could be seen in greater comfort. The Union Company allege that they make every arrangement for the convenience of the trippers, and they do make some attempt to do the thing well *for the colonies*. But the skipper is just about as bad a man for such a business as they could possibly select; and colonial notions of doing a thing well do not come up to European. The Captain ought to be conversational, bright, cheery, obliging; all of which he is not. The Bluff might well have been reached in time to catch the train for Dunedin; but the Captain most accurately timed his arrival to be just one quarter of an hour too late for it. So we all had to steam on to that Scotch capital of Otago; and there at last broke up the motley crowd of the First Sounds Trip. Let us hope that the "Pantomime Fairy" came to no harm in her flirtations; that the Bear Leader without his Cub ("wise cub to desert such a leader," said Our General) came to grief (for we deemed him unendurable) in his overt matrimonial approaches to the Unlovely Heiress; and that all the good fellows and nice women that we saw no more had a good time of it ever after. We had seen the Sounds not quite at their best; for Wet Jacket Arm in rain (and we saw it in fine bright weather), George Sound in sunshine (and for us it was all in cloud and drizzle), are said to be perfection. But the beauty of the view up Hall's

Arm, and the grandeur of Milford Sound are things ever to be held in admiring remembrance.

Dunedin proclaims by its name its Scotch origin, and maintains its Scotchness unimpaired. Indeed all Otago and Southland are Scotch. I do not think any one but a Scotchman could conveniently live in the bleak cold that holds part of Southland even in midsummer; how much more then in midwinter? But Dunedin, as I saw it, is not cold. It is, however, said to be fickle. And it is very prettily situated. I met a man who remembered it a generation ago; all the hills around bush-covered, and not a building in the place but scanty plank shanties. Now the hills are nearly all cleared, only patches of bush remain, and country seats, such as Larnac's Castle, crown the heights, while the town boasts of the finest buildings in New Zealand. In the bright clear air, it is a charming drive along the Upper Road to Portobello, and back by the Beach Road, or out to the Taieri Valley; and the road to Blueskin (if that be the right name, for I never can remember whether it be not Bluerift, or Bluedrift, or Blueshirt or skirt; however, I think it is Blueskin, after some fellow who was tattooed blue all over—as blue as a "woad"-ed Ancient Briton): I say the road to Blueskin takes you up over a pass of some 2,000 feet into sight of long ranges of hills (the only way to Christchurch in the old days), that are yet covered with unbroken bush. Looking down on the harbour, one is reminded somewhat of Nagasaki; it is the same long narrow inlet, hill-surrounded, with the town at the extreme end of it. But there are differences enow; here are the hills less steep, less varied in outline, softer, more rounded; here is no natural waterway, but a channel patiently wrought and incessantly dredged; here is a chain of promontory and island (Quarantine Island) that almost closes the inlet from Port Chalmers to Portobello, to which Nagasaki affords no parallel. It is pretty, as are all New Zealand ports that I have seen, except the Bluff; but not beautiful as Nagasaki. Taieri is a long and fertile valley between fine grazing hills. There is much cultivation as well as mutton and wool-growing about Dunedin. Let us go into this Meat-freezing Factory. Sales of beeves and sheep are busily going forward in the yard close by; here we may see the latter congealing, to reappear in London as best Welsh mutton. The first chamber is at a temperature of 26° F.; the carcases have only just been put in, and are still tender to the touch, and meaty to the smell. The second chamber is at 18° F.; and here a blow struck on the stiffened body rings sharp and metallic. The amount of cold put into the sheep depends on the distance it has to go (by rail) to the refrigerating chamber aboard ship. Beef cannot be frozen so well as mutton, owing to the necessity of cutting up the carcase, thereby losing much of its natural juices, so that when unfrozen it eats much poorer than the mutton which is frozen whole.

Some of our "push" decided on reaching Christ-church by sea in the *Rotomahana* (Rotten Banana

Our Humorist would call it); but Our Enthusiast preferred the rail, and so did I. And it is, in truth, a very pretty bit of road as far as Blueskin, and some little way beyond. The line passes just above Port Chalmers and round the promontory that ends the range which we drove out over the other day, and presents charming views of rock and sea, and cove and bay, of hill and gully, fern- or forest-clad or cleared for grazing. But do not let yourself be drawn into riding on the platform of the carriage, lest a tunnel (of which there are several, and one a long one) come suddenly upon you unawares, and you emerge therefrom as grimy as a coal-heaver, or as Our Enthusiast did. Oamaru, where you lunch, is a most striking town in one respect; it is all of stone, quite a curious sight after the long succession of wooden erections so almost universal hitherto and hereafter. It is the outlet of a most fertile country. On by Timaru to Christchurch, the scenery is much less interesting, not to say monotonous. The Canterbury Plains *are* plain, almost level, and, as I saw them, as brown and dry as an Indian plain. Indeed, the scene reminded me strongly of India ; the same hot weather haze hanging about the low undistinguished hills in the distance, the same interminable expanse of parched-up lowland, with here and there a little clump of trees, hiding in India the gaon, here a tiny homestead, or shepherd's or labourer's hut. About Christchurch itself, I am sorry that I can tell you nothing but what you will find in the guide-book; for I arrived at 9 P.M., and got no dinner—only a supper; and left next morning at 8 A.M. I can only say that it is as English and churchy as Dunedin is Scotch and kirky; that Warner's is a comfortable hotel, and the proprietor obliging and scrupulously honest (he returned to me by post, after I left, a modest two shillings which his clerk had unwittingly overcharged me); that the streets are ill-lighted, or unlighted, at night; and that there are hansom cabs, whose cabbies will show you the way about if you don't know it yourself. I was there only a short time; and have no more to tell you of Christchurch.

CHAPTER X.

THE OTIRA—THE BULLER—NELSON.

OF the coach drive from Christchurch to the West Coast, and thence to Nelson, I had heard conflicting accounts; some averring that the Buller is much finer than the Otira Gorge, others maintaining the superiority of the latter; one saying that the general discomfort that had to be endured rendered the trip unenjoyable, another that it was real good business. It seemed to me that probably the pleasure of it depended largely on two things besides the scenery; to wit, one's company and the weather. Now the former I had of the best all through, for Our Humorist and Mrs. H. were my fellow-voyagers even to Wellington; and the latter was at starting altogether beyond reproach. The first stage is by rail to Springfield, through country no more interesting than that seen the day before coming into Christchurch, except that those distant hills are getting nearer, more defined, more striking. At Springfield the railway ends, and one gets a lunch of the kind one is becoming accustomed to in the colonies: huge helpings of meat from the joint (an adult New Zealander eats 200 to 250 lbs.

of meat a year to the Englishman's 110, and the " portion " served out to you is, therefore, of course, enormous), pudding and tea! Tea at all meals, and at all possible hours outside meals, is a characteristic of Australasian civilization. Concurrently, as might be expected, there is far less "nipping" and consumption of alcoholic drinks than in places I wot of in the East and Far East. We got away from Springfield about 1 P.M. : two coachloadsful. Such lumbering-looking coaches, yet really not heavy, with enormous leather springs. On one coach went the Leader without a Cub, with the Unlovely Heiress, and all her female relations; we called them now the Raja and his harem. We Three took the upper box-seat on the second coach, and the great Cassidy himself was our driver. We went steadily enough until we got to the end of the plains, and into a gorge of the hills—such bare hills, almost as absolutely bare as the Remarkables, and not rock either, or rather volcanic rock all disintegrated and crumbled, grey in colour. Then after a fine drink of milk we walked up the long ascent of Porter's Pass—and very hot it was to us dressed for cold climates.

At the top, 3,000 feet high, the wind blows sometimes so strong as to upset the coach; at least it has been known to do so when the load was a light one. Then a long descent past little Lake Lyndon, amidst ever-changing views of bare mountains; rattling along, for Cassidy is a fine driver. He takes us gently over the open watercourses that cross the

The Otira.

road and all the rough bits; yet every now and then we on the box, at an extra heavy jolt, rise simultaneously from our seats, bow politely, and sit down again. A change of horses at the end of fifteen miles, and we speed along to Castle Hill, near which are a number of curious-shaped rocks stuck up in all sorts of positions and groupings, and at which are good tea and excellent scones to be enjoyed. The road crosses one or two snow- and ice-fed streams, lying in stony beds; one is very deep cut, with the banks so naturally and levelly terraced that it seems hardly possible that art has not come to the aid of nature. Yet there is no doubt that here, as at Lake Wawkatip, the terraced banks are merely the result of the lowering of the water-level. Then through a pass where the hills close in on us, and a splendid down-grade to Craigieburn (twenty-eight miles). Horses changed again, and we spin along past Lakes Pearson and Grasmere, and through a big grazing plain, some of it cultivated with oats. The road runs straight for a couple of miles; evening is closing in; cold blows the wind across the wold; the sunset flush fades from off the mountain-tops. It is already dusk when we reach the Waimakariri—a splendid scene. The river wanders over a wide bed of shingle, shut in, as it seems, by great mountains, black and silent, thick with birch forest, but bareheaded or snow-capped. The road crawls along the precipitous bank, now climbing 200 or 300 feet up, now descending almost to the water's edge; until at last we get on to almost level ground and arrive at

Bealey at 9 P.M.—forty-five miles. Dinner is a repetition of lunch; and the bedrooms, small as they are, are double-bedded. But early to bed, sound sleep, and an early rise see us cheerful enough in the nipping and eager air at the 5 o'clock start. For many a mile the track runs along, and mostly. in the bed of the Waimakariri and then of the Bealey River, and a fine jolting the rounded stones give us. Cassidy is not with us; but the silent Holmes is as good a driver, if a far less communicative and attentive cicerone. The sunrise is unluckily a cloudy one; the scenery looks all the more solemn for the dull grey light. At last we get clear of the river and begin the long ascent of Arthur's Pass. We are glad to walk and get warm, and welcome the sun as he breaks through the cloud veil. There on the right is the Devil's Punch Bowl—a small stream of water pouring into a rounded basin; little water, but a big drop. On the left Mount Rolleston, with a splendid glacier, seems close to us; mountains of six, seven, eight thousand feet stand about us, until at last we reach the top—the water-divide, the backbone of the Middle Island. The descent begins almost at once, but, just after it has started, has to cross a huge moraine: the greater part of the mountain-side on the right seems to have fallen into the gorge. Having surmounted this, we commence in earnest the descent from our elevation of 3,040 or 3,050 feet; and a very rapid descent it is. The road zig-zags down the terribly abrupt side of the moraine; it is only just wide enough for the coach, and at each corner it looks as if we must go over the edge. But horses and driver alike know their work, and only a foolishly nervous person need feel anything but the keenest enjoyment as we swing along at a real good pace. The gorge narrows and closes in on us; the road leaves the moraine and cuts in along the face of the cliff, propped up here and there with wooden stays where it actually overhangs the brawling torrent below. This torrent has to be crossed once and again, by stout black wooden bridges; note the colour of the snow-water, melted ice; a blue green that I should call glaucous. It is a tremendous fine bit of driving, this Otira Gorge, and one not to be missed. Drive down it; that is, start from Christchurch, not up it (*i.e.* from Greymouth), is my advice to any one who thinks of going that way; and don't fail to secure a box seat. After such an early *chhota haziri* at Bealey, one is quite ready for a good breakfast at the Otira Hotel, with fifteen miles left behind us. Already, as we came down the gorge, the character of the scenery had begun to change. The absolute bareness of nearly all yesterday's drive had yielded to black-looking forests of birch, and this in turn now gave place to the dense and varied jungle that clothes all the waste lands of the west coast. For thirty-seven miles the road is right through this bush; and very beautiful it is. Big pines (rima or red pine and others), big fern-trees, a wealth of varied vegetation. There is one twelve-mile avenue of unbroken bush. We follow the Otira river until it joins the

Teremakau and then along the course of that to Kumara. Here and there is a clearing—Jackson's, Taipo (= Shaitan; why so called I do not know), and others. The snow-capped Alexander is on our right; and the river brawls beneath it over a wide shingly bed. Gradually the hills become lower and lower; all are now wooded to the peak; here we pass a flat of rich land, undrained swamp, but capable of reclamation. Suddenly we find ourselves in Dillman's Town and Kumara—the face of nature seamed and made hideous in the search for gold. The townships are high above the river, and all around are vast water-flumes and masses of rubble and refuse. No quartz-stamping here, but washing for alluvial gold. A very bad lunch at Kumara, and then on (leaving the coaches to pursue their road to Hokitika) by such a funny little tramway: a one-horse affair; wooden rails of the smallest conceivable gauge; the tramcar a ramshackle box, a cross between a 'bus and a Black Maria. The line bores its narrow way through dense bush to the river; it is pretty, only we have had about enough bush for the day. Then the river has to be crossed in a cage which runs on a wire rope stretched from bank to bank; the fixed engine runs it smoothly across, and drives a sawmill in the intervals. Over the river the tram runs on to Greymouth, getting out of the bush on to a very ugly sea-beach cut up with diggings and washings for gold. We are not sorry to reach Greymouth after thirteen hours of travel; nor to spend there a quiet day of rest before resuming the road. It is a quiet little place; terminus of a railway that is to grow into a Midland, reaching to Nelson on the one side and to Christchurch on the other. We passed on the road surveyors at work on the latter branch at and under the Otira Gorge; we shall see the construction of the other branch actually in hand at both ends as we go to Nelson. How the line is ever to have the remotest chance of paying, it passes my wit to conceive. The line must be costly, and most of the country it passes through is unfit for agricultural and for pastoral industry, nor have minerals been found in it as yet. Where there are minerals—coal and gold—the railway already reaches, or will do when it gets to Reefton; and that ought to be quite far enough for it. But so long as British capital chooses to let itself be available, so long, I suppose, will works like this railway and the harbour at Greymouth (and at many another place) be taken in hand by the guileless New Zealander. Greymouth can, I should say, never be a large port; yet it has planned its breakwater on a most extensive scale. Not unnaturally it remains unfinished, and seems likely to remain so. A nasty swell breaks in over the bar, and the breakwater leaves off in mid-air, so to say, with rails rusting, and the weather or sea-face uncoped, undressed, unfinished. It affords, it is true, the one promenade in Greymouth—when it is fine; a rare occurrence, but one that came off for our benefit. There is a noble view from the end of it towards the ranges we have crossed, and away to the south of them appears Mount Cook—the monarch of New Zealand mountains.

The morning is dull as we start next day and rail past Brunnerton and its coal-mines as far as the line at present goes—Totara Flats ; and then coach on to Reefton. A good deal of the scenery on the way is very like what I have seen in the Malay Peninsula—except, of course, as regards the kinds of trees that make up the jungle. Much diversity of low hills, all forest-clad except where artifically cleared; interspersed with level lowlands, mostly swamps undrained and useless. Rice-fields, of course, are absent ; they are replaced by grazing clearings on the drier flats. Reefton is the centre of the gold-mining industry of these parts. There are several mines at work, and I suppose paying. The companies have the advantage over the Ballarat people in having ample water to drive their machinery for crushing quartz, and the pumping and shaft-work of the mine ; it is a lot more economical than steam. Hotel accommodation is hardly to be called magnificent at Reefton ; a very pot-housey dining-room, awfully shut in and stuffy. My English fellow-travellers, not less than my Anglo-Indian self, marvelled greatly at the way in which people in New Zealand keep their houses shut up, even in weather that they deemed warm and we found chilly. The first thing one had to do generally was to open the windows ; the next was, if possible, to get them to stay open—for many times we found them not built to stay open of themselves at all. The houses are nearly all of the same minute shanty kind that the up-country colonist seems to prefer. It is the fashion to speak of Japanese houses as "toy"; but these New Zealand dwellings have a better claim to that description. Look at that butcher's shop; it is exactly—joints and all—like one in a child's play-box. And some of the dwellings are so cramped, confined, and dirty, that no decent Japanese would dream of dwelling therein. The drive from Reefton to Longford is said to be very beautiful. I do not feel in a position to express a decided opinion. When everything is hidden in low, grey cloud, and the rain descends ceaselessly and soakingly, beauty disappears, and you who ought to be elevating your soul by the contemplation of it, are merely wet through, and dull, and cross. There is plenty of bush, but the clearing through it is not made pretty by fallen and yet standing logs all charred and burnt (no removal of them except by burning *in situ* appears to be ever performed in these parts). There are plenty of streams, of which most unbridged: thank goodness they are not in flood, else should we have to turn back to Reefton. There is really nothing to remark except the postal delivery—paper or letter flung down in the rain and mud by the driver as the gate is passed by the unstopped coach, to wait there until picked up by whom it may concern; until we reach the Inangahua, and cross it, coach and all, on a flying bridge, a big raft attached by ropes and blocks to a wheel that runs on a wire rope stretched above us across the stream. The current is so sluggish that we by no means fly: rather crawl insensibly; and not long after reach the junction where the Buller receives the Inangahua. Here we waste an hour and a half for no earthly perceptible purpose, for lunch takes but half-an-hour; and then drive up the Buller Gorge, for nearly seven mortal hours. It is impossible to say what the scenery around is like; the clouds have stooped from heaven and taken the shape with fold to fold, and a good many folds to spare, of mountain, and of everything except what is in your immediate vicinity; but the gorge is really beautiful. The river, narrowing gradually, as gradually we rise nearer to its sources, has worn its way through rocks that seem harder and firmer—less crumbly and disintegrating than in the Otira—real solid rock; the water colour is a fine blue, the rocks often red. Here the river rushes almost as tumultuously as in those rapids near Kioto, and the hill-sides are thicker with dense bush than those that rise above the Japanese stream. Steep is the road, and narrow, with here and there a sheer drop to the rocks and river below, down which should we fall (as the Bishop and his clerical companion nearly did in one place), coach and passengers would speedily be converted into matchwood and corpses. At the Lyell,—a straggling street of houses, each perching out half of it over the ravine,—a welcome cup of tea has to last us up to Longford, not reached till half-past 8 P.M. Along this drive there are, for the first time in our New Zealand wanderings, many birds to be noticed:

the parson-bird, with white choker and tie; green parrots (or parakeets), lots of them; finches; sparrows; Maori-hens—very perky and unafraid; large handsome pigeons; rakas—regular foolbirds, they say, of which if you shall shoot one, the rest will flock round to investigate and mourn until you have bagged every one, and there's none left to continue the inquiry and lamentation. At Longford we pig it much as we have done at the other "accommodation houses" on the road, yet are free from the wicked ones which some had led us to fear here; and sleep the sleep of the just after our all but twelve hours' coaching. From Longford we pass the junction of the Mangles River, a "romantic bit" (guide-book); near the Owen, "another fine vista" (guide-book again); Granity Greek, "very interesting" (as before), and the spot where the Rotoroa joins the Buller, "one of the wildest gems of river scenery that one could hope for" (really the last guide-book quotation). The guide-book is quite right; but I wish it would not keep on raining so, and that the driver would not take us along as if we were following the hearse at a funeral. Rapid motion through bright clear air, that is exhilarating, something to rejoice in; but crawling wearily through mist and rain! Why can't we get along a bit and have done with it? By the time we reach our sole change of horses in the whole day's drive, with lunch still two hours ahead of us, even Mrs. H., the ever bright and cheerful and pleasant, is more than half cross (the only time I ever saw her so). We are tired of noticing the "shady recesses that murmur at morn" of the little Hope River, up which we turned away from the Buller; the isolated single shanties, miles apart, of miners who prefer independence and bare subsistence in the midst of solitude to working for wages with their fellows on capitalized mines; the little scratchings and washings that they have made near their hovels in their search for gold; the else unbroken, unending bush; all we want is to get on. But still we crawl along funereally; it is exasperating. At length we climb the saddle, the central ridge, made hideous—as all clearings are—with charred logs and stumps unremoved and partially burnt, among which roam grimy sheep; the bush gets thinner, more forests of charred poles, then open country, cultivated or pastoral, low, treeless green hills, and a level road. But still we crawl; and it is only after seven hours of it that the landlady from the Orkneys (or the Shetlands, I forget which) gives us what she can at the Motupiko inn. We have still three hours more to do, crossing Spooner's Range—very bare and ugly, now being tackled by the railway, but with a really pretty view from the top over the Waimea Plains on to Nelson and the good old ocean beyond: a view that is home-like and charming in its rustic and fertile calm; and finally an hour and a half by rail, and we are in Nelson. About Nelson may be had, in the season, shooting of pig (tame ones gone wild for generations), deer (introduced from home), duck (I saw a few here and there), quail (Californian, fine big birds with strong and numerous broods of young did I see along the road), and (if you consider them game as the gentle sportsman who sat next me seemed to do), swamp-hens and rakas and parrots of sorts. A day of somnolence and placid strolling about in and around the town and the Botanical Hill succeeded our five days' coaching ; not entirely a day of pure enjoyment, for we were anxious to get on to Wellington—I *en route* to Napier, and Our Humorist to catch a boat for Auckland. But the Union Company, with that careful forethought for the convenience of travellers which so distinguishes it, had despatched two boats to Wellington the day before, and had none going to-day. "There'll be one to-morrow leaving at 5 A.M.," said the Agent ; and, when Our Humorist, in his suavest manner, remarked on the awkward distribution of their service, proceeded to get excessively irate. "I've been here twenty years," he raved, "and never heard such complaints made ;" and his wrath exploded in inarticulate ejaculations as Our Humorist remarked sweetly on the pity of it that this long experience had not led to better arrangements, and on the proof his statement afforded of the long-suffering patience of the travellers in New Zealand. The Union Steamship Company of New Zealand has a practical, indeed an absolute, monopoly of the inter-coastal service of the colony, and, like other monopolies that we wot of, is far too strong to be lightly assailed. But elsewhere, say on the Irrawaddy, for instance, the Flotilla Company does at least do you well on board: there are roomy cabins, with decent appointments, and food and service that need not be grumbled at. But this colonial monopoly puts four berths into a cabin barely big enough for two, and erects between each pair of cabins one single washhand basin for the use of the eight passengers; or it turns its saloon into one huge cabin with berths on and above the seats where, in daylight, you sit at meat, and the smoking-room as its deck-cabin to receive all that cannot be jammed into the saloon. The meals are of the plainest, and the attendance of the offhand and inattentive kind which is *not* exceptional in the colonies. Its steamers rarely (never in my experience) start in time; and when it does build a good-sized boat, she breaks down every trip (that is what the *Monowai* did, all I have ever heard of her). So we had two nights and a day in Nelson—a quiet place, with no industries to speak of; hops are not grown half, nor nearly half, as they used to be; yet two breweries are going, and there is fruit enough to feed two jam factories. It rejoices in a cathedral (all wood) and a bishop of its own; a number of people living moderately on independent means in charming wooden bungalows; a harbour to be entered only at high water, and then only. by boats of light draft; and a picturesque situation, surrounded by rounded hills of varying height and outline, green, though treeless, with a view of bolder ranges in the distance. By 5 A.M. we were duly on board the *Rotten Rower* (the Maori spelling is Rotorua), and of course she did not start till 6. On the way to the entrance to Picton Sound (that's not the name of it, if it has a name, as probably it has; I mean the Sound, long and narrow and deep, at the end of which lies Picton), you pass through a strait that truly deserves the name; a reef runs out and leaves the most exiguous space to pass in, through which the tide rushes at a best-on-record sort of pace; and then you enter the Sound—truly a very pretty one, with its little town charmingly perched away at the end, backed by pleasing hills. A little place with a little railway to Blenheim (how martial and patriotic our names are here, to be sure)! it lies dreaming of the greatness to come when its depth of harbour, its coal and gold and antimony, its mutton and wool and lumber, shall attract something more than the one sailing ship that lies by the little wharf (and has lain for weeks, and will lie for weeks to come), and the brief visits of the Union steamers. And so good-bye to the South or Middle Island, and across with a fresh wind (rather too fresh for some) to Wellington, the capital of the colony, too late for anything but supper and bed.

You will have noticed, perhaps, that, so far, the Maori has not received the honour of mention in these pages. That is his fault. I cannot, as a truthful pensman, write of what I have not seen; and I saw no Maori in the Middle Island. There are a few, I am told; but very few, and merged in the general population, not dwelling apart with some show of independence as in the North Island. The Chinaman I did see; right away south in Southland is the pig-tailed heathen present, but looking unnatural and preternaturally ugly in his European clothes. I do not envy a Cantonese living in the climate of Queenstown. And many a sight that is worth seeing have I also left out for want of having seen it: the Lakes of Otago and Southland, excepting only Wawkatip; Mount Cook (Aorangi, the Cloud-piercer) with its enormous glaciers, Tasman and Mueller and Murchison and more besides; all the east coast from Christchurch to Blenheim; the Buller from the Junction to Westport—the best piece, so they say, finer than what I did see, so far as rain permitted. People are fond of comparing the Otira with the Buller. There is no true comparison to be made; the styles are too different. The Otira grandiose, bare or gloomy with black birch, and big with mountain and glacier and immense moraine; the Buller graceful with the free rush of blue water through forest-clad ravines, alive with birds and varied and almost too profuse vegetation, beautiful but not imposing. The Otira strikes the imagination, the Buller charms the fancy. If I had to advise how best to see this part of New Zealand, I should say do the Buller from Nelson to Westport; return by sea to Nelson; get by land from Nelson to Blenheim and on to Christchurch— or by sea if that is too long a journey; do the Otira from Christchurch to Greymouth (or Hokitika) and leave that by sea. This would give you a rather large dose of Union Steamship discomfort ; but you would see the Buller and the Otira the best way about, and would escape the uninteresting piece from Greymouth to the Inangahua Junction—a day and a half's journey.

CHAPTER XI.

THE REGION OF UNCEASING FIRE.

WELLINGTON, I am sorry to say, I can tell you no more about than I could about Christchurch. It has a good harbour with a villanous reef of rocks barring the entrance, and a pretty situation encircled by hills. (You are perhaps getting tired of this phrase, or something like it, applied to each New Zealand port in turn. But it is true; each of them *is* pretty—except the Bluff.) Having delivered myself into the hands of Cook, and being bound (as I thought) to be in Auckland for a steamer on a certain day, I had of necessity to proceed as per programme—except when the Union Steamship Co. upset it; and it upset me out of the one day that I had destined to Wellington. So after arriving at 9 at night, off I went by rail at 6.30 next morning by one of the two private (*i.e.* not Government) railways in New Zealand. It is a pretty bit of country that the line passes through as far as Otaki, first up and through and down the encircling hills aforesaid, and then along the rocky sea-coast with the old whaler's island of Kapiti in sight. After that it is dull enough—swampy with much flax (looking like a kind of aloe) and bush—cleared and charred (as usual) in not a few places. Here and there a Maori settlement—very unnative and unromantic, both as to huts and as to garb of their occupants. A breakfast car on the train is a bit of good bandobast not before experienced. At Palmerston it was necessary to leave the train for the coach, the line constructed through the Manawatu Gorge being not yet open for traffic. Here reappeared Our Enthusiast and Scion of Noble House; and we coached on to Woodville. The gorge is said to have been fine once; it isn't now, the railway cutting has spoilt it. Nor is the road remarkable except for its narrowness. The only pretty bit is the entrance at the Woodville end. Rail again from 3 to 9 brings us to Napier—through country of bush at first, with many ugly clearings, the bush ceasing suddenly as we reach the eastern side, and giving place to wide grazing downs. The soil is of great fertility in this district, and carries certainly six—some say eight or even ten, but this is bluff—sheep to the acre. It could support a large population if it were held by many for themselves, instead of by a few who find their profit in growing mutton and wool for a distant, not a resident, population. For all that, Napier must go in for its half-a-million or so to improve its harbour, which certainly needs improvement; it has built itself a fine sea-face, and is aiding nature to reclaim by silting up the watery flats that almost surround it. The charming hillock on which its residences stand was evidently once an island;

streets and offices, &c., lie on the level at its feet. The climate is noticeably warmer than in the South Island. Only one day here, and then two days coaching to Taupo. People have tried to count how many times the coach crosses the stream up whose course the road runs before it reaches the uplands ; but as in the case of the stone Buddhas on the river bank at Nikko, no two computers arrive at the same result. It is somewhere about fifty ; and as the bed is rubbly, there is no lack of jolting. Fortunately nothing worse, no floods to delay us, or—more disastrous—to upset the coach. This did happen once ; the driver thought the flood not too high to cross, but, arrived at the farther bank, found it cut away and too steep to mount. Trying to turn the coach, over it went; and, while he saved his passengers, his horses were drowned. The chief characteristic of the uplands is fern ; miles and miles of hill, of outline bold and varied enough, covered with bracken (rapa, I believe, the native name). A bright fine day and pleasant fellow-voyagers in a coach not too full, with wide extending views back to Napier and the sea, make the morning pass away pleasantly ; but tiffin on utterly tasteless and leathery mutton is not so cheerful. Really this accommodation house at Pahui is the meanest in building and in board that I have come across. A long climb brings us to the top of the saddle, and then a fine down-grade and another long ascent on the far side. The latter part of the descent at Tikiakura is steep, the road narrow, looking right down on the stream ;

a wooden rail protects it. I cannot understand how any one can feel nervous in rattling, as the experienced MacAuley rattles his coach, down such a splendid bit of driving as this. Yet such men are. One, it is related, at the steepest and narrowest part, clutched at the reins, and, before the driver could check him, turned the leaders right on to the rails. Over they went; the driver, poor fellow, was killed, while the idiot passenger—of course—escaped. There is a second down-grade towards the end of the day—finer than the first. It is a glorious view in the evening light (the best of all lights for scenery) from the summit of Tauranga Kuma down into the deep-cut valley, with terraced banks, bare to windward, forest-clad in the sheltered ravines; we halt a while to gaze on it,—"the finest view in New Zealand," says the enthusiastic local man;—and then spin along, descending 1,500 feet in three miles and in eighteen minutes. A modest but clean and decent inn shelters us for the night in the hamlet of Tarawera (not to be confounded with the ill-omened mountain of that name), and off we go again at 7.30 next morning. The road at first is finely picturesque as we wend our devious way about and across these deep-cut terraced ravines; but before we reach the summit the bush ceases and yields to scrub or rubbishing grass; and at the top and on to Rangitaiki it is very desolate and drear: partly unwholesome-looking swamp; partly bare volcanic soil; partly tufts of useless ugly grass or stunted puny manuka. The solitary inn, where again we endure a starvation tiffin, is about the most utterly abandoned, God-forsaken-looking place you can imagine.

On to Taupo the country immediately around one is not much better. Not a sign of human habitation—none, indeed, since Tarawera, except that dreary inn (with the landlady mortal sick, poor soul!) and one, or it may have been two, Maori settlements, and those empty. No sign of life, except a derelict sheep from a mob, marching from the droughty plains of Napier (for that fertile land has its droughts, though as nothing to the Australian version, or the Indian, of that terror to beast and man) to the valley of the Waikato; and a few wild horses that stand and gaze at us afar off. (All animals imported here seem to lose a few which run and breed wild—horses, cattle, sheep, goats, cats, dogs, pigs.) The only beauty is in the distance: the great snowy shoulders and peak of Ruapehu, the smoking cone and long flat ridge of Tongariro, rise clear in the soft blue air; and soon we sight the blue waters of Taupo—greatest of New Zealand lakes. And so we enter on the Region of Unceasing Fire, generally called the Hot Lake District. As the lakes are *not* hot, while the fire *is* never resting, my name is not only better-sounding but also true.

At Taupo you command from the Terraces Hotel a fine view of the lake and mountains just mentioned, and close at hand are natural hot baths, in the hollow under the hill. There, too, is a natural black terrace, curious, but uncanny-looking, gruesome. Or, if you prefer it, you may go some miles on to Joshua's Sanitarium, where you will have no view, but find yourself right down in the hollow in the midst of the hot springs. In any case, you must not omit to see the geysers and hot springs on the bank of the Waikato, just off the road to Joshua's. The setting is picturesque, the strong clear river winding in a deep-cut bed between rocky banks; and the steam and hot water break out in a score of places for half a mile along, from the very edge of the cold stream up to near the top of the slope. The chiefest and best is the Crow's Nest. The stuff deposited by the water has formed a sort of cup—a hollow cone with the top cut off, and from this, at intervals, shoots up a strong jet of boiling water to a height of say 80 feet—not straight up, but slantin'dicularly. Then Wairakei is to be done; a little valley cramfull of splendid shows. The Champagne Pool, where the water is in a constant state of bubble and boil—a great cauldron that seems ever effervescing but never bursts up into a geyser; the Pack-horse Mudhole, said to have been made active by a pack-horse falling in (bad for the horse), where the black mud rises and seethes and spurts up in a miniature geyser of molten rock; the great Wairakei geyser, playing full and strong, but not very high, every six minutes, and forming beneath a small yellow terrace—model of the lost wonders, the pink and white Terraces of Rotomahana; the porridge pots, grey and cream-coloured and white, in which the ever-heaving mud is ceaselessly burst through by little spits of energy that form perfect-shaped smooth flower-petals, and throw up from the crater little pellets of mud; the lake of exquisite, turquoise-blue; geysers, the Twin, the Prince of Wales's, the Terikiriki—all gaily active; all these and more, and everywhere the richest colouring of red and purple and orange and yellow on the disintegrated rocks round blowhole and pool and geyser. Here is steam at work with the steady, regular, ceaseless sound of a donkey-engine; there is a mysterious pool where the waters seem to be sucked down and thrown up again from unknown depths. And all this in a little bit of a ravine that you could easily throw a stone across, from side to side, or, for the matter of that, from end to end too. It is a wonderful spot: an epitome *in petto* of the Region of Unceasing Fire. Another fine thing to see, between Wairakei and Taupo, is the Huka Falls of the Waikato. The river narrows to a channel that seems artificial, so clean is it cut through the rock, and down this it rushes in broken rapids to throw itself over a fall of some thirty feet only, into a wide pool. No great height of a fall, truly; but the hurry of the pent-up water, the delicious cool greenness of its colour, its volume and sound and spray as it falls—they are good to see and to linger over for a while. Our Enthusiast and I had heard that one might get in under the fall, and diligently scrambled and searched for a way, but found none. I am sure there is none; neither is the fall high enough, nor the river

The Region of Unceasing Fire. 213

rapid or full enough, nor the rocks steep or overhanging enough, for the water to shoot clear and leave room for man to pass.

From Taupo to Rotorua is some fifty-six miles, and this is done with only one change of horses; cruelly long stages they are wont to make them on these New Zealand coaching routes. A full coach, roads unmacadamized and made only of soft mud, good steady drenching rain all day long—no wonder we laboured sorely and often seemed as if we should stick fast or topple over in the mud; until at last we did stick, and all hands to the wheels alone set us going again. Weary and sodden were we after ten and a half hours of such a road in such weather. As we passed Whakarewarewa the steam rising from its many geysers, and the like, was immense. Heavy rain and a high river always, it is said, make them extra lively—and naturally enough. And such a smell of sulphur in all the air as we drove on into Rotorua. Our Scion gasped and groaned with disgust. Next morning it was not so bad by a long way; we lounged around Rotorua, and went all over Whakarewarewa. The Waiotapu valley we declined to go to—the place is twenty miles off, the Maoris there are extortionate, and with doing what we had done plus Tikitere on the following day, we thought we had seen enough of the infernal regions for the time being. Rotorua or Ohinemutu and Whakarewarewa are simply riddled with ventholes from the volcanic forces below. At each is a Maori settlement, and the occupants need not search for fuel. Scrape a bit of a hole in the ground and your oven is ready; drop your potatoes in that pool and they are soon boiled. Take care where you walk, or you may put your foot into a natural kettle of scalding water. Some of the pools are of only a pleasant warmth; troops of naked brats dive in them for coppers. I did not notice anywhere here the splendid colouring of Wairakei; the area is far larger and the sights less varied here than there. At Whakarewarewa there are two large geysers— Pohutu and Waitiki, of which I did not see the former play; the latter is placed high on a terraced platform of its own building, and throws a grand body of steaming water at least thirty-five feet high. Down by the river go off under-water explosions, now like a pistol-shot, now like a sharp musketry-fire, again (I was told) with the boom of cannon (but this last I did not hear). Here are large baths, knocked out of shape, some of them, by the Tarawera bust-up in '86; and near Rotorua is a regular bathing establishment with medical officer, and patients taking a regular course. The Priest's bath is said to be the most potent; Madame Rachel will enamel your skin and make it beautiful for ever; the Blue Bath is blissful to swim in. These places are all interesting, and if not all beautiful, at least not hideous—although Our Authoress and Our Scion turned back from Whakarewarewa, so sieve-like was the earth with fuming blowholes. Nevertheless we brought them through Tikitere—a place reached by launch across the lake of Rotorua and

The Region of Unceasing Fire. 215

a half-hour's coach drive on. This scene is indeed hideous. It is nothing but a collection of cauldrons, big and little, of boiling mud, black, bituminous; not boiling gently, calmly, but furiously raging, chafing to burst out and follow the clouds of steam that rise high over the rugged lips of the bowl. Elsewhere are sulphur beds which are known as Sodom and Gomorrah—desolate and ugly in the extreme, but furnishing excellent material for the chemical works away in Auckland.

A very pleasant day may be spent in the steam launch on Lake Rotorua, taking first the island of Mokoia. Here was Hinemoa's bath (the story has been told too often to bear repeating), a good deal upset by the '86 eruption; and the Skeleton in the Tree—which I would not go to see: the natives had a row over it a year or so before, *re* the profit made by showing the thing to the much-fleeced globe-trotter, and one party cut all the bones out of the tree; when peace was restored, the bones were fixed up again, *tant bien que mal*, and are now shown as if they had never been disturbed! It is a quiet little place, where a few lazy Maoris dwell at ease amidst their patches of yams and potatoes, common and sweet, and maize. Thence cross to Tengae for Tikitere, and after doing that devil's delight, get away to Hamarana, and lunch by the spring. Spring is hardly the word; in the midst of a thicket wells up through a large crevice, quite six feet by four, a regular river of the coldest and purest water—a marvellous contrast to the heated waters, impregnated with countless malodorous elements, that rise so freely such a little distance away. Hang over the chasm where this stream issues steadily and strongly up, and I think you will own that you have never seen such a magnificent colour effect. I certainly have not myself received such an impression of infinite unfathomable blueness as is given by the rich intensity of the blue that predominates in the iridescent and opalescent colouring of Hamarana.

You have, of course, to fee a Maori for gazing on this sight. The Maori as you see him in these regions is simply and inevitably detestable. They are said to have been a handsome people; if there be any beauty left in man, woman, or child, of them, it is hidden fast away out of sight of the passing voyager. Their garb in the old days, national, characteristic, was also sufficient, surely, for decency, and not wanting in picturesqueness; now it is—or if it is not, most successfully and exactly imitates— the broken-down, shabby, dirty Europe clothes of a white navvy or of a half-caste "loafer" in India. The women, rigged out in gowns of atrocious colour, and wideawake battered straw hats, are coarse-featured and coarse-voiced; and men and women alike having no work of any kind to do (the rents paid for occupying their lands, and the fees they extort for sight-seeing, amply keep them), are idlers and drunkards of the most completely developed description. In vain Sir George Grey gets them to sign with him an agreement, a bond, to refrain from liquor; they laugh and drink on. The otherwise

The Region of Unceasing Fire.

not uncomfortable Lakes Hotel is made hideous with their howling in the bar—a spot just opposite the dining-room door and in close proximity to the passage and the smoking-rooms, where residents in the hotel must needs pass. It is beastly, and a disgrace to the hotel and to the place. The 'Arry out for a 'oliday sort of tourist, however, likes it and encourages it; stands 'em drinks and makes them dance and sing. Often, too, he also makes an exhibition of himself. Here is the story of a man of whom some of us saw much more than we wished. Dead drunk in saloon of P. and O. coming out, fell asleep head on lady's shoulder; carried out most neatly by two stewards. Twice, having placed all his luggage on board, got drunk and missed his steamer. Drunk and riotous in dining-room of Grand Hotel, Dunedin; had to be suppressed. Reappeared at Whakarewarewa and appropriated our buggy; when our Authoress and our Scion (as before noted) turned back and wished to occupy that vehicle, refused to quit, or to listen to the driver; being drunk, had to be forcibly ejected by three men. Found drunk, coatless, collarless, in hotel passage by front door at 8 A.M. Got to Auckland somehow; drunk and disorderly in street, passed night in lock-up, fined next morning, and then packed out of the colony by Cook's agent as too utterly unendurable. Fine sort of specimen of an Englishman to go travelling in our colonies, don't you think? He is at least a startling exception, thank goodness; whereas that the Maori around Rotorua should be a more or less drunken loafer is the standing rule; if there be exceptions, they did not come under my notice. Thus it was that when I heard that the departure of the mail steamer had, without warning, some ten days only before the fixed date, been postponed for five days (surely a pretty tall order, isn't it?) and thus doubled the time I intended to spend in Auckland, I determined to go and see the Maori away from the regular line of tourist travel: a week's journey on horseback and in canoe, with only so much kit as my horse could carry on the saddle in front of me. But first I wished to see something of the desolation wrought by the eruption of Tarawera in 1886. The uncertainty of the weather, with the want of a companion, (for Our Enthusiast couldn't come,) prevented my going right away to Tarawera; but I rode with Macdonald, the guide, to Wairoa. You may read what kind of place this was, and the way on thence to the Terraces, and what they were, in Froude's *Oceana*. Now—*quantum mutatus!*—the Lakes of Tikitapu and Rotokakahi that charmed Froude with their colour are of a ghastly grey, thick with pumice mud; the road that runs by them is broken with earthquake-riven rents, or buried in mud; so bad is it that here and there we have to dismount and make a way to lead our horses over. Wairoa was buried in twenty feet of mud; and of all the houses, huts, hotels, mission church, manse and school, but one hut is standing—Sophia's, in which crowded all that were saved that night. All that smiling valley and lakelet behind Wairoa is a waste

AT WAIROA AFTER THE ERUPTION.

The Region of Unceasing Fire. 219

of mud ; the waterfall is shattered by earthquake shocks ; Lake Tarawera is of that same unlovely hue as the upper lakes ; bush is devastated, ruined, or buried in the all-enshrouding mud. Of course in the five years and more that have passed since then much of the mud has washed away into the lakes (hence their colour), and here and there appear the points of palings, the seats and tops of the wheels of a buggy, the broken remnants of hut or house or school. Sometimes other things come up. But a few days before, Macdonald had followed up the end of a blanket laid bare by the rain-wash; it led to the corpses of two children. Yet is this grey and smothering mud most fertile. How the Cape thorn has spread itself over the surface ; grass, too, good grazing grass, has come up ; the mission orchard—walnut and quince and damson—is bearing gaily ; here are dog-roses in blossom ; the blue-gum is beating even itself in rapidity of growth ; down below fern-trees are enlarging their fronds. We see Tarawera in the distance, utterly bare, sullen-looking ; still so hot, they say, that you can thrust your stick into the soft summit of him, and bring it up charred and too hot to hold. Nine craters opened up in that long flat ridge, and behind it broke open a chasm of I forget how many miles in length, that swallowed up Lake Rotomahana and its exquisite terraces, and has left in place of them chaos and ancient darkness, the abomination of desolation. It is not my intention to tell you all about the eruption ; I only want to tell about what I have seen. If you travel this way, you can hear all you want from those who were through it all, if you ask McRae at the Lakes Hotel, Rotorua, or Sophia, the guide (lame now, poor woman), or one of the housemaids at the Grand Hotel, Auckland (name unknown to me).

CHAPTER XII.

THE WANGANUI—AUCKLAND.

I DO not think many tourists make their way from Rotorua to Wanganui. Macdonald, the licensed guide, had not taken more than three parties through before me (one included a lady, who rode cross-saddle); and one had come up from Wanganui. It is rather an expensive trip, as you have to pay for your guide and his horse and your own horse, and, *besides*, find them not only while with you, but also while returning to Rotorua. For one travelling alone, it comes to £3 a day (or a trifle more or less) for nine days. Then a special canoe down the river—one day or a day and a half, is £4, and your expenses from Wanganui, *viâ* New Plymouth, to Auckland, will be nearly £5. In all, some £36 for a trip that took me just nine days; *i.e.* £4 a day. And it is doubtful whether you get quite your money's worth. I was at any rate disappointed in my expectation of seeing the Maori unwesternized; indeed, for much of the way, I saw no Maoris at all. I do not think you will see any remnant of the old Maori, unless in the Urewera country, which is not easy to enter. Even the

Governor does not go into it unless invited by the Chiefs; and their letter of invitation struck my Anglo-Indian mind as a singularly free and equal-to-equal sort of communication. Fancy an Indian Raja—who is at least nominally independent, while these Maori home-rulers are at least nominally subject to the Queen and her representative—fancy one of our Native States signifying to an Indian Governor that he couldn't come to visit it just then, because the chiefs were engaged on business; but that he might, if he pleased, come later on, when their business was over. And this letter seemed to be considered quite a delightfully acceptable one; begged from the Governor, and carefully stored in the Public Library at Auckland. Or perhaps in the King Country may be found some traces yet of the Maori as he was. For here, in a colony of the British Empire, is still a gentleman who calls himself King; and has lands, and retainers, and a country that is called by his name. But my route lay far from the Urewera country and touched only the edge of the King country. The first day's ride was 30 miles, the second 26, then in order 37, 52, 27 (much of this last very bad road); passably good going for the same two horses carrying our kit as well as ourselves. To Atiomuri, my first stage, the road is the coach road to Taupo; this time fair overhead and decently dry underfoot. Horohoro is a big hill that we pass, connected with Hinemoa's story; a curious white rock in a green nook looks exactly like a good old single-pole tent ready pitched : red rocks look down on it; and Atiomuri, with the rocky-banked Waikato in front, has a regular Deccan hill-fort kind of rock behind it. And a fort the old Maoris made of it, as they did of many another isolated summit, being (*teste* the Pakeha Maori) extremely well up in the art of fortification. I wondered, as I looked on these "pas," as they are called, how the garrison kept itself in water. But when I read "Old New Zealand" I understood that it did not require to provision itself for a siege. If supplies ran out, the beleagured one would be re-victualled by his friend the enemy, so that the fighting might go on. You see, the principal business of man was to fight; and as it is evident that a man cannot fight if he has no food or water, it is ridiculously clear that you must —if you wish to fight him—supply him with them when he has none. When you have killed him you have your reward ; for then he furnishes you with a meal—you eat him, and consume with his flesh the *virtus* or valour that was in him, and which you thereby annex and add to your own. (Of course, if he kills you, he gets the victuals you gave him and you and your valour too, and the sum does not cancel out quite so smoothly. But it is your business to prevent that ; else for what are you born a man, and wield a spear?). The modern Maori is said to be rather ashamed of his ancestors' (or, in the case of the older men,—*his own*) anthropophagic taste. Yet I found the guide at Whakarewarewa by no means bashful in pointing out the natural oven that was specially reserved for cooking chiefs' brains in. It was quite like an altar of sacrifice; but cold now, its fire dead. At Atiomuri (sweet-sounding name) was the Governor in camp. Not quite the style of thing of an Indian Governor's camp. But nothing in the colonies is in the same plane for style, even for comfort, much less for display, with our Indian way of life. My second stage on from Atiomuri is still the coach road to Taupo; rather dull and uninteresting. Still it is curious to notice a settlement of Mormon Maoris—for even thus far has that singular superstition sent its proselytizers (we shall find them on the Hawaiian Islands too). Farther on we cross Poison Creek—there is death in the draught to whoso drinks of it, man or beast. There is a poison bush, too, which starving or inexperienced cattle eat unwittingly, and go as mad as march hares. Taupo is an exceedingly small and quiet place. One policeman looks after it and all the district round; one of the waifs of society, a 'Varsity man, a gentleman, rusticated to a place where there is no work to be done, and his demon will hurt no one but himself. Work there used to be here, in the old war days; the Fort, a standing memento of those times, is just exactly one of our outposts in Upper Burma.

Fine brilliant weather for our next stage; all round one side of Lake Taupo to Tokaänu at the farther end. New ground again, and a thoroughly enjoyable ride. Through what a deserted country, though! only two tiny native settlements in all the thirty-six miles, and Tokaänu quite a small place in the thirty-seventh. And though much of it is poor land enough, much more is fair to good — yet all alike waste, useless. The scenery is pleasing, as the road winds now on the margin of the lake, where a few wild duck paddle slowly out from shore, now through a narrow gorge made up of old extinct craters, again down a wider valley with sheerdown walls of white, across level lands and hillocks and swamp, with ever in front of us, afar off, the snows of Ruapehu and the steam of Tongariro. Then the Waikato has to be forded near its entry into the lake—luckily not so full as to be impassable, yet full enough to give some little trouble. Close over us is Pihanga, an extinct volcano ; and this is the legend concerning her. Once she was a lovely maiden, and the giants Tongariro and he that is now called Taranaki fought for her. And Taranaki was defeated and fled, and the track that he fled by is the Wanganui River. |But he fled on to the seashore and stayed there, and they called his name Taranaki. And Tongariro won Pihanga for his own. And ever on still clear days men may see the smoke from the long sharp cone of Tongariro, that is called Ngaruahoe, float over and fill the bowl-shaped crater of Pihanga, and know that Tongariro and Pihanga are wed.

There are more hot springs at Tokaänu, and a country inn to put up in, and a waterfall fair to see. Hence may be made excursions to Lake Rotoaira, up Ngaruahoe (7,481 feet) and Ruapehu (8,878 feet). But our way lies right round the base of Pihanga and of these—a splendid ride in splendid weather. The track runs at first broad and good, ascending gradually, with the bare mountains on the right, while the slopes we cross are grass or fern-clad, and the Waikato flows down in the hollow far on our left, beyond which rises a fine forest-clad range of hills—I forget its name. As we get beyond the road surveyor's work, the track diminishes to a mere bridle-path, and soon we get to a region where it can hardly be called a path at all. Down from the blasted and riven ridge of Tongariro—one mass of extinct craters—and its smooth, grey, smoking cone that stands apart, and down from the snows and glaciers of Ruapehu come deep-cut huge ravines and gullies, in which you get a fine variety of rock, whole or disintegrated, mud and stone, and a path that is unvarying in its excessive badness. I suppose a man might ride down them all; but certainly not a man with any consideration for his beast. We led ours in and out of all the big ones—nine in number, I think; and the space that they covered, which Macdonald called seven miles, was the longest seven miles I ever rode (except perhaps marching at night through Burmese mud to surprise a dacoit camp). By the time we are past them we are ready for lunch, having taken five hours over twenty-five miles. And oh for the neat little Jap lunch-boxes! We have to be content with clumsy sandwiches wrapped in paper. An hour's rest and on we go, soon reaching the Desert. Truly a desert—bare sand, volcanic rock, and old igneous formations disintegrated by years of snow and frost. No snow or frost now, thank goodness, but good cantering ground on the level up at the top of the water-divide—when down goes a saddle-bag and in it our sole bottle of whisky. Barely enough is saved with which to drink, in Waikato water, perdition to the soul of him who made those straps of perished leather; for not a drop of liquor shall I get now until Wanganui, three days away! The Waikato comes down from the sides of Ruapehu, and we cross it as it flows eastward to Lake Taupo; and immediately after we strike the Wangae as it flows westward to the Wanganui. Then many a mile of good going on gently descending downs through the sheep-run of Karioi.

The nags go free on the springy turf, as if they were beginning and not ending the day, and so we finish our fifty-five miles by a quarter to five. Karioi is a big run, over 15,000 acres, but it is poor soil, and carries only some 46,000 sheep. The owner lives away in the South; but the manager is courteous, and shows me over the washing and packing of the wool (shearing is all done). And the lodging at the accommodation house is passable, but the board exceeding poor. And the morning and the evening were the fourth day.

A very few miles on the fifth morning brought us into the bush—that bush which is so thick on the western, as it is so thin or absent on the eastern, side of the water-divide. Out of sight go those mountain masses that we have had in sight for days past, and down we go through fine forest by quite a good track for nine miles—to the Government "whares" at Wai Merino. Now there had been heavy rain in these parts—even the rain that fell on us all that day coaching from Taupo to Rotorua, and more besides, so that there were rumours of floods and fears of swamps being impassable; wherefore we sought to inquire at the whares, wherein dwell two men whose part it is to mend the road. But we found them not, and we rode on past Akuni, a native settlement, and ever the road got worse, so that we rode heavily. Howbeit, when we had paced on three hours and more, lo! those two roadmen jogging homeward, smoking the pipe of contentment.

"The road? Oh, all right. You'll find a bit—four or five chains—that you'll need to get off and drive your horses through. The rest's all right, we've just been out patching it up a bit. Going into Karioi to-morrow."

Whereat we were well pleased and rode on hopefully. Nevertheless, I would that I were the Executive Engineer of the district in which these men dwell, or that they were the children of Israel and I Rehoboam, or they Spanish Protestants and I Inquisitor-in-chief. "Road all right except four or five chains!" It is not a disgrace to any country to have a bush track knocked out of shape by heavy rain; but it is a disgrace to a country that claims to be civilized if the men employed by it neglect their work, and no one supervises them or sees that they do it. Here were these two men, drawing good fixed wages, and a full week elapsed since the destructive downpour—surely time enough to render the track in some sort passable, and to ascertain if any damage were done beyond their power to repair. Yet for the swampy part, within easy reach of their free quarters (comfortable and well furnished), the repairing done amounted to just nothing; and for the ghat portion, some way off, they were in complete ignorance that seven miles of it were rendered utterly impassable by countless landslips! and next day they were going to take a holiday to Karioi! Verily, those who work for a free and enlightened democracy have a far easier time than the servants of a bureaucratic despotism; and the free and enlightened democracy aforesaid seems to be well content to be swindled. We had the best part of two hours driving our beasts through the swamp: not clean wholesome mud, but a mass of water and earth, and decaying vegetable stuff, and twisted and contorted roots, most vile to pick a way through. Tommy, the Rat (my nag) lost a shoe and sprained his fetlock; and glad we were at noon to strike the camp of a Government surveyor—one hospitably inclined, who supplemented our poor sandwiches of sardine and cheese with mutton chops and most super-excellent spuds, and with endless libations of tea from the billy. He, too, wondered vaguely why his brother, gone for stores days before to Piperiki (our point for the night) had not yet returned; but neither to him nor to us did the truth suggest itself. So we rode on, past the Italian's solitary hut in the bush, until we came to a deep nalla—bridge washed away—sides cut perpendicular by the flood, rocky, impassable. And we blessed those hard-working roadmen, and off-saddled, tied up the horses, cached the gear, shouldered the "swag" ($=$kit) and footed it. And evermore, as we went, we praised those roadmen; for lo! landslip after landslip had piled tons of mud on the track, or carried whole sections of it away to the bottom of the "kora." There were places where men could hardly pass without footholds cut for them (we met the surveyor's brother cutting them), and these so slippery that McD. fell and hurt his foot. So it went on right through to Piperiki, where we arrived at 7 P.M., only to find that the floods had swept away the Government store, and smashed up the accommodation house; so that there was no one to put up with save a half-caste boatman, who should hire me a canoe next day. So he turned out of his bed, and my guide and I shared it; and we had for dinner, tea and bread-and-scrape and apples. In fine weather and with a decent track it would be a very pleasant ride, this from Karioi to Piperiki; it is a splendid fertile soil much of it, and a glorious forest; there are views down the ghat part of it that are really fine where the path runs along the edge of a good 800 foot drop into the gully below. But with that Kaikatea swamp and the poor feeding and boarding, it was perhaps more varied than pleasing. The nine-mile walk at the end I found very enjoyable after so much riding. At Piperiki I said good-bye to McD., who went back to pick up his horses and return to Rotorua in time for the races (for even that exiguous township has its autumn meeting), and started off in canoe down the Wanganui.

The river is not so deserted as the road. All those fifty-two miles from Tokaänu to Karioi there is not a single vestige or sign of any human habitation whatsoever: except only the temporary huts of a Government surveyor — and these empty. And for the thirty-six miles from Karioi to Piperiki there is only one Maori settlement (a small one) and the solitary hut of an Italian. Karioi itself has nothing except the buildings and inhabitants required for the sheep-run. But along the river are a good many villages. I landed at the first. All the huts, as at Piperiki, are of English fashion; the clothes are of English cut and cloth; every man I met spoke to me in English, and insisted on shaking hands English way. Here, no more than in the Region of Fire, is the native unspoilt by the veneer of civilization. I asked the name of the village; "Jerusalem!" and farther down are Corinth (Koroniti) and London (Ranana) and Athens (Atene), and a lot more idiocy of that kind. The missionary is abroad in the land; and all these Maoris are Christians. I don't think their religion makes the least difference to their lives. They gamble and drink, and live lewdly just as much under a Christian profession as when they were simple pagans, and change from one sect to another—Roman Catholic, Protestant, Dissenter of several species—as easily as they did from the darkness to light (if the missionary's cant phrase may be used). Quite a centre of life this new Jerusalem : here I met the Roman Catholic padre;—the Church of Rome certainly sends out, as a rule, missionaries much more suited to the work and much more acceptable to the general public than does any Protestant sect ; here also, the Italian squatter, friendly but unintelligible in a patois of English and Maori and the tongue of Dante. I went on, and landed at no more settlements that day. Some have good native names, such as Tauwiti nui ; but all are unnative in outward show. At one there is wailing over a death, a man drowned in the flood a week ago ; in another a big piece of red rag with a union jack in the corner hung upside down half-pole high: also for a death. The scenery is good enough in the upper reaches of the river ; bold precipitous banks, profuse bush, hurrying rapids ; but lower down the banks are commonplace, the bush cleared away, the river slow.

The weather turned wet, too, about 3 P.M. ; and as at 8 P.M. we were still seven miles (quite two and a half hours at our then rate of progress) from Wanganui, I stopped at Upokongaro for the night. Bedroom tiny, but clean ; food decidedly poor. But what can you expect for four shillings and sixpence

The Wanganui. 233

per day? It took me till nearly noon next day to reach Wanganui, there being a strong head-wind and squalls; and wet and squally it continued all day. I fled next day by rail to New Plymouth, through a country of no remarkably interesting feature until Mount Egmont comes in sight. But even as the road had played me false with its swamps and landslips, and the river had with head-winds and rain taken one and a half day over a day's journey, so the railway was determined to have its little joke too. The train was a mixed one (I never saw one that wasn't in New Zealand), and a bag of grass-seed thought fit to drop out of a leading truck, get under the wheels, and derail that truck and the two that followed it. We were going at top speed; but that is only about twelve miles an hour, and the place was on the flat—no cutting or embankment—so no harm was done except a delay of three hours while they got back those extravagant and erring trucks on to the line. New Plymouth is hardly so pretty as most New Zealand ports. It has, of course, its costly breakwater and its railway—the former causing a silting up, and the latter of consequence only so long as there is no through line from Auckland to Wellington. The great feature of the place is Taranaki, without which it would be nought. Much, indeed, in the history of the Maori wars, for here and hereabout was much fighting; but nought scenically. Taranaki is neither so high nor so beautiful as Fujisan, but, like that jewel of Japan, it stands alone, the lesser hills bowing themselves lowly afar off; on its head is a "morion, washed with morning," of shining snow; about its feet, the rocks are "encompassed by the inviolate sea." In New Plymouth is a member of a family with many well-known representatives in the Western Presidency; and he is mine host of the White Hart Hotel. Glad to replenish from his stock my exhausted supply of trichis. The Union Steamship Company run twice a week, on the arrival of the mail train from Wellington, a steamer to Onehunga, whence it is a short rail on to Auckland. This, therefore, is the quickest route from the largest town in New Zealand to the capital town, and through it to all the South Island. Naturally, there are a good many passengers. Equally, of course, the Company meets the traffic with a boat of under 300 tons; and you find the saloon one vast dormitory, the smoking-room full of beds, the meals a scramble. Luckily, the weather is fine, and even the often boisterous entrance over the Manukau bar is gentle to us. And so Auckland at last, and comfort and good quarters at the Northern Club. Here, for the first time—since when? I hardly remember, it is so long ago—I have *dinner:* a meal served at a reasonable hour, and of a sort and in a style that deserve that too often misapplied, unmerited designation. There are many good points in Auckland, of which the hospitality and excellence of this club is not the least. It has, like every other colonial town, however small, a Free Library and Reading Room; but it has them far better than most others, enriched by valuable gifts from Sir George Grey. The Museum is not a very great show. But the town is a pleasing one, and the view from Mount Eden is charming. This extinct crater commands a prospect extending from the Manukau bar over all that bay, and the narrow isthmus on which Onehunga stands, right across the fine harbour of Auckland, and islands and extinct craters galore. Certainly a finer view than anything which it was my fortune to see at Sydney. The climate of Auckland is delightful; and the suburbs, with many charming bungalows and compounds dotted about them, are good to look upon. Altogether it seemed that New Zealand had (in the matter of towns) kept its best until last. It is sad to think that so fair an exterior hides what is (I heard in more than one quarter) financially unsound in every direction— public, municipal, business, private. Anyhow, with no less than nine of our No. 4 "push" met together again, the time passed pleasantly and quickly away, until seven of us embarked on the *Mariposa;* and the Third Part of my tour and the eighth month of my leave began together.

CHAPTER XIII.

AUSTRALASIA.

FROM the date that I touched at Port Darwin to the date that I left Auckland is just three months. Not a long time to spend in any country, if one wishes to know all about its institutions and its people. But I did not come with any such wish; I came merely to amuse myself, and I brought no letter of introduction that should open the doors of "society" to me. I did not write my name at any Government House; and I contented myself with just such companions as my travels brought me into contact with, such openings and introductions only as their courtesy provided for me. And so I do not think any very serious weight can be attached to my opinions on men and matters in Australasia; they are about as solid as a butterfly's may be imagined to be on the flowers that he flits among. Yet, as it amused me to form them, it may amuse you who have wandered thus far with me, to hear what they are. If any Australasian reads me he will probably feel a desire to kick me; for there is nothing so sensitive to criticism as your "Cornstalk." And I would not wish to be kicked by him; for he is usually a man of robust physique, long limb, and strong muscle. Nevertheless, I will venture to say that most of the criticism that Froude in his *Oceana* hints rather than positively makes on Young Australia is fully justified. There are, of course, great differences, for the Australian community comprises many distinct classes of men. I do not mean classes as against masses; I mean the three divisions of—first, native-born Australians without European training; second, native-born Australians with such English training as a visit to the old country gains them; and last English-born immigrants. Now the Froudean criticisms—many made, mind you, not by Froude himself, but to him by men themselves belonging to the community criticized, and merely reproduced by him—apply with less and less accuracy as we advance from the first to the third division. Speaking of the first division only, and weakening the remarks down to nothing as we get to the end of the third, I should say that the Australian manner is the most self-conscious, self-assertive, inconsiderate of others, unpolished, that has yet been developed. Of the soundness of the heart, the thoroughness of the sentiment that may underlie that manner, it is not now question; I am speaking only of the outside shown to the passing observer. It was a native-born Australian lady, transplanted by marriage to another part of the Empire, who said to me that all those remarks in *Oceana* on the Australian native were perfectly true. I met in one city two brothers, English; one in the army, stationed in India, the other on a sheep-run up country in Australia. Now, the manner of the former was that usually seen in a British officer ; that of the latter was a great contrast—loud, boisterous. I do not see how in the existing environment any good manner is to be born in Australia. Up country the hardest of lives and the least of society, in the capital a society of plutocrats only, everywhere a devotion to money-making and absence of leisure that render superfluous, impossible, any style but the self-assertive and the pushing. " Good dressing, quiet ways, low tones of voice, lips that can wait, and eyes that do not wander, shyness of personalities . . . to be *light in hand* in conversation." Is the Professor at the Breakfast Table right in considering these "a fair capital of manners to begin with " ? " As a rule, vain, ignorant, underbred, without dignity, without courtesy, and with a conceit that was unbounded." So Froude describes Young Australia ; I am told rightly ; from my own seeing, I should say rightly. Good manners do not, *as a rule*, exist except in those who have come out from England, or who, being " natives," have been to England long and often, the longer and the oftener the better. One youth, hearing I was from India, remarked that he did not think I was dark enough in colour. Did he expect me to be black? or did he mean to say he didn't believe me?

In one respect I go farther than Froude. He says the purity of the Australian pronunciation of English is complete. I should say it is not. I do not know that there is anything to be ashamed of in an Australian accent, any more than in a Scotchman's or Irishman's brogue. But it is there; and it is not, to my ears, a pleasing accent. A cross between an ultra-Cockney and an American twang. A few Americanisms in the language too—"so long" for good-bye—and a good many native-born colloquialisms: "a dead bird" for a dead certainty; "swag" for kit; and "swagger" for a man who walks carrying his kit; "sundowner," which it would take long to describe—you would know all about him if you read Boldrewood's *Squatter's Dream;*—"push" for party, and more besides. But many Americanisms are not there yet, thank goodness; so that one can still speak of the railway station (and not the railroad deepo), of "just behind" (and not "right back of"), and need not interlard one's discourse with "I guess" and "I tell you." Of course these remarks on accent are subject to the same limitation as those on manner; they are less and less true as you proceed to the third division of men. And both sets of remarks are subject to the further limitation that they hardly apply at all in New Zealand. A great difference between each Australian colony and New Zealand lies in this, that in the former there is a distinct colonial type forming, and in New Zealand there is not. There is in New Zealand no sole city the head and centre of the colony; everything is provincial, and each province retains the type (the general manner and accent) of the part of the old country from which it is colonized. I cannot see anything distinctly colonial in Southland and Canterbury, only Scotch and English; and any New Zealander will—the chances are—have the accent (midland or northern or what not) of his ancestral county at home. It follows that any one emigrating from England will in Australia (himself probably, his children certainly) become Australian, in New Zealand provincial. Neither fate appears to me specially desirable; in each, absence of culture and high-bred manner is sure for the children. But the provincialism of New Zealand jars less than the colonialism of Australia.

The newspaper press of Australasia is enormous. Every little bit of a township has a paper or two, and the leading organs in the big cities are extremely well got up and well managed. Their weeklies beat any of our Indian weeklies; their dailies are more full of cablegrams (as they call them) than the *Pioneer* (though I don't know that that is saying very much: our leading paper is hardly the fullest in its telegraphic news). And of all the papers, I think the Sydney press has the best. I do not forget the Melbourne *Argus* and *Age;* but the Sydney *Herald* and *Telegraph* appear to me better done on the whole; and the *Bulletin* is far cleverer than the Melbourne *Punch.* You will notice in the columns devoted to domestic occurrences crowds of entries under the heading "In Memoriam." This will be new to you. It would appear that many colonials, on the anniversary of a relation's death, insert here a notice conceived in the following form, or in words to this effect: "In [sad, loving, or sad and loving, or sad but loving] remembrance of my dear [father, brother, &c.] [here insert name], who died [here give place and time, and also any details that may be of interest, and deceased's age at death]. [Add a verse of Scripture, or several verses of doggrel at discretion.] Inserted by his [daughter, sister, &c.] [here give name in full]." Anything more snobbish and detestable it does not seem to me that one could easily devise. Many omit the verse of Scripture and the doggrel—generally, indeed, except in the Melbourne *Age*. Here there are often columns of the feeblest verse. We were unfeeling enough to hunt for these columns in search of a laugh; for who could help laughing at such rhythm, such sentiment, such rhyme, such choice of words? I give you one specimen from memory:

> From life she is forced to depart;
>   Her troubles and sorrows are o'er;
>   Her weary and grief-laden heart
>   Is heaved by affliction no more.

(This last line I am sure of.) Here is another, copied verbatim:—

> It is just two years ago to-day
> Since my dear mother passed away;
> God loved her best; it was her fate!
>   Inserted by her daughter Kate.

Is it not pitiable? Scarcely less objectionable are the funeral notices, in which the undertakers are permitted to advertise themselves with full names and addresses under pretext of publishing day and hour at which the recently deceased will be interred. In some of the smaller papers you will find whole pages where larrikin idiots are allowed to disport themselves. Under the name of each of a score of parishes in turn will be found a dozen such items as these :—"Where did Tom get these new collars from?" "I wonder what Ella would say if she saw how Dick is carrying on with Etty?" "Harry is getting on well with his dancing, especially when he sits out." Where is the wit in these things? Of what conceivable interest are they to the public? It appears to me to be just one more, and perhaps the most ill-bred, exhibition of the colonial love of self-advertisement which appears in all the journalistic vagaries that we have been speaking of; and in other ways besides.

  The Australian does not, as a rule, it would seem, care to make himself comfortable. I do not mean that there is no comfort in well-found houses in all the colonies. At their homes the well-to-do make themselves comfortable enough, I do not doubt. But out of his own house he is content with rough and ready accommodation. From the time I left Hongkong until I reached the Northern Club in Auckland, I never saw a finger-glass at table (if one asked for one, there was none), and I was never in a bedroom of decent size. Attics of the narrowest kind at the Grosvenor, Sydney; so at the Grand, Dunedin; and everywhere else the most modest space conceivable. The table at hotels in Melbourne and

Sydney is good enough; but elsewhere it is anything from passable down to impossible. Generally enormous portions of meat, and wedges of pudding, with no variety, no cooking. I took a walking tour once in the midlands at home, in all sorts of out-of-the-way places; we put up in any roadside pub. that came in our way. On the colonial main tourist routes we fed much the same as on those remote rustic roads, and were penned at night in far more crowded and less comfortable quarters. In the public baths at Rotorua, even the most exiguous bathing dress, the veriest figleaf, is dispensed with—unless you like to be singular and bring your own. (I speak only of what I know—the men's baths.) Everywhere, however, they provide in the bedroom a hairbrush and comb for you. I wonder they do not add a toothbrush. One man I found complaining because the steamer had not provided a hairbrush and comb for the four-berthed cabin. Evidently the colonial travels light in the matter of toilet. I suppose this is the result of the style of life that most men lead or have led. I have read with much interest some, and with much tedium others, of Mr. Rolf Boldrewood's works. I presume they describe with accuracy Australian life as it was lived in the fifties and thereabouts. Some allowance must, no doubt, be made for the novelist's heightening of colour and deepening of shade to emphasize his contrasts. But that allowance made, it seems clear enough that the usual colonial life is to slave unceasingly, living like a pig the while, until you have made your pile. That is how the Miner lives with his Right, the Squatter with his Dream, and the Reformer as he gains colonial experience. The pile made—what then? The answer is a little vague. But *back to the old country*, if not for good and all, at least for long and frequent intervals, is what it sounds to me. And a very good answer too. Coming from a Colonial, as I believe the author is, it is singularly confirmatory of my own opinion that the colonies are a good place to live out of. From what I have heard of up-country life in small townships, or in back lots in Australia, from what I have seen of remote locations in New Zealand, I had much sooner let my enemies live there than abide there myself. Indian stations, where you find yourself the sole white man, or sole but one, are bad enough; but to my mind better than colonial isolation. And much as its servants are wont to growl at that fearful and wonderful organism, the Government of India, still it is far better to live under than the full-fledged democracy of the colonies. The Government of India is at least one and consistent; it is—as governments go—fairly honest; well-intentioned, and with a very tolerable power to carry out its intentions. Now I do not think any one of these characteristics—which together make a tolerably good government, and the absence of which an extremely bad one—I do not think any one of them can be found in any one colonial Government. One? By no means. There being no natural parties, there are artificial ones, and ministries are formed—generally mighty short-lived ones—in all manner of coalitions and shufflings of the cards. And of course each ministry plays for its own hand, and away goes consistency. As to honesty : I only said that the Government of India was fairly honest as governments go—for it has its little jobs and little bits of backdoor management, nepotism and the rest—but the colonial Governments leave the modest and secret little peccadilloes of India far behind. They job openly and unblushingly. It is a one man one vote country, and every man gives his vote for the best consideration that he can get for it, and the elected candidate votes in the House merely and solely to catch the votes of his constituents for next election. If he catch them not, away goes his £300 a year—or whatever else may be the honorarium by law fixed for his remuneration.

These are opinions not my own, but expressed by Sydney men in conversation in which I took mostly a listening part. And in New South Wales I am inclined to fancy the public jobbery is least, as in New Zealand it is most. I was in Wellington just about the time of a change of ministry. The outgoing ministers grabbed a piece of patronage that it would appear simply indecent in them to assume—the appointment of members of the Upper House, while the incoming ministers (a ministry of bootmakers and other artisans) held a session of a week and voted (by their supporters) for that protracted session the full remuneration for a year ! The railways of New Zealand have cost millions, and they have not one decent through line in the country; nothing but a crowd of little broken bits that lead nowhere; all due to jobbery, for the initial scheme of railway construction provided an excellent system of through lines and feeders, which little pettifogging local interests were by jobbery allowed to break up. Certainly I never heard corruption so freely assigned as a motive or cause as I did in New Zealand. It shows a pretty low estimate of the public probity when it is stated —as in conversation I more than once heard it stated—that the Maori War might have been concluded far more speedily and more satisfactorily than it was, had not the holders of good billets and the contractors found it more to their profit that it should not end. Altogether, the opinion which I also heard expressed—that New Zealand had got its constitution far too early and could have done far better with a strong Crown colony government —seemed to me a very sound and sensible one. How any decent government can have left the Maori question in the state in which it stands it passes me to conceive. There is a whole tract of country where the white man cannot enter, and vast areas more where, though he can enter, he can do no good, owing to the asinine and anserine manner in which the native land question has been dealt with. The Maori, with his very fluid ideas of property in land, has been allowed to cavort round, land grabbers have snicked in and swindled, and Government has been too weak or too dishonest to deal with either;

so that even existing titles are all doubtful, and no man dare touch a piece of native land to buy or lease. And thus many miles of good land lie idle, which the lazy native won't, and the desirous white can't, touch, all for want of a little strong, honest, clear-headed government. But the Government has been so taken up in borrowing millions and spending them, and quarrelling over the spending them, and then in designing ways and means of meeting the burden imposed thereby, that it has had no time to attend to a matter of such vital importance as the native land question. Some say that the natives are dying out, some say not. It would be better if they were, so the problem would solve itself. They were a terrible lot of savages in the old days, and most of the sentiment lavished on them by some folk seems to me to be sheer waste; while as to what they are now, hear the Pakeha Maori— one who knows the race well, and likes them in a way:—"The present generation of Maoris are a stunted, tobacco-smoking, grog-drinking, psalm-singing, special-pleading, shilling-hunting set of wretches." True, every word. They would, I doubt not, be glad to drive out law and the pakeha, although they are represented in Parliament, and many are rich, and many have intermarried with the white. Their old customs are mostly gone with their old costume; and a good thing too; for cannibalism and the "utu" and the "muru" and the "tabu" are not lovely in themselves nor admissible in good society. Nor was their tattooing beautiful. Not content with scoring the body from waist to knee, the face also (of the men) was thickly lined with multitudinous tattooings, deep-cut, of a dark dull green colour. You still see some of the older men with this disfigurement fully developed on them : I saw one at Tokaänu, who was further made beautiful with wounds received in fighting against us, which dragged his mouth out of shape, ruined one eye and dilapidated an ear. The women were scarred on the lips and chin ; many are so still. They look as if they had been chewing something and the olive-coloured juice were all over their lips and trickling down their chins. The men are now rarely tattooed, at least on the face; I suppose not lower down either. The old Maori fashion has passed away, yielding place to new; except in the North Island the Maori himself has passed away, and now he is but one in fifteen (say 40,000 in 600,000) of the population. He does not seem to be capable of decent civilization, and the sooner he passes away the better, leaving this most English of colonial lands for the white man. For New Zealand is more English than Australia, not only in its people (as before noticed) but in much of its natural scenery, and in its climate. The aspect of much agricultural country, and of many a stream bordered with weeping willows and osiers, seems to one looking thereon merely a part of home, in a way that no Australian landscape can ; and nowhere here is the monotony of endless forest of a single kind of tree, though the blue-gum, once imported, grows as gaily here as on the Blue Mountains of Sydney or of Madras.

But all this is somewhat of a digression, and I want you to return for just a moment to our comparison of Indian and Colonial governments, and dispose of the last of the points mentioned above—intentions, and power to carry them out. It seems to me that the intentions of colonial governments are just such as are dictated by the apparent interest of the class that happens at the time to be dominant —that is, as a rule, the working class. They are not intentions formed on a basis of careful inquiry and consideration of facts, and aiming for the good of all, but on a basis of self-interest and class-jealousy. Parties in Australia, as they appear to me, are merely a war of class against class. The landless wish to get the land; the labourer wishes to monopolize the labour market and all the fruits of labour; the manufacturer wishes to be freed from competition. And besides land and labour and trade, I don't know what other questions there are— save one great one. These three questions the colonies have not solved yet. Land is—I should judge—as burning a question yet out here as in any old country; labour had been having a fine old set-to with capital just before my visit, and, while I was in New Zealand, was proceeding in Queensland to rioting that required suppression by military force; trade is still quasi-free in New South Wales, heavily protective elsewhere. And that one great question that remains, what is it? What but Federation?

As I left, the colonial representatives were meeting in Sydney to discuss it. There is some talk of "loyalty" to the British connection. It seems to me very foolish talk. What does it mean anyhow? The colonies will gladly maintain the connection so long as it is to their advantage, and if we can arrange that it will always be to their advantage, it will be maintained for ever. But if we cannot so arrange, then it is hardly to be expected that some vague sentiment which some choose to label "loyalty" will avail to counterpoise the dead weight of material disadvantage, and the connection will go—unless we should enforce its maintenance; which is absurd. Therefore it is merely for us to see how it can be arranged advantageously; and the immediate question is whether Imperial federation is aided or impeded by intercolonial federation of the Australasian colonies. I cannot see myself how it could be other than aided. Only I would not include New Zealand in the new Australian dominion. It is too separate, too different; it should continue to stand on its own basis. But a federation of the continent of Australia with Tasmania is devoutly to be wished. And as to separation, the colonies will have to be much better fitted to protect themselves than they are now, before they *dare* separate. Why, China would annex in no time a free Australia unprotected by Britain. She feels the exclusion of her pig-tailed sons pretty well as it is; and, if she had a free hand, would simply swamp the new independence with swarms of celestials. Separation is not a question of practical politics at all, at present. And may it never become so, notwithstanding the screeds of certain papers, which serenely assume it to be not merely practicable but desirable now and at once. Australasia is a splendid reality, with a more splendid future before it. Rich in minerals, rich in huge areas of fertile soil and of soil fertilizable by irrigation, what though it grows (as certain cynics assert) fruits without flavour (or if with flavour yet with less than in the old country), flowers without scent, birds without song, a fair sex more distinguished by size than beauty? Does it not grow fruits bountiful in kinds and in quantity (cherries, strawberries, pine-apples, peaches, apricots, bananas, were all on the hotel table, daily, at Sydney; and grapes that make most potable wine, the red much better than the white to my taste); huge herds (I should say mobs) of cattle and sheep; horses of great shape, speed, stamina; pigs, goats, any blessed quadruped that you choose to import; almost any wealth-producing or beautifying item of the vegetable kingdom that you choose to import too; and most of all, plenty of men of muscle, full of energy and self-confidence, strong of will? The old motto, "Advance Australia," has been acted up to; now the new one, "One people, one destiny," is to be worked out. One not merely for the Australian colonies, but one for them and the old country together.

PART III.

FARTHEST WEST

CHAPTER XIV.

HONOLULU—HALEAKALA.

"THE Paradise of the Pacific." That is what the guide-book calls it. We call it the Sandwich Islands. The people who live there call it the Hawaiian Islands. As they ought to know best what their own country's name is, I shall call it by that name, notwithstanding its christening by the great Captain Cook, who died and is buried there. It is twelve days' steam from Auckland, even in the *Mariposa*, which is about the fastest boat at present on the line. The flag is American; so are the officers—most of them; so is the style of feeding. If this be a fair sample of American comfort in travelling, why, the American is no better than the Australasian. The deck-cabin has, it is true, only two berths, but it has no sofa or anything to sit on except the floor; the wash-hand basin is so arranged that you can't get your head into it, without imminent risk of breaking the water-reservoir, or more probably your skull; the bath-rooms are dark and hot, and only two in number, not fitted with shower-baths, and half way through the voyage the fresh water ran out. Steerage passengers have all the deck around the aft deck-cabins, and the food is execrable. The bill of fare is very long, but the same day after day, and when you have struck out the dishes that are ill-cooked, or uncooked (" rare " they call it, American for just not raw), or bad, there is precious little left to eat ; and what there is, is not nicely done, appetizing. The weather treated us tolerably on the whole ; but there was generally enough wind—at first N.W. then N.E.—to keep us rolling a good deal, and there was none of that lovely halcyon weather that I had associated theretofore with proximity to the equator. We crossed the 180th meridian on a Sunday ; and not hankering after two Sabbaths in succession, we doubled the Monday, and had two March 2nd's ; and on the 7th I, for the fourth and last time, crossed the equator. Notwithstanding discomforts, it was in many respects a pleasanter voyage than any previous one related in this journal. For we had no awful " Young Australias " of the Frondean type on board, nor yet any of the objectionable style of Yankee ; the colonials and the American passengers were mostly of a good sort, and some particularly nice. The "bounders" were, I fear, mostly Britishers. The daily lottery in the run went well, thanks to an excellent auctioneer ; the committee for amusements did all they could (Our Enthusiast was indefatigable) ; and our " push " played shuffle-board (a kind of bull, only better), to the vast admiration of the Catholic Church in the person of a colonial bishop on his way to Rome. Flirtation was not so obvious as often it is on board a P. & O., only one pronounced "mash" being observable. Howbeit, there were two whom Our Humorist called "the Dream of Fair Women" and others "The Seven-Footer" and "Goggles." The vessels of this line call *en passant* at Tutuila, one of the Samoan group, and pick up and set down the Samoan mails. Usually a crowd of canoes comes off, and natives—men and women—sell fans, and curios, and dive for coin. We were much disappointed at only two boats appearing, with only two men in each, and a scanty supply of fans, which was soon disposed of. The guileless natives did not refrain, however, from accepting silver, even when they had nothing to give in return for it. A passenger came on board here, from whom we learnt the cause of the small show of natives. It appears that on the farther side of the island there was a cricket match in progress, to which all the population had flocked. Indeed, the greater part of the population must have been engaged in the game, for there were—he said—105 men on one side, and 88 on the other. It must be a great game to see,—a Samoan cricket match. The bat is a cross between a club and a croquet mallet. The bowler bowls from either end, wherever the ball may happen to be; as each ball is delivered, there is immense shouting and clashing of Samoan music; the striker smites the ball (an india-rubber contrivance with a wooden core), and the hundred or so of fielders pursue it as it bumps and meanders gaily among the cocoa-nut trees. As I understood,

s

there were, when we passed, some 90 wickets down
and the score was over 500. The match promised
to last for quite ten days. The men whom we saw
were fine athletic-looking fellows, light brown in
colour, with hair cut short, brushed straight towards
the front, and coloured a sandy red. The chief
occupation of the people seems to be to play and
enjoy themselves, find wives (?) for the white men,
and—in the case of chiefs—do the white man's
washing! Tutuila is a lovely islet, brilliant in
verdure and in colouring. How I wished to stay
and wander about these isles of the Southern Seas
for a month or two—or six.

But here we are at Honolulu. It is night, and we
are anxious for a good solid supper after twelve
jours maigres on the *Mariposa*. Hotels here,
however, do not consult the convenience of passengers to the extent of finding supper for them,
and we partake gaily but unsatisfyingly of coffee
and cakes and bread and butter at a restaurant.
Next day we devote to business, to taking stock of
our new position, and to seeing off our friends who
stay not here, but go on with the *Mariposa* to
'Frisco. And a good see-off they get, with plenty
of "leis," band playing, hearty good-byes, and pro-
mises to meet in England. Honolulu is a pleasant
enough place to stay in. I do not feel inclined to
enthuse about its tropical magnificence in the way
that that most globe-trotterous Miss Bird does in her
book, but it is beyond question a charming situation. The town is not much; streets of no great

width, and with no fine public buildings, if we except the palace and the Government offices. The former is a tolerably big and handsome mansion, standing in grounds nicely laid out (the father of the Heiress-Apparent has a pretty taste in gardening), and the wall around them is low enough for a man to hop over. Before the rebellion—yes, rebellion : this mighty monarchy has had its rebellion ; it is true that it lasted but a day, and was suppressed with a minimum of bloodshed—before the rebellion in 1887, the walls were high, exclusive walls ; but as they interfered with the shooting in that fierce insurrection, they were lowered to their present diminutive stature. The gate-posts and entrances were still draped with the black with which they and all the town were hung when the late king, Kalakaua, was buried—an event that took place shortly before our arrival. The new Queen, Liliuokalani (pronounce Lily o' Killarney—it is quite near enough), seems to be a woman of will. She made her Cabinet resign, whether they would or no, and they no-ed until compelled, and then she appointed whom she would, including the Prince Consort, one Dominis. Our Humorist and Mrs. H. were received by her in audience—a form of amusement into which I did not chip in. They tell me the Throne-room is not badly got up. The fixings in it were, however, being squabbled over (so I heard on good authority) by the queen dowager, who claimed them as Kalakaua's private goods and chattels, and the queen regnant claiming them as State property. The Government offices might all—Treasury and Parliament House and Secretariat and Supreme Court and all—be put away easily in the Sydney Post Office or the Bombay Secretariat; but they are big enough for a kingdom of 90,000 souls with a revenue of four million dollars (say £800,000). The statue of the Egbert of the islands, who made the kingdom from many petty chieftainships into a single united whole—Kamehameha I.—stands in front of the building, and is goodly to look upon. Sentries guard the palace, supplied by the army of sixty-three men. The band is nearly as strong, and is a State band. Moreover, the hotel is State property—built with public money, and leased to a manager. I have heard or read of it as the best of all conceivable hotels. Bluff, my dear sir, bluff. The food is served American fashion, and is not more than average; wines high in price, and nothing special in quality. The place is a decent enough caravanserai, and the bachelor finds liberty in the cottage-rooms or the basement; but it is nothing magnificent to boast about. The noise in the dining-room is awful until you get used to it, as all the knives and forks and spoons are cleaned in it after each course, and the boys (Chinese and Portuguese) wear resounding boots. The guide-book details other public buildings which may be things prized by the Honoluluites: they are not worthy of notice in themselves. But the private residences are, in many instances, charming little bungalows—all wood, set in compounds radiant with flowers and palms, and grass of a greenness to make an Anglo-Indian gardener die with desire. These are most numerous on the Nuuanu Avenue, and on the road to, and at, the seaside suburb of Waikiki. By the first you go to the Pali (precipice); at the last you may bathe. The Pali is the one point to which all go who pass by Honolulu, even those who go on by the same steamer; for it is only six miles out, and a good driving and riding road. And the view is certainly very fine—when the mist and cloud are good enough to let you see it.

In the gap that nature has left in the ridge of mountain lying "betwixt windward and lee," the trade wind, of course, plays freely, and he keeps his gambols constantly hidden by drifting and driving vapours. They are worse to look at than to go through; so don't turn back (as Mauritius and I came near to doing), merely because the clouds in the gap look threatening. After all, their presence only adds one more change of colour to the landscape, and variety and richness of colour are the special characteristic of Hawaiian landscape and seascape. The brilliant orange and purple, and red, and yellow, that we saw staining the decomposing rocks near the active blowholes of Wairakei, seem to be scattered and diffused all among the disintegrating volcanic rocks and dead lava of which the Hawaiian Islands are composed. Grasses are on the hill-side in various stages of greenness, yellowness, brownness; in the ravines trees supply many more tints and tones of green;

the sun catches the vapours drifting along the ridge, and paints them with rainbow hues. Altogether I have never looked on a view so splendid in colouring as Honolulu seen from the sea on a bright afternoon in March. (I think I have already mentioned that the afternoon light is the best of all lights to see scenery in.) At Waikiki the sea comes rolling in over coral reefs, and within them is yellow sand, and safety from sharks, so that one may bathe here at one's ease. (I fetched the Japanese bathing-woman completely by talking to her in her own language. By the way, how terrible a Japanese woman looks in a "holoku." Designed for the big fleshy women of the Sandwich Islands, this nightgown for day wear is outrageously unbecoming on the petite female of Japan.) Further, at Waikiki are royal residences and lanais, and a public park and racecourse lying close under Diamond Head—the great bare dead giant that shuts in the bay on the East. A "lanai" is, according to the idea which I have acquired from a visit to one, a large wooden building of the size of a barn—and a big one at that —filled with all the accessories of a Western drawing-room. Its floor is level with the ground, and its roof not raised any great height. The size of it crowds other rooms into tiny little corners, or clean out of the house into separate buildings. But for a dance or an entertainment, nothing could be better. The owner of quite a modest mansion built lanai-wise would have a royal, or at least a gubernatorial, ball-room. Within the same grounds that held this

DIAMOND HEAD, HONOLULU.

lanai, I saw also a grass hut of the old native fashion. The walls were extremely well woven, and the roof thickly thatched; the Hawaiian seems to have had a very fair idea of how to keep out weather. But this hut, being royal property, was better than the average. I saw some much poorer things up-country.

And up-country it is time to betake ourselves. Our Enthusiast's brother, the Reverend, has kindly supplied us with letters, and the date of our sailing has come. So we bid farewell to those good friends, and the *Claudine* carries us away from the shores of Oahu, past Molokai and Lanai, to Maui. (If you wish to know, Oahu is the island of the group on which Honolulu stands, Molokai lies next it eastward, and is the island on which the leper settlement is; Lanai lies in the channel between Molokai and Maui, the next island eastward; and Hawaii, the largest and eponymous island of the kingdom, is to the south-east of Maui. *Vide* any decent Geography.) The *Claudine* and the *Kinau* are the best of the steamers that ply amongst the islands. But they are small, and, as the wind blows free through the passages between the islands, they are gamesome and lively; *robur et œs triplex* may be defeated in these choppy seas. It was only "after much debate internal" that I decided that I could see it through; and I did. Under the lee of Molokai we had peace. The leper settlement is on the north side of the island, "walled in with rocks like an inland island." I did not go to see it.

Perhaps, in time, that mighty entity, the Government of India, may take heart of grace and follow the example of this twopenny-halfpenny kingdom. Every leper is compulsorily segregated, and something like a quarter of a million dollars are spent yearly on stamping out the plague. No small sum when the revenue is only four millions. There is some chance—nay, good assurance — of leprosy ceasing to exist in Hawaii. In India there is a good solid certainty of its spreading with great regularity and no small speed. I should like to take a Member of Council or two round a few Burmese villages that I know, and show him the extent that it has already reached. Apparently it is worth while to raise religious riots in the centre of Hinduism for the sake of a water supply ; but it is not worth while to take any steps to eradicate a general pest, until a Commission shall have inquired and reported. It would have been of some interest to see what the arrangements are for dealing with the compulsorily segregated ones ; but I preferred to let it slide. Enough and too much has been written about Molokai ; and very much sentiment has been wasted on it. The gush of the *Gutter Gazette* over Sister Rose Gertrude's start for the Islands was sickening ; and renders all the more lamentably laughable the polite cold shoulder that she got when she reached them. It is a fine example of sentimental cant withered up by working good sense. I saw this "Sister Rose Gertrude" in the Hawaiian Hotel ; as I understood she is doing nursery governess business. And a good sensible business too! Let her and others leave the lepers to those whose business it is to manage them.

Kahalui is a port on the north or windward side of Maui; and at Kahalui we arrived at 6 A.M. on the 17th. Maui does not reach the size of Gaul, and is divided into two parts only, East and West. Kahalui is on the isthmus uniting the two. Thence we drove up, partly along the sands, partly by a good made road, to Wailuku, on West Maui; and there were received at Mrs. Yarrick's Boarding House. It is not a splendid hostelry. We are not yet educated into appreciating our meals American-wise; and when they are so served, and moreover immensely and incredibly bad, we become even as men that starve. "Alas, poor Yorick!" thy "hash-house" is, of "all places that the eye of heaven visits," the one that I least wish to see again. Now, after we had feigned to eat breakfast, Our Humorist and I took a walk towards Waikapu. (I protest that, by myself, I am not so insane as to go taking walks in the sun for pleasure where the shade thermometer is 87° in a moist climate.) And we cast our eyes towards East Maui, where there was a long long slope upwards from the sea on the north, and again a long long slope from the sea on the south; and they went on up and up until the whole island was filled with them. And I said, " Surely this must be Haleakala (pronounce Hally Ăkălāh), the House of the Sun, whose height is ten thousand feet." But Our Humorist doubted, and I wavered; yet, after much consideration, we concluded that this was even so. This much I will say, that for so well-grown a mountain, he carries his height remarkably well. It hardly looks over 6,000 or 7,000 feet ; until you realize what enormous sloping sides those are, and how high they carry up until they meet. The absence of any distinctly marked summit-peak, or cone, or what not, assists in the deception. Now Haleakala is the largest crater in the world. It is extinct ; but that is no matter ; it is a crater, and the largest in the world. And to see it we had come to Maui. Wherefore, after presenting to an Englishman a letter, and being kindly entreated of him, we left the hash-house of " Alas poor Yorick!" and rode forth to Haiku. In view of the custom of the country as to the manner of ladies' riding, and of her inability to conform thereto, Mrs. H. had borrowed a side-saddle ; Our Humorist and I got such colonial saddles as were to hand ; and Joe, the guide, used a Mexican. With our kit for several days, and our coats and waterproofs strapped on to these, we started, making a gallant show. And we passed by the railway that runs from Wailuku by Kahalui and Spreckelsville (euphonious name) to Pahia—even for six miles ; and on until we came to Haiku. Now, the road at first is by glowing yellow and golden and orange sands of an intenser colour than any sand I have ever seen ; and over a red red, road, and past miles of green and yellowing sugarcane, in sight of the polyphloisbuoyant one, green and blue and foam-flecked, on the left ; and the huge hill of Haleakala on the right.

A feast of colour for the eye. That evil-sounding name aforementioned belongs to perhaps the biggest of all the sugar-mills and estates on all the islands; you may read all the figures in the guide-book, if you feel like it. Past Pahia, the road is more up and down; we pass over cliffs where the green one is more phloisbuoyant than ever, down into a gulch (by which hideous name these poor people are wont to speak of a ravine), and up again, and across uplands where the all-prevailing sugarcane grows, until we reach our host's house. Now for simple, unaffected, unadulterated kindness and hospitality commend me to Our Host at Haiku. Not content with our staying with them on our way up the hill, with doing all they could for us as to how to get up, with obtaining for us the use of a house—furnished and unoccupied—at Olinda, the highest on this side of the hill, Mr. and Mrs. Dickey pressed us to stay with them on our way back, and did entertain us most friendlily for so long as we were able to stay. And we saw what life up-country in the islands is, as we could not have seen in any other way. But of that hereafter; our present business is to get to the top of Haleakala, and there see the sunrise. So Mrs. H., politely accepting a carriage to drive in, and secretly wishing she might ride, and Our Humorist and I on our gallant steeds (awful gamelegged sluggard his was, to be sure), by the direct route, and Joe by a way round to go and get the keys of the house at Olinda, set forth provided with bread and meat (in tins—I should say cans), and such necessaries as we could think of, and rendezvoused at Mrs. Alexander's, the highest house in Makawao, itself the highest township (colonial) or settlement (American) or station (India) on the hill. Anything up higher is only single house or station (colonial).

The road so far is a driving road, in good enough order except in one portion, and with only one "gulch" to cross, and that not a severe one. When at last loaded up, on horseback, with all our kit, saddle-bags, and holdalls, and parcels of bread, and canteens, attired in clothes befitting the situation, we presented an appearance that might have made even a Bengali Babu laugh, if he were not unprovided with the risible faculty; such a crew of unprincipled brigands returning from a raid did we seem to be. From Makawao the road is a bridle track only across the grazing run or ranch, constantly ascending, yet nowhere severe, until at Olinda we are 6,000 feet up. Olinda might be called the House of Rainbows. It is just on that corner of the hill at which the clouds that drive across from East to West Maui break off from the former, and just at that elevation where the sun catches the flying vapour at the proper angle. We appeared to be continually riding into a perfect arch that grew beyond the half-circle until it seemed that it would become a whole one, yet never quite did it; so close to us and so complete down to the ground that it was a marvel to see. And whenever we looked back at Olinda there was a rainbow somewhere around. We reached the house at sunset, and, none of the keys seeming to fit, Our

Humorist effected a burglarious entrance. Charming little rooms, plenty of furniture ; but, horror! no lights, and we have brought none! At last a few lamps, each with a little oil, are discovered, and blank darkness shall not envelop us. So Joe hews wood, and I draw water, and Our Humorist lights the fire, and Mrs. H. combines the functions of chef and maid-of-all-work ; and we peel potatoes and open tins and cook food. Then to wash and brush up for dinner. Alas, no towels! Scraps of window-curtain and spare handkerchiefs have to serve instead. So we feast gaily, and discourse plaintively about lights and towels with Mr. D. and our actual though absent host Mr. Baldwin. They are some way off, but that is no matter ; for is there not a telephone? (Honolulu and Maui are the most telephonic places I ever came across. Mr. D. is the pioneer of telephone enterprise in the Islands, and has planted them all over the place. There seems to be no spot in Maui to which you cannot talk along the wires from any house that you may be at. As for Honolulu, it is not content with one company, but must have two. Their wires are all over the town in huge quantities, and form one of its most striking features. Here endeth the digression about telephones.) Huge razais formed our bedding ; and up we got at 2 A.M. and started for the top. A fine clear night, luckily, and a growing moon that lighted us for nearly two hours. The path not difficult, nor the air so very cold. Even the last hour's climb in that darkest, and chilliest, hour before the dawn is not so bad; the guide was doubtful of the way at one spot only, and fell only once into the ditch. We did the march in just three hours, and at 5 A.M. already there was a premonitory low red line in the east, and the morning star shone with exceeding brightness. We could only guess at the crater on whose edge we stood; all was dark down there; we knew only that earth ended and space began. So, wrapped in ulsters and rugs and stamping up and down (for at 10,000 feet elevation the morning breeze is chill even in the tropics), we waited for the day to dawn. That narrow, low, red line lengthens all across the East, "under the opening eyelids of the morn," and the sombre blue softens to pale grey:

> Once more the old mysterious glimmer steals
> From thy pure brows and from thy shoulders pure
> And bosom beating with a heart renewed.

And while I repeat to myself that exquisite idyl, the red light retreats farther and farther into the northern and southern limits of the east and spreads uncertainly up to the zenith. Full in the east the sky becomes pure saffron, with a luminous intensity in the midst of it foretelling the point where the sun will appear. And from the mountain-side, a couple of thousand feet below us, stretches upwards (as it seems) to the immeasurably remote horizon an illimitable ocean of clouds. Here they are piled in cumulous masses, there teased into the shining smoothness of a wind-swept snowdrift; or blown into gauze-like veils of exceeding tenuity, they hang between us and far-reaching ranges of mountains filled with gloomy chasms and serrated ridges and black or snow-capped peaks. They seem to be motionless; one looms dark in front of that centre of brightest light. Suddenly a touch of fire kindles its topmost point, and runs out along the ridge in red and gold and yellow of brilliance indescribable. And then comes forth Hyperion from "his palace bright bastioned with pyramids of glowing gold;" and day is born again. The huge masses of cloud are seen to be in motion; they seem to be pouring down from the very threshold of the dawn against the sides of Haleakala, and under the slant rays they glitter with a brightness hardly to be borne. As they strike the mountain they part, half winding round the eastern and southern sides and half moving in slow majesty along the northern coast, whence they stream disorderly across the bay of Kahalui and re-form their broken masses on the mountains of West Maui. It is a scene of unsurpassed grandeur of ever-changing form and density, that we stay all day to gaze on. Glimpses of the blue sea and the green cane-fields come to us on the west; in the south-east far above the clouds are Hawaii's still snow-capped volcanoes, Mauna Loa and Mauna Kea. They slope up gradually and, as it seems, evenly to nearly 14,000 feet, with as rounded an outline as the back of a porpoise when you see him gambolling alongside the steamer. Only on Mauna Kea's summit are some broken peaks and cones. In the afternoon those cloud cohorts that encompassed the south of

Haleakala creep up the western side, but above Olinda they are turned back by the column moving along the north, and you see them piled southwards in serried ranks, from which an upper current bears them off north-eastwards, that they may be in their places at His Majesty's portals when he rises next morning.

We did not go down into the crater, it is too much to attempt in one day—the getting down and about and back again. The walls are from 2,000 to 2,700 feet high, perpendicular for hundreds of feet—not smooth, but broken and jagged, and then slope steeply down to the floor. Remember that the crater is seven miles across, and that these walls run in a kind of V shape for twenty miles. All about the floor of this huge hole are lots of small craters, each 600 or 700 feet high, but looking like molehills. From their rims, red with cinders and grey with ashes, run flows of black lava, and there is no scrap of vegetation to be seen. At either end of the arms of the V the walls of the great crater have given way—have been swept clean out, and huge gaps give exit to the lava flows. At the point of the V is the highest top of Haleakala—three piles of cinder loose and weary to walk on—and hither I scrambled along the edge of the rugged walls, passing not a few tracks of wild goats in the ashes, and finding ice in the crevices where the vapours had left a little moisture. From the summit a long steep slope affords the only practicable descent to the bottom of the crater; and from it you get the finest view up each arm of the V. Whether it was from tire and from sleeping in the sun, or from mere mountain sickness, I know not, but sick I certainly was that afternoon, and did not feel fit again until we had ridden without further adventure back to Olinda and had cooked and eaten our camp dinner. Joe departed early next morning, but we idled the forenoon deliciously away, and passed votes of thanks to one another for our domestic services, and especially to Mrs. H. for hers as chef. I have never tasted such excellent sausages and fried potatoes as we had for breakfast that morning. And then we rode back well-pleased to Haiku.

CHAPTER XV.

KILAUEA.

"Suns that set and moons that wane
Rise and are restored again."
Are ye, molten lava lakes,
  Gone for ever out of sight,
  Passed "afay in die ewigkeit?"
Or will ye, when Pele wakes,
  In her fiery vast domain
  Rise and be restored again?
    Visitors' Book, Volcano House, Kilauea.

BEFORE we left Honolulu there were rumours of the bottom having fallen out of Kilauea. (That was the expression used; most inappropriately, as it seems to me; for the pit of Kilauea would rather appear to be like that one mentioned in Scripture, and which the flogged school-boy, being exhorted to emulate the great Pitt, said that he wished he was like—bottomless.) Kilauea, you must know, is the largest active crater in the world; it is, according to the descriptions that one reads and the pictures that one sees of it, full of lakes of fiery lava, in constant turmoil and ebullition, a sight terrific and most magnificent to behold. Now if, indeed, "the bottom having fallen out," the crater was left empty and silent and cold, we should miss one of the wonders of the world. And ever the rumours grew, until hardly room for hope was left. Yet I refused to give up hope until I should reach the crater and see with my own eyes its blankness, its extinction; and Our Humorist and Mrs. H. were of the same mind. So we tarried at Haiku but two nights and a day, most joyfully accepting hospitality so freely offered, and thereby escaping for a space the horrors of the hash-house. And we played billiards with our host—that American form of the game: four big balls on a small table without pockets, where a cannon counts one and a double cannon two, and thirty-nine is game; and suffered grievous defeat at his hands. Also whist we played—we two against our host and a dear old lady from New Zealand, and must have earned the reputation of practised card-sharpers; for we fell upon them and routed them, even though seven made game and honours were not counted. Strange whist, where we could not help winning, for the innocent eagerness with which the adversaries played their best to help us. But was it not all for love? (Howbeit, I love not whist where the game is seven and no honours!) Then, in the morning, family prayers before breakfast! It seemed so strange, after—how many? say a score—of years since, in childhood and schooldays, the rite was a daily experience. After breakfast, it being Sunday, we must to church. Two children of my host (I was staying with a relative and next-door neighbour of our first host, with whom the H.'s still were) drove—a he of seven (I think) and a she of less—in their own neat pony-carriage with two smart ponies; a perfectly charming picture. And the rest of us in buggies and breaks. A buggy is not a buggy of Bombay, but vastly more pretty and comfortable; and a break is not a break, but a tum-tum or bamboo cart, neither pretty nor comfortable. A five-mile drive to church; a fine day luckily, for I am but a fair-weather Christian, and do not yearn for church through five miles of rain. The church a plain (or should I say handsome? for so the parishioners deem it) plank building, yet adorned with organ and some stained glass windows. And the service congregational—so they told me; it seemed to be rather a go-as-you-please sort of arrangement. All the seats are ranged amphitheatrically; the padre has a platform to himself and no pulpit; behind him the organ and choir. And it is strange to hear Americanisms and the American accent which one associates mostly with humour and would-be witticisms—to hear them used seriously and solemnly in Divine service. The preacher proche on the woman healed of an infirmity who "glorified God," or, as he expounded it, "glorified God right there." In the afternoon many neighbours called (including one who wore his *pince-nez*—when not in use—on the top of his right ear), and we sat in a vast circle in the drawing-room and talked. After dinner more conversation, and then an early bed. I am not sure, though, whether it was dinner—I think not; dinner came at midday on Sunday. But each meal was so exactly like the other two, that whether you call it dinner or tea or supper makes not the smallest difference. No liquor appeared at any meal, nor at any other time either (neither, by the way, did our hosts smoke); breakfast was distinguishable by starting on " mush," *anglicè* porridge, whether of " cracked wheat," or of an unholy white stuff called "hominy," or the more familiar oatmeal, and by continuing on hash or steak or stew, while the dinner or lunch went in for joint (or poultry in place thereof). But hash or joint, the wonder was the quantity of wadding that went with it in the shape of dumplings and corn (*i.e.* of course, Indian corn) and peas and potatoes and biscuit (*i.e.* scones)—terribly filling, and yet hardly satisfying. Breakfast ended with hot cakes—sort of pancake eaten with "surp" (I spell syrup as pronounced in America); dinner and supper, or lunch and dinner, with something equally indigestible. Water your drink at each meal until quite the end, when you were allowed one cup of coffee or tea, and no more. A prolonged course of such diet would send me to an early and dyspeptic grave. Next day we were quite sorry to bid adieu to our hospitable entertainers, and rode back to our hash-house. Thence might we not escape for yet thirty-six hours. So we called for horses from Joe, whereon to ride into the valley of Iao—a most picturesque spot in the heart of the hills of West Maui. It is to be reached only after fording a stream that once ran red with blood and was choked with corpses, when the conquering Kamehameha routed the kings of Maui

We asked Joe if it were fordable after the rain that had fallen. "You will see when you get there," said Joe pleasantly. And so we did. Our Humorist's game-legged sluggard all but went over with him, and my war-horse, after ducking me almost to the seat, came out where he went in and would by no means go in again. We tried up stream and down stream, but our nags knew better than that; so we remained in much the same position to Iao as Moses did to Canaan—t'other side of Jordan. Then we rode back and out on the Waihi road, cantering gaily across the bridge. As we walked back across that bridge, Mrs. H. read to us a notice affixed thereon: "The fine for crossing this bridge faster than a walk is five dollars," or words to that effect. I said we should be run in, sure. Prophet of ill! As we rode through the main street there came one behind me who said, "You owe me fifteen dollars." I asked "How?" ("How?" is American for "what?" but I only meant, "How do I owe you fifteen dollars?") He said, "You three cantered across the bridge; fine five dollars a head; three times five, fifteen." I explained that I had not seen the notice, nor had any of us until returning. And suddenly off he went at score in French! I was content to listen, and left Mrs. H. to continue our side of the conversation. He was, it seems, the road overseer and a Frenchman; a polite little man and friendly withal, who accepted a composition of apologies and nothing in the pound in full settlement of his claim.

The *Kinau*, bound for Hilo, the port for Kilauea, calls at Maalaea—seven miles across the isthmus from Wailuku—any time between midnight and dawn; there is no telephone (marvellous to relate) between Wailuku and Lahaina—the port of call next preceding Maalaea (pronounce this as if you called your mother a fabricator—Ma-a-liar); so there was nothing for it but to drive there by midnight and wait. It was just about full moon; really a beautiful drive in the tropical moonlight, close under the West Maui mountains with huge Haleakala on the left and the wide-mouthed bay in front. We reached the Deceitful Parent by 10; a very stuffy, ill-smelling shed to wait in. I rolled myself in ulster and rug, and, with holdall for pillow, slept on the sand until, at 2 A.M., the *Kinau* appeared and we made ourselves comfortable on board. No sleeping on deck cheek by jowl with the natives, *à la* Miss Bird, but cosy bunks in roomy two-berthed cabins. By noon next day we were at Mahukona—a dreary-looking place, with a strong wind blowing dead off shore. Here we remained twelve mortal hours, uncomfortable, but too chastened to complain much, while the business of the owners of the ship and of the little railway and the store—that is to say, of all Mahukona—got itself transacted. Next morning we were rolling gaily on the windward side of the island of Hawaii. How that ship can roll! It was impossible to do anything but fix oneself firmly in one's cabin and read, and look out of window at the island coast. It was worth looking at. I woke up opposite

Waipio, a wide opening in the rocky cliff that all along this windward side forms the edge of the land, and (according to Miss Bird, the guide-book, and other word-stringers), a valley of great beauty. Thence all the way to Hilo—a distance of sixty miles —there is, raised off the sea by the rock-barrier, one or two or three hundred or more feet high, a ribbon of green canefield, sloping gradually up towards the mountain—the mighty Mauna Kea. The ribbon varies from a mile to, say, three miles in width; it is cut pretty often by great gulches that come down from the mountain to the sea. Higher up the slope is forest, sad-coloured against the vivid green of the cane; and above all, the crater peaks of Mauna Kea, cinder-red, ashy-grey, lava-black, or dazzling white with snow. Some ravines (I can't use that word gulch again, it is too ugly) cleave the seaward barrier right down to the ocean's edge, others turn their waters loose over the unbroken crest of cliff, and delight the eye with waterfalls of all kinds—solid and thunderous, gauzy and graceful, cataract and cascade. Here, at every few miles, is a sugar-mill, and flumes (water-conduits) run into the mill from all parts of the plantation, bringing in the cut cane. We halt at only too many places down this coast; for we have a lot of Japanese emigrants —contract coolies—on board, and are distributing them to their various employers. Yet, at length we reach Hilo, famed for its beauty; but to-day it is all veiled in grey mist and drifting cloud-wrack. It is really quite tropical; I could almost fancy myself back in some little town on the Tenasserim Coast. We were very eager to see the "surf-riding" of the Hiloan bathers—a most graceful and skilful sport, they say; but there was not surf enough, and we could not. (Yet, how that ship did roll! What in thunder would she have done if there had been a good sea on?) So we merely stroll around, and start next morning for Kilauea—thirty miles away. Even yet we are uncertain whether we are going to find an active or a sulky volcano. There is a goddess who presides over volcanoes, and her name is Pele (drawl both e's, like the Burmese e in *hle*, a boat—not *hle*, a cart); she lives in Kilauea. Once before, "in a respite of slumber, in a lull of the fires of her life," the volcano went out—five years ago to a day; and before that in legendary times she has let the fire run low. That was when she went fooling down to the sea to bathe (she'd want it after a year or two of active stoking down below), and to try her hand at surf-riding. And as she disported herself she heard the sound of far music, and became anxious to see what it was. Wherefore she left the human form that she had donned, and followed the sweet strains "on from island unto island," even to the uttermost limit of the farthest island, the island of Kauai. For the magic musician of the king had sent his strains so far to find her. And behold the king was holding a nautch—I mean a hula-hula; and as she looked on him she loved him. Thereupon she appeared unto him as a most exquisitely lovely girl (rather fat, probably, and cocoanut-oily about the hair), and King Lohiau, being no Joseph or bashful Adonis, straightway fell in love with her. And she stayed away so long (her servants down in Kilauea not knowing where she was, and being afraid to wake the human form which she left asleep on the shore by the sea), that the fire at home got very low indeed. There is a lot more of the story—how Lohiau got into very hot water—hot lava, rather—with his burning lady-love, and got out again; but you've probably had about enough of it; and, indeed, I've forgotten exactly how it runs. Anyway, the road runs from Hilo for thirteen miles in a tolerably well-made track (cost 30,000 dollars, they say) over lava of kinds—aa and pahoehoe, they call them—and through bush of strange trees, breadfruit and ohia and lehua, until it ends abruptly in mid-forest, and we have to take to horse and the horse-trail (*anglicè* bridle-path). A Burmo-Japanico-Serbonian bog is this trail to begin with, and then chunky and angular and slippery hard lava. Consequently seventeen miles take five hours to accomplish; and I am of opinion that a Mexican saddle is an atrocious thing to ride in for five hours. My Virginian (for there was also on this trip a youth from West Virginia, whom I call My Virginian, inasmuch as we chummed somewhat together) thought the same of an English saddle; but then he was riding a moke. (Not that he called the sagacious beast a moke; he did not know what the word meant.) In a Mexican saddle you cannot get a seat at all, can't sit down in the saddle; you have to stand in the stirrups (such clumsy stirrups too), and ride on the fork. Luckily it did not rain, and we skated over the humpy lava and plunged through the puddles merrily enough. Then a nice track gave us a mile or more's brisk canter up to the Volcano House. There we learnt at last the full measure of our misfortune. The bottom had indeed fallen out, with no chance of its falling in again for many a day to come. I saw no fire at Kilauea, other than the cheery wood fire that burned at night between the dogs on the great hearth in the Volcano House. A comfortable hostelry, for up-country, with good food and a kindly and communicative host. Mr. (or Colonel) and Mrs. Maby have probably left there by now, as the old order (and Company) has changed, yielding place to new; and, of course, in things American, with every change of administration, office-holders change too. May future guests be as well looked after as were Colonel Maby's. Now, I think that if we had seen Pele's house in all its glory, I should still have refrained from inflicting on you an attempt at description, and should have referred you to Miss Bird, or to the Visitors' Book, wherein is much verbiage even stranger than Miss Bird's, or to your own imagination of the conventional hell. But as we saw the goddess's abode when she was out of town, I can only tell you what the place is like when the light is out. On the slope of that 13,800 footer Mauna Loa, at a height of 4,000 feet above the sea, is a big hole in the ground. I suppose the circumference is some seven or eight miles, and the height of the almost perpendicular sides about 1,500 feet. The dimensions are respectable, are they not? Somewhere about the centre of this enormous crater is the House of Fire, the active crater which has had the mishap to its bottom. From the foot of the outer wall to the edge of this inner pit stretches a slightly rising field of lava; and it is about one mile and a half from foot to edge. You walk over solidified waves of what was molten rock, here heaved into mis-shapen mounds, there rent by great fissures, black, vitreous. Solidified? well, hardly; the rock rings hollow; it is solid-looking, but full of big caverns and tiny air-bubbles shut up by the rock that hardened as it cooled. Down in the crevasses the sides are brick-red; snow-white and yellow stuffs are found in the caves. A hardy fern or two tries to grow in the crannies near the edge of the field. All else is black, bare lava; yet, not all black, for as we search we find blown threads and fluffy-seeming ringlets of Pele's golden hair. When the lakes of lava are lively, the wind catches the spray and foam of fiery molten rock, and blows it out into long thin thread-like spun glass, faintly yellow, with black beadlets strewn in where less fluid atoms of the vitreous matter have refused to be extenuated; and these threads are carried and dispersed all about the surface of the lava. Are they not the hair, the combings of the locks, of the goddess Pele? Remote from the pit, we find them in little huddled patches in the crannies; they look soft as floss silk, but the threads are as brittle as a lover's vows. But all about the edge the newer lava is covered thick with the hair blown out in single threads, so interlaced and so glittering that the rocks shine like burnished gold. And the rocks as you walk on them crackle crisply, and every now and then cave in beneath your weight; and a sweet-smelling vapour of sulphur rises hotly from the cracks, and from the surface all round you, and you may (or you may not) see the sullen red glow of yet uncooled lava a foot or so below the surface. And so you come to the edge of the pit—a hole about a mile round, and five hundred feet deep, with sides sheer, but shattered and crumbling, for three hundred feet, and then sloping steeply funnel-shaped down to—well, down to the "house of unquenchable fire." A mist of white steam covers the entrance.

The subsidence of the Kilauean lakes in March 1886 was followed, in June 1886, by the terrific eruption of Tarawera. *Post hoc* or *propter hoc?* And if *propter*, where will the vent take place from the subsidence of March 1891? Who can tell?

There are plenty of sulphur blowholes on the top of the outer wall of the big crater, along by the hotel; you can have a sulphur vapour-bath if you wish. (I didn't find any other and more common and desirable kind of bath to be had.) And not far off—a pleasant ramble among the lehua and ohelo, with its pretty clusters of red berries—is the very dead crater of Kilauea Iki; a bed of black lava at the bottom of a hole 1,000 feet deep. And again we sat round the fire in the Volcano House at night, and wrote our names in the Visitors' Book, being the last visitors that should visit and write under the old dispensation. And when My Virginian saw that I broke into verse, even the verse that stands at the head of this chapter, he marvelled, and Our Humorist wondered, and none spotted that the first two lines are a quotation, nor did I tell them. And My Virginian queried what "die ewigkeit" might be, and produced a verse of marvellous construction, to which (I own with shame) I gave him the last line :—

> The goddess Pele, a lady of high rank,
> Was daughter of fire and a mud bank ;
> The mud bank it busted,
> And Pele she dusted,
> And now she is——— ——— ———
>   blank !   blank ! !   blank ! ! !

Such are the results of a Harvard education.

My Virginian and I swapped saddles going back (but I did not bone his moke), and we made a little better time—some four hours for the seventeen miles. Near Hilo there are many pretty points—Cocoanut Island (very poor show of the "coco's drooping crown of palms" : not in it with Penang and Malaya and all the islands of the East), and the Rainbow Falls, and the Boiling Pits. To the last two we walked, My Virginian and I, through much mud. There was no rainbow at the Falls, nor any pit or hot water at the Boiling Pits. Nevertheless, I will not deny that they were pretty sights ; the Boiling

Pits are really fine : water that "dashed downward in a cataract" into a pool whence, finding no superterranean outlet, it bubbled and gurgled up underground into a lower pool, and again in like subterfugacious manner into yet a lower pool, all hemmed in in narrow space by lava "rock and crag, with many a jag." In the way of lava it is a cheerful country. The hill-side opens out now and again, quietly, with no unnecessary fuss, and pours out a good strong stream of real hot lava. The outer surface cooling and hardening, the stuff makes itself a tunnel as it proceeds (like a column of white ants does) and the liquid rock goes a long way scorching hot. The stream, awhile ago, made straight for Hilo, and got so near to it that it seemed little would be left of it "in the coming by-and-bye." But the Governoress of those days, being of the Royal Family, rose to the occasion. She put her Christianity in her pocket (a very small pocket would hold it all, or, indeed, all the Christianity of all the Hawaiians), and went forth with pomp and ceremony to meet the advancing lava-flow. And she prayed to Pele and the gods, the old gods of Hawaii, and offered sacrifice of pig, the sacred pork, and I know not what else ; and even when and as she prayed, the stream stayed, and Hilo was saved. This is no legend, it is fact ; and the black lava stream stopping dead half a mile short of Hilo is there to this day to prove it. Near the B.P. (Boiling Pits, not British Public ; there is no pub. nearer than the Hilo Hotel), we ran—or rather stumbled through mud and rock—into an unsophisticated Hawaiian hamlet. Quite Irish in the domesticity of its pigs, dirtier and more tumble-down in its grass and palm-leaf cabins than even a Burmese dacoit-village in the rains. An old man whom we found to show us our way ought to have been interned in that sequestered nook on Molokai. The uncivilized Hawaiian of old time may have been a fine fellow; at present he is most unromantically unclean and unsavoury.

CHAPTER XVI.

THE HAWAIIAN KINGDOM.

THE N.E. trade is all but permanent nine months in the year in Hawaii, and keeps the windward side wet and green while the leeward is dry and brown. Now and again comes a southerly wind— a "kona"—which is very muggy and relaxing— takes all the starch out of everyone. At all other times the climate is perfection on the leeward side. A shade thermometer that in Honolulu never reaches 90° and never (or hardly ever) falls below 55°, and has an annual mean of 75° ; sheltered from the too great force of the perpetual trade wind, yet irrigated (artificially) by waters brought down from the windward side or up through artesian wells ; with the bracing air and bright cold of mountain altitudes easily accessible on Maui and Hawaii islands, that are made up, mostly, of volcanoes whose heights run up into five figures, and of their enormous ejects of lava ; a rainfall of usually some thirty-five to forty inches, excessively heavy at no season of the year: what more would you wish for when you are still a couple of degrees within the tropics ? The Hawaiian Islands, it may be necessary to remind some who forget their geography, are not South Sea Islands, but extend from under 19° to over 22° north of the Equator. Yet, tropical as they are, one can— owing to the natural causes just sketched—enjoy quite a temperate climate, and go about all day in the sun, in a small hat, as no one who was not a lunatic, or desirous of speedily becoming one, would think of doing in the same latitude in India. What wonder if the natives are happy, soft-natured folk, easily led, thoughtless of all but the present, sensual, slothful. And what a wonder would it not be if such a people, brought into sudden contact with Western civilization—and that in an active American and missionary form—did not die out? It is a pity, but inevitable. I say it is a pity, for the people are a very different lot from their cousins the Maoris, whose speedy extinction, I said some way back, would be a good thing. These Hawaiians, though their islands be not in the South Seas, yet are South Sea Islanders. There seems no doubt that they came from the Samoan or Society Islands in the sixth and eleventh centuries A.D., and there does not seem to be any reason to believe that they found any indigenous people on the islands when they first landed. Thus their language is not mixed, as Maori seems to be, with unoriginal elements, and it has only twelve letters in the whole alphabet. Nor have the Hawaiians ever contracted, as the Maoris of New Zealand did, the taste for human flesh. Human sacrifices there were, but not cannibalism. The victim was placed on the altar;

and left to natural causes to dispose of. How, after grand sacrifices such as the great Kamehameha offered when rebuilding the heiau (temple) of Puukohola at Kawaihae, the high altar must have stunk! It is curious how ideas vary as to what is an indignity and what is not. The bones of chiefs were most carefully concealed—after being stripped of the flesh—in order that they might not be made into spear-heads, fish-hooks, or the like, which would have been a terrible disgrace. Yet once, when a faithful friend entrusted with the bones of the alii-nui (chief) Kualii, to find a safe place for them to rest in, could find none, he ground them into powder and mixed this royal bone-dust with the pudding (poi) which the funeral guests were given to eat. Thus, as he elegantly explained, his master's bones were buried in the bellies of his mourning friends. So it is an indignity to have your bones converted into something useful, but none to have the flesh hacked off them, and themselves ground up for kitchen use. In the matter of *tabu* (or *kapu*, as it would more properly be written here, there being no true *t* or *b* in Hawaiian), the Hawaiian custom was, as I read, much the same as the Maori; but I have not read of anything corresponding to the New Zealand "utu" and " muru." On the other hand, the making of "kapa" (fibre-cloth) and "awa" (liquor), while common in Hawaii, was unknown in Maoriland. About matrimonial arrangements there was, of course, a charming simplicity, and that monopoly of one another by a woman and a man, which is so fixed in our ideas of marriage, was conspicuously absent. Not only might a man have several wives, but a wife might have several husbands; polyandry as well as polygamy. And a man handed over his wife to another easily enough, if such stories are to be believed as that of Kaikilani, who, being the loved wife of Kaualoa, was by him handed over to Lono, merely because she liked him better; or as that of Kelea, whom her husband with equal facility let go to Kalamakua. These "meles" or legends of the chiefs show further that, except mother and son (query : and father and daughter), any two might intermarry; the offspring of brother and sister took the highest rank (alii niaupio). Yet, it does not appear that the women were in any particularly evil plight. They were debarred from many things by the kapu; but they had no small influence, and were not forbidden even to take part in men's proper business of fighting. (So in Burma, the king regularly married his half-sister, and matrimony is a far from indissoluble bond; yet are the women free and independent enough.) From the old "meles" it would seem, too, that for all the laxness, devotion to one sole partner was neither unknown nor unadmired; for Kaaialii is sung of, who followed Kaala into the sea-cave whither her cross-grained father, Oponui, had dragged her, and refusing to leave her, even though his king the mighty Kamehameha commanded, dashed out his brains with a stone, and so died by her corpse; and Mauono, who died on her husband Kekuaokalani's body, fighting for the kapu and the old gods of Hawaii; and the lives and death of Makakehau and Puupehe. That abolition of the old religion and dethronement—nay, destruction—of the old gods is a strange story. It followed, it is true, intercourse with the white men, but preceded any, the feeblest, attempt at missionarizing; and was brought about by wine and woman (nothing strange in their upsetting a man's religion), and (what is strange) by the high priest of the falling creed. For King Liholiho would not have ventured so far as to utterly efface the old faith, but for his wife and the high priest Hewahewa, and for his being well-primed with export gin. Soon after, in came the missionaries and gave them a religion in place of the vanished worship. And now all the natives are Christians—" nominally, I suppose," I remarked to The Reverend, and he answered with a half-amused sadness, " Very nominally." Certainly, as one sees the Hawaiian of to-day, it is impossible to imagine him taking anything seriously. I mean taking anything to heart, so as to feel deeply about it. He is light-hearted, one might almost say light-headed, his feelings ephemeral, his stability *nil*. Fond of flowers —and most pretty is their custom of decorating themselves and their friends with leis (garlands of flower and leaf); fond of feathers (worn bandwise on the hat), fond of music (the white man's guitar is now the universal instrument), and of dancing (of course, much of it is indecently suggestive), and of pleasure (notwithstanding prohibition laws, and the

Seventh Commandment), and of feasting (a luau—or picnic—is delightful, if you like raw fish and poi), the Hawaiian seems incapable of fixed feeling, seated sentiment, thoroughness of thought. Religion, love, friendship, gratitude,—such things they have the outward show of; but behind it all is an absolute absence of reality. Reality in such matters is impossible without some recollection of the past, some forethought of the future; and the Hawaiian lives in the present only. It is as well, perhaps; for there is practically no future for him. The Hawaiians have dwindled to well under 40,000; and how many of these, I wonder, have no intermixture of foreign blood! Very few, I warrant. Their royal family is full of it; and the heiress-apparent—Her Royal Highness Princess Victoria Kawekui Kaiolani Lunalilo Kalaninuiahilapalapa— (I take some credit for remembering that name)— might more simply be called Her Royal Highness Miss Cleghorn, and will doubtless marry a white man, as her half-sister has done. (She is being educated at school in England; chance for any bachelor wishing to become a Prince Consort.) The Hawaiians have always received foreigners kindly. You can hardly call it through unselfishness: it is merely easy-going flabbiness. Japanese were, it is legended, wrecked here centuries ago, and later on Spaniards; and this flotsam married into the highest families. That Cook was killed at Kealekeakua Bay was merely the accident of a trumpery quarrel. Davis and Young (adventurers of sorts), who came soon after, became progenitors of royalty, and the missionaries were received open-armed. And didn't they make a good thing of it! Trust the missionary—more especially the American missionary—for that! Houses and lands, wealth and position, these are the portion of the descendants of the missionaries of the early years of the century. The people they came to convert are, it is true, rapidly dying out. Ah, well, there is the more space for the padres and their offspring! The mixture of races in Hawaii is curious. Of capitalists and employers of labour, the American first, the English a bad second, and the rest nowhere. Of labourers, Portuguese from the Azores, Chinese, and of later years Japanese in thousands. The foreign population outnumbers the native (half-whites thrown in). Now, some would like a few coolies from Madras, Bengal, Bombay, as cheaper than the rest; and cheapness in labour is much desired by the capitalist now that his sugar has to compete in the States equally with all other sugars, instead of being, as of old, free while they were taxed.

But Indian coolies in a foreign state are much trouble to the British representative in that state; and the British representative does not like to be troubled. I fancy the planters will have to do without Indian labour for a while. The sugar industry is the only one on the islands worth speaking of; the capital in it is some twenty-three millions of dollars American, about five millions British, and a few odd thousands others. In mills and machinery they are a good way ahead of Mauritius; so a planter from there told me after seeing some of the estates here. This disintegrating lava, once it has water, seems most fertile; and water they spare no pains to supply it with where natural supply is wanting. Most of the flower and foliage that make Honolulu beautiful is fed by water artificially obtained; for the leeward side of the islands is by nature very bare and singularly poor in vegetation. Even on the windward side the jungle—all that I have seen—is nothing like so all-pervading and so dense as in Java and the Straits. But with water splendid flowers are produced in abundance; John Chinaman plants his paddy-fields, and the natives their *taro* (as it is usually written; *kalo* as it should rather be). It is an insipid but filling sort of food, this kalo, taken natural; but it is capable of being made up into tasty biscuit, or by the natives into their staff of life, yclept *poi*. This is a dirty pink stuff something of the consistency of arrowroot—that is to say, very thick or thin, as you choose to make it; flavour subacid, slightly fermented, not particularly pleasing to a white palate, but not atrocious, abominable, like ngapi or dorian. Fish the islands have of many kinds, but only the mullet pleases Western taste, and the natives prefer their fish raw. Pig was all the flesh they had before the white man came. Now there are ranches with cattle and horses, and an island or two filled with sheep. The diet they eat seems, anyway, to have raised a fine big race. Their legends speak of men of six-and-a-half feet

HAWAIIAN WOMEN.

as quite common; and there seems no doubt that the old Hawaiian was a splendid animal. The race has degenerated somewhat, no doubt, in bulk as in numbers; but even now they run to a great size. Catchweights over 300 pounds would be about the correctest figure to give for ladies of the royal family; and the women-folk generally are big-faced and big-bodied, though not especially large-limbed. Many of the men are of quite "ornery" size. I should not call any of the men handsome or the women beautiful: large dark eyes are the only redeeming features in broad heavy faces. The costume of the women—the "holoku"—does not set off any figure they may have; it is a long night-gowny sort of arrangement of ample dimensions unconfined at the waist. Men wear coat and trousers and shirt à l'Européenne, or rather à l'Americaine. Both sexes favour wide straw hats adorned with lei of flowers or feathers—peacocks' and pheasants' feathers for choice. As to voice, they are not to be despised. The language having but seven consonants (k, p, three liquids, an aspirate, and w), of which no two ever come together or ever end a syllable, the words are nearly all vowels, and the people seem to have a natural aptitude for music. I have listened to the "vowelled undersong" of a girl singing to her guitar alone, and thought it charming; I have heard the Quintet Club play together banjo, guitar, mandoline, and a flute-like thing, and sing in parts their Hawaiian songs, and I have joined heartily in the applause; and I have heard the Royal Band play both wind and string (the latter poor), and fully endorsed the high reputation that it has (as a brass band). The band-master is quite a personage, for to him (a German) all its excellence is due; and when the phonograph was displayed in the Royal Opera House (really a decent little theatre), the band played into it the Liliuokalani March, and it was delicious to see on the happy maestro's face the smile of rapt beatitude that sat there fixed while the machine rendered his strains clearly and well, and he knew that his music was recorded for ever to be played in places which his band could not reach. It was not my chance to see any dancing. At entertainments got up at private houses even, "hula" dances are given, and are (as I have been told) apt to be embarrassing from their too realistic pantomimic representation of things not done in the open; even as a Burmese pwe sometimes is, for instance the one given at the palace at Mandalay one evening in the Christmas week of '87. If you want to get up a "hula" for yourself, it is a matter of secret arrangement by night, and a trip to an island in the harbour, and plentiful gin to the flower-clad (else mostly nude) danseuses. The thing is not allowed by law, but that does not make much odds; laws exist in Hawaii chiefly for the purpose of being broken. Dances of that kind are not worth seeing when degraded as the hula here and the haka in New Zealand are; I do not care for such things unless they are performed naturally, spontaneously, by a people not yet ruined by the veneer of civilization. The Hawaiians are great riders, many in Mexican saddles—which seems to me absurd, where there is no lassoing or rounding in of half-wild cattle to be done; many in colonial or English. And the ladies have long ago decided the cross-saddle question; all ride *en cavalier.* Even the white ladies on the islands have—many or most of them—adopted the same fashion; and riding in ample well-adjusted skirt (no folly of coats and tunics, breeches and boots displayed, but just in good long skirts properly arranged) they look extremely well. It seemed to me elegant, becoming, sensible. And my friend Mrs. H. thought so too.

The white population is so much American that it seems to be all so. Even the English in Hawaii speak with that dulcet twang and use the strange provincialisms of the American language. But the Government is of English fashion, and the royal family, with English blood in it, has decidedly English leanings and preferences. It may be that the islands came, once, very near to being incorporated with the country of the star-spangled banner (the most beautiful flag on earth, an American tells me; creditable to his patriotism but not to his artistic taste). And I don't, for my own part, see that it would hurt any one in particular if that should be the ultimate fate of the kingdom. The U.S.A. have secured a naval station in Pearl Harbour (near Honolulu) already; and what further benefit they would get, or harm we should suffer, by the kingdom becoming a state of the Union it does not occur to me to apprehend. But I don't think it is likely to happen.

Ah, well, it is a pleasant place to linger in, this cluster of volcanic islets separated by thousands of miles of sea from all other land (2,100 from San Francisco, 2,300 from Samoa, 3,400 from Japan), and the people are cheerful and bright—what matter if they be shallow and insincere?—and they speak a sweet-sounding language, and take life easily—both this one and their thoughts of the next. Aloha oe, Aloha nui, Hawaii nei.

CHAPTER XVII.

THE PACIFIC SLOPE.

THE steamer service between Honolulu and the Coast (I never heard San Francisco and the Pacific slope spoken of by any other name in Hawaii) is not well arranged. Instead of a regular weekly service, which they might easily fix up, you have an interval of twelve days between one boat and the next, and then a space of only two days before a third follows. And the boats might go much quicker than they do; the *Australia* had to slow down for the last two days of the run, for no other purpose than just to consume the regulation seven days allotted to her to make the passage in. We had a tremendous see-off—"leis" galore, band playing, big crowd—the usual thing on the departure of the steamer from Oahu ; a very pretty and lively sight. I cannot say that I enjoyed this voyage. We rolled a good deal in the bounding billows, and "bounders" on board were far too numerous for comfort. There was no fun in the lottery, it became a put-up job ; seven-point whist without honours is deadly ; (piquet is a fine game though) ; flirtation "gross as a mountain, open, palpable," is not even amusing to watch when it is rather more than less rowdy. The smoking-room was cramped and creaky, groaning with package on package of plaintains loaded on the roof; and as the tobacco-chewers (that is to say, nearly every American man on board) invariably shot wide of the spittoon (pardon; I mean cuspidor), the floor was a terror to see and to walk on. From a careful observation of the common or garden American that one meets travelling, I should say that he washes his clothes rarely, and himself never. The bathman on the *Australia*, when I descended for the matutinal tub, was evidently much surprised at seeing any one in search of a bath, and his astonishment was unbounded when I said "Yes" to his wondering query, "Do you wish a bath *every* morning?" Evidently it was a most unusual thing, almost unprecedented in his experience. I observed later on in "sleepers" (sleeping-cars on the railways) that the shirts of my fellow-passengers were usually excessively grimy, only the cuffs and dickeys and collars being (for outward show) comparatively clean. We certainly did have a mixed crowd on board. Hawaiians of various shades of snuff-and-butter colour; Hawaiian Americans, coast Americans, opera singers and managers, downy ones of singularly ill-veiled downiness, and I really don't think one gentleman in the whole blessed crowd. (Of course, I reckon Our Humorist and Me and My Virginian as not of the crowd—merely onlookers.) The Ancient Downy, owner of thousands and thousands of acres (fifty-six was it? or fifty-seven thousand ?) in Killarney, or Blarney (or Cockaigne, or Limbo, or where?) wandering round searching island-rocks for guano for a living ; the Younger Downy One simply found—cheating is an ugly word ; let us say—taking undue secret advantage at cards, yet, after brief expulsion, taken back to the bosoms of the players; the moneyed man with enormous diamond stud in frilled shirt-front, tie carefully drawn on one side, and tucked into the front above the stud, that the latter might shine resplendent—the types of character on board might be enumerated at length, but none would be found charming. Wherefore, I was well pleased when at length we came in sight of the Californian coast, and neared, and reached, and entered in through the Golden Gate. This name is pretty-sounding, but its exact appropriateness I do not grasp. Nevertheless, it is a good name ; the sweet sound of it in the ear recalls a scene that is certainly delightful to look upon. The morning was fine, and the green hills on the south side of the entrance, the sand and rock on the north, the vast expanse of bay and island, and wide-extending shore, dotted with cities and backed by hills, that lie within the Gate, were bright and cheerful in the clear spring sunshine. It is splendid in size, and beautiful in form and colour, this harbour of San Francisco. Not very powerfully guarded; an antique Spanish Presidio is the only defence visible, and there are no more. Navy ?—good, what there is of it, perhaps ; but how shall such an exiguous fleet suffice to protect the seaboard of so vast a dominion as the United States of America? But bother politics, especially in the States; we are not come here to touch pitch, or to be defiled therewith, but to enjoy the pleasure of life, and see fine scenery, and make good friends. There is Nob's Hill—Snob's Hill—which is it? and here is the wharf and Market Street, and the bustle and push of life more "bruyant," more energetic than we have seen since —well, since (ages ago) we were in the good old City of London. San Francisco is very new, and hasn't learnt to pave its streets yet. Its sidewalks are hardly so vile as those of New York, but its streetways are worse. The moral of this is that you should walk or else ride in a cable-car, and avoid all hacks and 'buses. I don't see that the cable-cars (most excellent invention) have the call over the Melbourne system; they're as good, and go up hill and down grades as steep as Hongkong's Funicular, and in and out and round about the city in every direction; but I don't know in what way they're better. Perhaps more striking as a sight, from the comparative flatness of Melbourne and the great variety of steep hillocks and sand-dunes to be surmounted in San Francisco. But our independent cousins' City of the West leaves our colonial cousins' City of the South a bad second in one respect. For the number of pretty female faces that you will see in an afternoon's promenade, send me back to 'Frisco. No other city that I have seen in my wanderings is in it with her: Kearny Street is a joy to walk down, and Market Street in its best portions, and is it Sutton Street too? But that is enough.

I was told that at the Palace Hotel you were a mere item lost in a crowd of items, indistinguishable, ill-served, ill-waited on. So I did not go there. But I was told wrong; for Our Humorist found it good in all respects. However, at the Baldwin I was as well off; I growled only at the extreme casualness and dilatoriness of the negro, mulatto, almost (but not quite) white, table servants. Around the walls of the dining and lunch rooms at "Lucky Baldwin's" Hotel are plaques painted with head and bust of types of female beauty; and My Virginian pointed out to me, with admiring pride, that the necklace that each lovely one wore was not painted, but actual glittering stones—real diamonds he averred them to be. I forbore from stating my opinion that it was hideous taste, whether the stones were real or paste; worthy of a half-barbarian Burmese artist who sews bits of tinsel on to his painted pictures. But let me not grumble; for certainly here was hotel comfort, throwing into the remote shade the "accommodations" (as Americans call them) of Australian hostelries.

San Francisco is a pleasant place to wander about in except for the wind, which is gustatious and (in April) chilly. Fog also is said to be around at times; but I came on none. So that when I went out to see the Presidio, and the Seal Rocks and the Golden Gate Park, I saw them and not fog.,

And the Seal Rocks are neither particularly curious nor at all lovely; just a few disjunct rocks on which crawl and roar many sea-lions and a few seals. They look like a mass of—well, what they most look like, seen from the distance from which alone you can see them, is (the simile is Shakespearian) "life in excrement"; just a crawling lot of dirty worms. But the view of the Golden Gate and back over the Bay is good, from the hill above the Seal Rock House (or whatever the little pub. calls itself); and the Pacific Ocean stretches before you for I forget how many thousand miles—a good deal farther than you can see, anyway. The Golden Gate Park is not of great beauty; but it is worthy of admiration as a triumph of somewhat formal art over an extremely formless nature. A vast waste of wind-swept sand-dunes is not a promising place for arboriculture, horticulture, or any other culture (unless it be that of a great thirst). Yet, on such a site has 'Friscan capital created half a park; and the only interest is that which townsmen and strangers take in it. Grassy lawns have been laid down, wide drives and walks completed, spacious arenas, and casinos, and conservatory, and what not else provided, groves planted, lakes and streams laid on. And in the other half, as yet mostly unreclaimed, is plenty of room for this new western energy to go on laying out and planting and adorning.

For the rest, San Francisco has no special showplaces, unless you reckon China Town as one. The

THE BAY OF SAN FRANCISCO.

city proper has big buildings, of brick and stone, where were modest cabins and plank shanties; and it is a child of vigorous growth since the days of '49. And its suburbs—Oakland and Sau Salito, and the rest—are pretty and pleasant to live in; and life is lived rapidly (I will not call the city a fast one—but it doesn't go slow). For theatres it does itself very fairly well. I tried comic opera, which wasn't much (but one had the comfort of smoking, and—its usual accompaniment, as at a music hall); and American comedy—extremely good; and adapted French—quite good enough. The real French arrived about this time, even the great Sarah; and from the opening of the ticket office for days on end the side-walk at Baldwin's was blocked with queues of patient Westerners waiting their turn. But I thought it was about time that I went to some of the visitable places in California; and off we set, My Virginian and I, for the Yosemite. There are plenty of places nearer, if you wish to see them; Stanford's Stud Farm at San Paolo, the Naval Yard, the Lick Observatory. I did China Town and saw nothing that I had not seen in China, except that I had not there gone to a theatrical show. It was not so noisy as I had expected, and I did not find anything particularly noticeable. The chief marvel of the place is how men who live in such crowded, dirty dens, can turn out so clean and respectable as John usually does. To Monterey, most charming and delightful of seaside resorts (Mrs. H. quite ecstacized over it), I had not leisure to go.

The American "sleeper" (what we call sleepers they call ties, and with them "sleeper" denotes sleeping-car, even as "smoker" denotes smoking-car, though "diner" is not used for dining-car, as logically it should be) is good in many respects, and unsatisfactory in others. I do not like being shut up behind curtains in berth or section, as one needs must be when men and women have the same car to sleep in and not distinct compartments as in our preferable Indian fashion; the cars are overheated by the steam-pipes by day and very draughty at night, whereby I acquired a villainous cold; and when there is no dining-car attached and meals are merely served to you in your "sleeper," the dinner you get is a very scratch affair. Sometimes the negro porter is civil, sometimes he isn't. It takes from 4 P.M. (first half-hour by ferry across the harbour to Oakland) until 6 A.M. to get from 'Frisco to Raymond, which is absurd; the distance, 200 miles, could easily be covered by that time if one left 'Frisco after dinner—say 10 or 11 P.M. At Raymond you get breakfast and then a coach, or rather a stage; for "stage" is the vehicle you travel in, not the distance it travels between two stations or changes of horses. And precious slow these stages go. From Raymond to Wawona, thirty-six miles, took us ten hours actual going, plus an hour's halt for lunch. True there is a pass of some 5,000 feet to get over, and the road was sloppy and rutty with winter and bad weather. So from Wawona to Stoneman House in the valley, twenty-seven miles, took six and a half hours; down the long descent from above Inspiration Point to the Foot of the Bridal Veil we just crawled; none of that dash and go with which we came down the Otira Gorge. Coming out it was even worse. Some one had complained of the jolting on the road—and it was pretty bad; My Virginian kept trying to punch holes in the roof by leaping up and striking his head against it; and because of these complaints the drivers got orders to go slow. That is why it took seven and three-quarter hours to Wawona; and on a drying road and a down-grade nine hours to Raymond. April is a little early to go into the valley. The first tourists got in this year on March 30th, but after that they had a good deal more snow, so that even on April 20th there was plenty of it lying on the top of the passes on the way in, and so much of it on the mountains around the valley that the track to Nevada Falls was cut through a five-foot drift, and Glacier Point and Eagle Peak were inaccessible. Around the Mariposa Grove of Big Trees it lay thick and even, even the coach road being deeply encumbered with it. About the middle of May would, I should think, be the best time; all the tracks would then be clear and in repair, while patches of snow would still be lingering in ravine and sheltered nook or on lofty crest, and the waterfalls would be at their grandest and best, full-fed with water from melting snow-fields. And if you intend to stay for a few days, put up at Barnard's—it is cosy and half homelike, whereas at the Stoneman there is no great comfort, and the table is bad.

And what shall be said of the Valley? Well, I don't think I will say anything descriptive. I suppose a good deal of word-spinning has been done about it, though, to say the truth, I haven't read any; and I don't see any need for my adding to the mass. Besides, I fancy I've made a good many shots already in that line in this journal, and you've probably had about enough of it. Moreover, and finally, I don't feel equal to the occasion. The theme is a bit too big for my pen; even as it is too big for any camera to do justice to. What good is there in talking about walls of cold grey granite that stand in huge bulk 3,000 feet sheer from the floor of the Valley as they do in El Capitan? Can you realize what they look like? Or if you hear how the Great Yosemite Fall pours a stream thirty-four feet wide straight down over the edge of a perpendicular precipice 1,500 feet high, the base of the fall half hidden in a cone of ice, and thence goes rushing in broken cascades down a fall of 626 feet to drop into the Valley by another sheer descent of 400 feet—if you hear all this, can you form a picture of it before your mind's eye? I don't believe it. Nor could I by any description convey to you a true idea of the serene yet wild beauty of the valley below the Nevada Falls with the vast Cap of Liberty and Mount Brodrick and the rounded southern side of the South Dome; nor of the great yet graceful Vernal Falls, nor of the charm of the changing views of Cloud's Rest and Star King (are they not pretty names?) and many another mountain giant, that you get as you wander about the narrow valley shut in all round by these Titanic masses of granite. There are plenty of waterfalls (without at least one, of course, no show scene is complete), but I do not greatly care for any but the Yosemite and the Nevada and Vernal. The Bridal Veil is all very well, but I own it did not particularly fetch me; the Widow's Tears soon dry up (hence the appropriate name); you can't get to the Illillouette without a lot of trouble. Mirror Lake is a biggish puddle of dirty water. It does its duty as a mirror very well, and there is a good deal worthy of reflection within its reach; North Dome and Mount Watkin and Cloud's Rest, and the precipitous north side of the Half or South Dome. It is strange to watch the sun creep up over the edge of the latter, and to note in the water a perfect rainbow round his coming, while in the sky there is visible only a blinding blaze of bright white light. And the Cathedral Spires—really most cathedral-like—and Sentinel Peak and Sentinel Dome, and the Royal Arches and Three Brothers, of whom the highest is Eagle Peak—if you want to see just the shape and position of them, look at photos; but if you want to know what they are like, to see a scene of most marvellous magnitude and magnificence—one that will not disappoint even an eye that is becoming a little weary of sight-seeing—why, do as I did, and go and see the Yosemite in cloudless fine weather, at the time of full moon, before the snow is all gone, and before the valley gets too hot to be comfortable.

The Big Trees in the Mariposa Grove are taken on the usual tourist round after your return to Wawona. This entails, at the funereal pace that obtains here, a very long day's staging; 6 A.M. to 8 P.M., with only about half-an-hour halt for lunch. But don't miss them; they are worth some trouble to see. When you hear of thirty-three feet in diameter, 100 in circumference, all but 300 feet high, you feel rather inclined to be sceptical; or if credulous, to think that such bulk will be curious only for its size—ungainly, unlovely. Not a bit of it. The measurements have been made and are true; and the trees are extremely handsome. Perhaps the Grizzly Giant must be excepted from the last epithet—he is too battered; and many of them are marred in part by the scorching and burning of fire. Nevertheless, their stateliness and cleanness of growth, the rich red brown of their thick bark, their symmetry as well as their size, render them beautiful as well as grand. And I think the deep smooth carpet of unstained snow that lay all around them on that April day when I saw them rendered them in their stillness and silence more impressive and sublime than they would have seemed in garish midsummer. And so we drove through one of them (as per advertisement) and round and about many more; and did not feel tired as at last we rattled home on the down-grade under the frosty moonlight to Wawona. (Frosty is only an exaggeration of a degree or two; it was very near 32° at night.)

My Virginian deserted me, and I went on to Los Angeles alone. It is not a pleasant journey. You have nearly four hours to wait at the junction at Berenda up to nearly midnight, with no decent place to wait in ; and next day the ride is through a very dusty and uninteresting country. (I say ride, for in America you ride not only on horseback, but in a carriage, on a car, in a boat. One day in Honolulu I proposed to My Virginian that we should ride, and he went and ordered a buggy, or, as he called it, a hack. When I explained that wasn't quite what I intended, he said, " Oh, you mean *horseback* riding.") Once through the desert of Mojave (pronounce *j* as *h* down here, please) the country improves, and around Los Angeles there is great fertility. I stayed here only too short a time, for the kindness and good-fellowship of the men, and the pleasantness and hospitality of the Club, would have made one happy for much more than a couple of days. I spent one in going around and about Pasadena. I don't quite know what fruit is not grown here—except cherries ; these, I was told, do not do well. But for the excellence of their oranges and olives I can answer; and the quantity ! An orchard of orange-trees in full bearing is a splendid sight. Apples and peaches and apricots innumerable were only just coming into blossom ; in miles of vineyard the vines were pruned down close. Some three or four years previous this part of the world underwent the usual malady of growing young cities—a land boom. Great blocks were laid out for building, avenues and streets named and signboards put up, and prices were exceedingly lofty. Of course the re-action came, and now the price of land is back to its old level, and though the names of streets and avenues remain on the signboards, the ways themselves are mere occupation-roads, and the blocks are converted into orchards and vineyards. I drove round by Sierra Madre and Baldwin's Ranche and San Gabriel. The Sierra Madre was once a hotel; now it is private, but that did not seem to be any bar to my wandering around where I would. At Baldwin's there is quite a pretty country box, and at San Gabriel an excellent hotel. Here also there is an old Mission Church, with adobe huts about it, old (for America), quaint, not lovely.

The best view of the valley is from the Raymond Hotel—an enormous structure, set on a hill. It is a pretty scene—a line of abrupt hills covered with thin scrub jungle runs all along the left; the snowy top of old " Baldy "—more respectfully San Antonio—looks over the far end of them, with the more distant snow of San Bernardino in the middle background, and farther yet San Jacinto gleams white through the haze. The haze of heat is thick enough on the right, too, to hide the sea, and the island of Santa Catalina looms but faintly visible. But all the centre is full of sunshine and fertile valley, with the wide shallow river-bed running through it, and dry nalas cutting down to it from the hills. The Raymond is open only in the winter months ; in summer, manager and the whole estab-

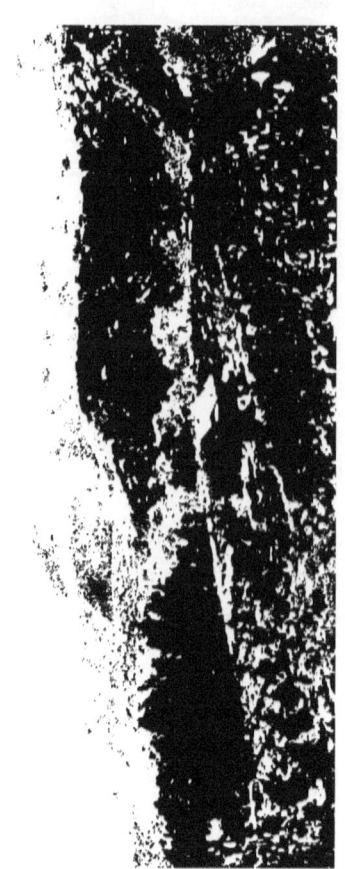

lishment move off to the White Mountains in New Hampshire—the other side of the Continent—to open the house there that remains closed all the winter. And on Sunday my friends took me down to Santa Monica (a little place by the sea, with a big hotel), and we bathed, and ate fish, and drank bock beer, and lay on the sands in the delicious warm sunlight, and had a thoroughly idle and happy day. Twenty-two hours of rail, with fine dust that penetrated everywhere, notwithstanding double windows closed and ventilators shut, and a terrible stuffiness in the car in consequence; and with no dinner (verily, their arrangements are not perfect even in America), and we are in 'Frisco again.

There are many ways from 'Frisco to the East; and Mr. Mackay, the agent for the Burlington Route, will do anything for you by any route. (I don't recommend Cook's; they are n.g. in America, and I speak from experience.) I chose the road north, past Mount Shasta, over the Siskiyon Range, by Portland, Tacoma, and Seattle to Victoria, B.C. It is fine scenery—I think the best. Certainly, the railroad all up to Sissons, at the foot of Mount Shasta, is very pretty, ever rising up through the narrow canon of the Sacramento River and winding through "the savour and shade of old-world pine-forests," with occasional glimpses of the big mountain that we have to circumvent, to get round; until at last at Sissons we are about at the summit of the pass, and the great snow-clad sides and peaks of Shasta are full in front of us. It is distinctive of the ranges, north from 'Frisco, that they run at only moderate elevations all along parallel with the coast, with here and there an immense solitary peak, snow-clad, standing as it were as sentinels along the line, Mount Shasta, Mount Scott, Mount Hood, Mount Adams, Mount Tacoma, Mount Baker. From the side of Shasta we run down again to the foot of the Siskiyon, and then have to climb a pass some 4,000 feet high. It is a good piece of engineering, and fine scenery. From the summit we say a last good-bye to Mount Shasta, now afar off, and plunge down, by a series of wonderful curves and tunnels and tressel bridges, into the valley of the Rogue River, and are in Oregon. Night comes down, and in the morning we are in Portland. Here you may spend the day, and rail by night to Tacoma; or, if you prefer, rail on to Tacoma, and stay the night there. I chose the former, and considered myself repaid by the view from the height above the town. I wandered to the top of Fairmount and overlooked this go-ahead and growing town of 100,000 souls, and across the Williamette River saw the Cascade Range with its two far apart "pinnacles of silent snow," Mount Hood and Mount Adams, and the Columbia River winding broadly on, now near the sea. Tacoma appeard to me dirty and mean—but then it was a pouring wet morning, and I was cross after a very jolty night-journey (the only one I experienced, and I rode by rail many nights), and a late train (also an exceptional experience ; common enough—even the rule—though, on the Northern Pacific, so they say) ; so that perhaps Tacoma is a very nice place really. Thence steamer carried me down Puget Sound, past Seattle and Port Townsend, and out of American territory and waters to good old British soil in Victoria, B.C.

California and Oregon and Washington and the States on the Pacific slope are go-ahead. My Virginian would not allow me to speak of them as American, at least not without qualification. He said they were as much American as Sydney and Melbourne are British ; as much so, and no more. My Boston-taught Southerner professed to find them as colonial as our "cornstalks" appeared to me. I can't say that I can see so much difference myself. But then, I am not a New Englander, nor educated at Harvard. He even, with withering sarcasm, expressed a wish that these Westerners would speak English. Of course, I know that we unfortunate people in England cannot speak English so purely and sweetly as the cultured inhabitants of "the hub"; and that, I suppose, is why I could not for the life of me make out any great difference in accent, or twang, or in general phraseology between the Eastern and the Western. (There are idioms peculiar to each, I know; as I mentioned when I wrote about Old Phil and the Nebraska Sportsman.) And in manners? Well, I don't know much about it. When you travel abroad, you meet men with good manners, and you meet men with bad; and when you travel at home in England, do you meet only men with good manners? I trow not. Anyway, I can't say ditto to that clever and well-known Anglo-Indian who has made public his criticisms on things American. That "wide-eyed young Ithuriel" (so an American writer—feminine, of course—styles him; fancy Mr. R. K. as an archangel; gods! it would be enough to make one join the rebel hosts and take the consequences)—he, of course, had a reputation for smart writing to sustain. I haven't, and so I can afford to be truthful. Smart or not, and unveracious or not, I'm sorry that an Anglo-Indian who is certain to be widely read should have descended into bad form, as (to my taste) that youthful angel of light with the well-skinned eyes has permitted himself to do. The Bohemian Club is a pleasant one, and when you are entertained at it, is it good form to guy your hosts and their guests? Of course, there are some things American that please not us. I suppose there are things English that please not them. We do not prefer a salt-cellar to which there is no salt-spoon, and in which the eater as he eats dips his *fork* (mind, the fork with which he is eating) at each mouthful; and not all Americans do this, but many do. We prefer to have each course separately; but it is not grievous if the gentle American prefers to have all together in a score or two dozen little platters around him at once, taking here a little and there a little from each and all indiscriminately. We do not care for tobacco-chewing, and for making bad shots at the spittoon ; and not all Americans do, but many do. Where was it that the notice was stuck up " Gentlemen will, and others must, make use of the cuspidor ? " The free and public use of a wooden toothpick does not, even if it be a woman who uses it, appear to strike American hotel-goers as inelegant, any more than gum-chewing strikes us as elegant. It is rather a jump, no doubt, from the deferential and humble service of the East to the freer independent manner of those who serve for hire in the West. But if your stomach is not too proud to swallow the difference in manner, you will get plenty of service, and in many cases obliging attentiveness, and in some cases none. (Tip *before* service is the American plan ; and don't forget it : it makes a difference.) I can only say this : that all in, I found the Western preferable to our colonial cousin down South. There are many English in California, and much English capital ; and there are many of all the nations of Europe and Palestine (or Jewdom) ; and what they are going to amalgamate into, it is much too early to say yet. They believe in their country, anyway. The President came round on progress, and they fêted him lustily. There was a padre on the train going north ; he was a man with a great and varied knowledge of the world, and recounted anecdotes thereof with much verve and gusto. Of course, being a padre, he cannot have ever wavered a hair's-breadth from the truth. Yet will I refrain from stating his version of the outturn of wheat and fruit per acre in Washington State. He said this : "Immigrants come in, sir, at 1,000 a day into my State." "That didn't last long, I suppose?" queried some one. "Continuously for two years. Yes, sir, for two years. The resources of that State are inexhaustible. Why, sir, I tell you, if the Pilgrim Fathers had landed at the mouth of the Columbia River instead of at Plymouth Rock, the Eastern States would have been uninhabited to this day." It is evidently a fine country, and grows very big products. This padre was one of them.

CHAPTER XVIII.

THE C.P.R. AND U.S.A.

THE weather cleared as we came into the wide sea-lake from which branch out Puget Sound and the Straits of San Juan de Fuca and the Gulf of Georgia, and I thought the prospect a splendid one. The chief feature is the great snow-clad Olympian range on the left. Victoria is so hidden away behind the crest of the hill on the right, as you steam up to the Island of Vancouver, that you do not see it at all until you round the corner and enter the little harbour. There is neither width nor depth enough for big ships; these are to be found at Esquimalt (pronounce Eskwīmalt) four or five miles farther up, where H.M.'s ships of war lie at anchor, and there are docks dry and wet. Victoria can hardly be called a big place yet. I suppose 25,000 is a liberal figure to give for the number of its inhabitants. An American in some book that I read called it a "quaint old English town." The first two adjectives are hardly appropriate, but there is no question about its Englishness. There is quite a different style, a different atmosphere, from that of American

Y

towns, far more English than anything I have ever seen in any other even of our own colonies. And Victoria is growing fast. I wandered out and about in all directions, and in every direction found new houses going up just as fast as they could be built. Mostly wood; the stone and brick age has not yet come except for some of the stores in town and for one particularly ugly residence on the top of the hill and another set in pretty grounds low down. The four days that I spent in the capital of our only Pacific province were very pleasant to me. It was perfectly delightful to find rest from hotels and from sightseeing in the comfortable home of an old-country friend and relative, settled out here, getting on well in his business, and (lucky man) married to a charming Columbian lady. We drove around over the hill (there is a splendid view across the Gulf of Georgia to the Cascade Mountains, with their big snow-sentinel Mount Baker) and back by the Gorge—a charming inlet, where the sea runs in far back from the harbour until it passes beyond Esquimalt Harbour, with but a narrow portage to separate them; and by motor-car to Esquimalt. I do not greatly like motor-cars—electric tramways. The car lurches along, pitching like a ship in a headwind, and the noise it makes is awful—like a sawmill screaming in agony. The driver is called a "motorneer," a word to make a purist shiver. Esquimalt is pretty—a landlocked harbour with a narrow entrance: defences there are none that I know of. There were only two ships there, and one of them in dry-dock. And I went shopping with the lady of the house and rummaged all over a shopful of Red Indian curios; and lived a domestic and peaceful existence until it was time to set forth again with face set eastwards and homewards. The day was vile—cloud and drizzle and rain and bitter cold, and I saw but little of the Straits up which we steamed to Vancouver. And at Vancouver it was no better. I walked hard for an hour-and-a-half about the Stanley Park—a large reservation that is still for the most part pine-forest with drives and walks cut through it. I suppose it may be beautiful in fine weather. Some of the trees are very old; some one said about these (or it may have been about the Big Trees of Mariposa) that they were here before Christ. I said I hadn't heard of Christ having been here at all; all I got for reply was " Never said he had." Vancouver had two houses standing some five years ago —burnt out. It has now about 10,000 inhabitants; but it is a very new place yet. Houses lie scattered about as if shaken out of a big pepper-pot, and great gaps yawn on the straight main streets and side streets that cross at right angles. But it will be a big place some time. Why? Because close by the wharf is the terminus of the Canadian Pacific Railway, and at the wharf is lying the *Empress of India*, a fine vessel of (*nisi fallor*) 6,000 tons. She can do from Yokohama to Vancouver in twelve days, and the Canadian Pacific Railway can (and did—just to show it can) rail you on to Montreal (3,000 miles) in ninety hours. Just add a good line of steamers from

Montreal or Halifax to the old country, or make the Allan wake up a bit, and you have a real fast high-road to the East—all British. You do not see much of the prosperous agricultural part of the country as you go through by rail. There must be a good deal, for hardware stores sell a good many agricultural implements and machines; but little comes in view except forest and river, which supply lumber and fish—the main supports of Vancouver. And the river—the Fraser—I saw very little of. How can you see when it rains incessantly with clouds low down, hiding everything? I had to take the Fraser Cañon for granted. Next day was more like April—shine and shower; but still clouds hung about so heavily that I was done out of large portions of the scenery I had come to see. And much of beauty is passed at night. Undoubtedly the best way to see the grandeur of the Canadian Pacific Railway is to get fine weather in the first place, and then to go from Vancouver to Banff, stay there a bit, and then return to Vancouver, stopping off at Glacier if you like. Beyond Banff there is little to see; and by the plan suggested you would see all you want. From Revelstoke, reached at 10 A.M., there was in the transient sunshine something of a view; the Albert Cañon, which the train halts for you to get out and look at, is rugged enough; and then there is the mighty climb up to Glacier. Glimpses of scenery, gleams of sun, rendered this part interesting and aggravating—superb what one could see, exasperating not to see all. Glacier and Selkirk

ON THE C.P.R.: LEANCHOIL.

summit were up in the clouds. Going down Bear Creek Gorge to Donald there was more sun, and a fine view there and up the Palliser Cañon, and a splendid view of the Chancellor some way on. Up the steep ascent to Field and Stephen the great glaciers and snow-peaks gleamed ghostly, and the dark forests loomed weird through the gathering dusk and the drifting masses of vapour. Ever since leaving San Francisco, the scenery has struck me as cold. I look for and find not that warmth of atmosphere which I love in more southern scenery. Even in bright sunlight, such as I had on May-day in Victoria, the landscape does not seem to waken and smile back to the clear blue heaven; it remains cold, austere, impassive. And these Selkirks and Rockies of the Canadian Pacific Railway—they are immense. Pine forest cannot look gay; it is always solemn. And the vast peaks of ice and snow—they are not savage. No, their grandeur is not of the wild or terrible type; they are overwhelming in sublimity, silent, seemingly immutable, everlasting. I found their lofty austerity impressive; yes, but so utterly unresponsive to light, so sad in colour, as to be not exhilarating but depressing. I admired and shivered, and felt better when I was through. And then came a whole day across the prairies—vast stretches of undulating upland, bare of everything but thin poor grass, void of man and beast. A small station at Medicine Hat; a cheery police commandant carrying a bottle of whisky in his pocket in this strictly prohibition country; some

Indians selling buffalo horns (poor specimens—not in it with a good Satpuda bison's); a terrible prosy old general, who did make one feel tired; a few local men getting in and out—good, even splendid, specimens of robust health and physique. Such were the incidents of the third day. I haven't much to say about the Indians. I saw one or two in the Yosemite. Those in Victoria were all in European clothes, and not in any way noticeable. At Medicine Hat they had something of their old style of dress; seemed very lazy—the most unpushing salesmen imaginable. The men big-featured; the old squaws ugly; the girls not unpleasant-looking; all dirty. And the fourth day took us through the wide wheat-lands of Manitoba, leaving behind the haunt of the buffalo. All the buffaloes are dead now, killed off so that not one is left alive, which happy consummation the far-seeing Government has met by making it a criminal offence to kill one! In early May, Manitoba is under the plough, and the scenery is not cheerful enough to make one sorry to reach Winnipeg, and get a night's rest in a bed after three in a sleeper-berth. Not that there is anything to complain of on the Canadian Pacific Railway. The berths are wide and lofty and comfortable—better than on such American lines as I chanced on; there is even a bath on the car, but so little used that it is stuffed up with rubbish of sorts, and you cannot get the use of it. The feeding is good and moderate in price; the track laid well enough for the train to run with most satisfactory

The Canadian Pacific Railway. 327

smoothness ; and the number of roadmen constantly looking after the safety of it render an accident from land-slide or fallen bridge almost impossible. (Not quite, though, for one occurred just about this time : forest fire, trestle bridge damaged, roadman inattentive ; enter train, collapse of bridge—smash up, death.) Winnipeg had in 1871 one hundred inhabitants, now it has 30,000. I do not know what there is in it besides one wide street, and a town-hall and memorial monument. It is a flat, unlovely country, and bleak enough in early May. Hence I turned south, and crossing the line (the International Boundary) passed through more prohibition States (Dakota) to St. Paul. Very rich-looking black-soil country all along the road. On to Chicago there is choice of routes. I went by one that clings to the Mississippi all day long. It is quite pretty in many places, with a placid rural prettiness in the English style, with now and again reaches and bays of more ambitious character. Down the stream go huge rafts of lumber, not content to float placidly down as on the Irrawaddy, but shoved behind by pushing little stern-wheelers. By the time we leave it, the river has grown into something wider and bigger than any English river. And at last, at night, Chicago.

That Anglo-Indian to whom allusion has before been made pours forth vials of contempt and condemnation on Chicago. To me it is a wonderful place. A low flat mud swamp on the shore of Michigan converted into a city of over a million people, with trade and wealth enormous. What if the pursuit of the dollar be here keen, persistent, supreme? Is Chicago the only place in the world where men make haste to get wealth? or spend it freely on wine and weeds and women? And Chicago has done what she can to make some bits of beauty on a most unlovely location. Are her parks and tree-bordered boulevard to count for nothing to her credit? And those large fourteen, fifteen, sixteen, twenty-storied buildings—are not many of them not merely triumphs of architectural skill, but worthy of admiration for the finish of their fittings and fixings? To me there was something fascinating in the rush and activity of life in this newest of *fin-de-siècle* cities. It is more rapid than in any other place I have seen anywhere, East or West. The elevators run you up and down the floors far faster than in New York. In the Board of Trade (Corn Exchange I should rather have called it) what a babel broke loose as business opened; what an endless traffic of cable-cars and trains and steamers; what hurrying to-and-fro of pedestrians! I say Chicago is splendid, for all the smoke and grime that makes her look old and dirty, even as London looks. And jolly good fellows are the men you meet there; busy chasing the cheerful dollar, yes; but none the less with time to take their pleasure with the same gay dash and go that they give to their business. With only a day and a half for Chicago, I had no idle minute, and not one dull or uninteresting. About to offices and shops and calling, out to park and boulevard and the site of the World's Fair—a scene of apparent chaos and immense activity of engine and man and beast; to the theatre, and after that—well, up again next morning all the same, and off to the Board of Trade and the old Chamber of Commerce, and by rail to the stockyards to see butchery wholesale. I wish I had timed one pig right through from the moment he is strung up by the hind-legs until he leaves the room duly cut up. The bristle-scraping machine is just perfect. Then the sheep: a somewhat less speedy business, each beast having to get its neck broken as well as its throat cut, and the skin having to be taken off by hand. It is a tremendous business—sickening to any one who cannot stand the sight and smell of plenty of blood, but interesting to whoso is callous and admires ingenuity and skill. Then a merry lunch in an underground restaurant, and hurried packing up of baggage and off by rail to Niagara.

I think I ought to stop here; when you are east of Chicago you have done with Farthest West, and are amongst places too well known to bear writing about again. Still, just a few notes by way of epilogue, as it were. First, don't come too early into this part of the world. The Clifton House (hotel on Canadian side at Niagara) is not open till June, nor is the Cave of the Winds accessible, nor are steamers running down the Thousand Islands of the St. Lawrence, nor on Lakes Champlain and George, nor by daylight down the Hudson from

Albany to New York. All these I had to leave out, albeit Cook's in 'Frisco had issued me tickets for them, knowing that I was booked from New York on the 27th, and not knowing, as they should have done, that the steamers did not run until after that date. Early May is also a little too soon for Vancouver and the Canadian Pacific Railway. As for Niagara, don't you believe any one who says the falls are disappointing at first sight. They are not; they are magnificent at first and every sight. Only, how hideous that Cataract House is, which obtrudes itself hatefully on the sight just above the American falls viewed from the Canadian side; how atrocious those factories—flour and paper-mills—just below the falls; how annoying the photographers (fotografers they often spell it in America) and curio-sellers! If only the Queen Victoria Niagara Falls Park and Prospect Park had been extended far down and back from the river. As far as I can make out, Captain Webb was last seen alive in some six different places down the rapids. I loitered and strolled and smoked a whole afternoon, doing nothing but look at the rainbow and the evening light on the splendid cataract.

Toronto is quiet and staid, as all Canadian towns are compared with American; yet not wanting in handsome buildings and fine streets. Lacrosse is evidently more popular than cricket and football: a crowd watched the former, cheering lustily; no on-lookers gathered about the latter. Still, Toronto appears to be English. Montreal does not; it is

The Canadian Pacific Railway. 331

more than half French. As a town, it cannot boast of fine streets; all are narrow and many mean. Dominion Square is the only decent one in the town; the big cathedral thereon is huge but hideous; Notre Dame is meretriciously gaudy. There are some fine public buildings, but not well shown off—cramped in too small space—and a fine tubular bridge across the river. But the glory of Montreal is its Mount Royal Park, on a hill behind the town. It is charming itself, and gives charming views over city and river and smiling champaign. Quebec is far Frencher than Montreal; the English language makes some sort of show in the former, but caves in in the latter. If used at all on public notice or signboard, it comes second, French first. I wandered about the Citadel and the Walls—a most wide and pleasing prospect therefrom—and to the spot where Wolfe fell, and the Governor's house, and all about the town—most quaint, un-English, provincial French, or rather Breton.

Here I have one growl—the only one—against the Canadian Pacific Railway. It books you through from Quebec to Boston, and carries you through, but leaves you dinnerless. This is unpardonable. There we were three—English, Scoto-Indian, Anglo-Indian—deprived of food : save late at night some bread and buns, bought at a stall and devoured in the train. And no drink either! Boston is disappointing for a "hub." I imagined a centre of sweetness and light, made lovely with the effulgence of culture. I found a busy manufacturing seaport, crowded in its narrow streets, full of smoke and noise and jostle. True, there is a beautiful avenue—Commonwealth Avenue—and a spacious common and public garden. But the associations of Bunker's Hill, with its very "ornery" column, are not so grateful to the patriotic Britisher as those of the Heights of Abraham. Harvard is a big place, and its memorial hall is fine. From Boston to New York the greatest comfort is by the Fall River line—rail and steamer. And in New York I had a good time for six days, refusing to be dragged off to Washington for a day, and doing all the sights in a thorough globe-trotting fashion. Here turned up My Virginian, arrived *viâ* Panama; and here also Our Humorist and Mrs. H. And the *Germanic* bore us off for England and home.

I don't know that I particularly wish to visit America again. If ever I do, it shall be at a later season of the year. And I think it would be highly advisable to bring letters of introduction with one, especially if one intended to stay "quite a little" time (*i.e.*, a good long time). I had very few, and went through with a rush; so that I had the best opportunities imaginable for forming hasty superficial opinions on American life and manners. They are good fellows—many of them—that you meet on your travels; and many of them are awful bounders. But in ordinary travel it is easy enough to avoid the latter class. Even amongst the former there are habits and customs that do not please the insular British taste (some of them I noted in my last chapter), and curious prejudices will be found fast-rooted in the American mind. One of these is against the use of a single eye-glass, or "monocle." Our Enthusiast carried one, and frequently brought it into play to assist his vision; but in America he had to lay it aside, to such remarks did his employment of it give rise. The skipper of the *Mariposa* was a courteous man enough. (When he first met Mrs. H. he mistook her for a former acquaintance, and addressed her accordingly. On discovering his error he apologized, saying, "I feared you might think I had been a little previous.") Yet he did not think it an unbecoming jest, when seated at dinner in the saloon, to stick a dollar in his eye in mimicry of friend B., who wore a "monocle." And K.—a most decent and intelligent Easterner—stated, as a matter of fact well known to everybody and indisputable, that the "monocle" was only plain glass, of not the slightest use, and that the wearing of it was mere foppery and snobbishness. It was evident that he sincerely believed what he said. I did not experience (thank goodness) any excessive spread-eagleism in my American travel-companions; and to suppose that they call all English "Britishers" is just as incorrect as to call all Americans "Yankees." The Canadians are just English (using "just" in the American sense: English and nothing else), except, of course, the French-Canadians; and these latter are certainly not American. I should suppose that there is no stronger desire in Canada for absorption in the United States of

America than there is in the States for absorbing her; and that is very little, for all that certain papers may say. Nevertheless it is a result that may, in time, very well come about by the mere force of the attraction of a large body juxtaposed to a small one, unless the Canadians and England can make it to the advantage of both (and especially of the former) to maintain and strengthen the present connection. Talking of newspapers, I can't say that I see very much cause for magnifying ours at the expense of the American. The comic papers are distinctly better—cleverer, more comic—with them than with us. I think *Life* is unsurpassed as a comic paper. Their illustrateds are not so well done as ours; nor are their daily and weekly newspapers so well printed or on such good paper. But they are cram-full of matter; not so much European news—why should they be? but any amount of American, and not more stuffed with criminal and other unsavoury reports than ours are now-a-days. Occasionally they indulge in blood-curdling head-lines which mean little. "Made Rome Howl" prefaced the information that a magazine had blown up and done some damage in Rome. "X. Y. Z. (I forget the real name) on the Warpath—His Scalping Knife Drips with Gore and Yearns for More" (or words to that effect), merely indicated that Secretary X. Y. Z. had caused one corrupt subordinate to resign, and was likely to cause another to follow suit. Certainly if officialdom and the judicial bench are anything like as—well, let us say, amenable to extraneous influences, as their own papers make out, I would as soon be tried by a bench of honorary magistrates in Rangoon as by an American court—and that is saying a good deal. Yet at times the latter deals out speedy justice. From their hotel in San Francisco a thief purloined jewels and coins of my friends. Within a week the thief was caught, all the property except one sovereign recovered from half-a-dozen different places, and a swingeing sentence passed on the luckless lifter. But the powers of Judge Lynch are yet freely exercised: witness the famous New Orleans case. Witness, too, a case in which soldiers of the line broke into jail, took out and hanged a man. Some fuss was made about this, and the President ordered searching inquiry. But I don't know what came of it. The use of the pistol, too, in settlement of private differences is by no means in its decadence. While I was with My Virginian he heard of two friends of his in the chief town of West Virginia falling out, and the one filling the other full of lead in the public street; both doctors—men of education and position. And you read in the papers of a good deal of miscellaneous shooting. There are things in which the Americans have the call over us, but this is hardly one of them. And it is, I think, mostly in things material that they score. We have no city bridge to match with Brooklyn Bridge; their elevated railway is a means of locomotion far preferable to the underground (nor do I consider the air-lines ugly); their Central Park is, I think, finer and better laid out than Hyde Park or Regent's Park (though the Zoo in it cannot compare with ours). But if you notice the carriages and riders in the Central Park at the fashionable hour, you will perceive a very great falling off in style from what you are accustomed to see in the Row. The people are not so well dressed, not by a long way; the turn-outs not so finished, so neat, or notable for elegance, as a whole. So at the theatres the audience is far inferior, from a dress point of view, to that in any West End theatre in London. (The prices, also, it may be remarked, are more democratic.) The boxes in most theatres that I saw are characteristic of America. They are not withdrawn, curtained, closed in, affording privacy, as with us; but thrown forward, low-railed, conspicuous, so that the occupants may be well *en évidence*. It is the same love of publicity that removes high walls from around gardens, and leaves them fenceless or surrounded by a meaningless little curb, so that all men may see the show you are able to make of your house and garden. "Know thyself" is not an American motto; "advertise thyself" seems to be the guiding maxim. They do not care for private life. Such a city as London, with its interminable rows and streets of small houses and cottages, each the residence of one family, is an impossibility in America. Hotels and flats and boarding-houses, where many families live under one roof, suits the American temperament better than the little compact domestic home of the Englishman. As for the American girl, it is better to say nothing. Should you venture to say anything that does not brim over with enthusiastic and delighted adoration, and should what you venture to say chance to be read by a male American eye, such a torrent of scornful and withering contempt and derision will be poured forth on your opinion and on yourself that you will be sorry you ever spoke. Let us take her at the American valuation, as inimitable, unsurpassable, perfect. (Yet of all places where that nasal twang sounds ill, it sounds worst from "red lips fed with all things sweet," as Hafiz has it. He must have foreseen the days of tutti-frutti gum-chewing.)

Where the New Yorker is miles behind the Londoner is in street management. I don't mean in street building; I like the rectangular blocks and the numbered streets and avenues: they are so easy to find your way about in. I mean in the regulation of traffic in the streets. After the Broadway, the streets of London are delightful to walk in; for there there is no attempt to direct the traffic by the blue-coated Bobby—it just takes its own way. What the New York streets would become if cabs and hansoms plied plentifully in them as in London it is impossible to imagine. I have seen twenty tram-cars in a line stuck still in a jam on Broadway, and as many more stuck on the down-line. There is a street in New York yclept the Bowery. My Virginian told me (after I had done it) that he would not care to walk down it alone at night. Well, I did so one night, after the theatre; and I can't say that I saw anything to disturb one. Penny gaffs, cheap theatres, admission-free music-halls, crowds low-class, but certainly not disorderly: not so drunken and rowdy as any corresponding street that you may select in London would be at the same hour. I just strolled through as far as Printing-House Square, where I thought I saw as fine a bit of city picturesqueness as I have ever seen. A full moon hidden by the lofty buildings of the Press (*Tribune*, I think), the lower floors all dark in shadow, the upper ones (some twelve stories high) bright with busy light, the moonlit sky crossed by clouds of light white steam from the vent on the topmost roof. It struck me more than anything else I saw in New York. For I do not overmuch admire the Statue of Liberty, and my recollection of the general view of the city from Brooklyn Bridge is sicklied o'er with the pale-yellow of "Castoria," advertised on every blank wall and hoarding and roof.

And so, with a nine days' passage through head-winds and fog and drizzle, my ten months' tour came to an end. If any one who may read this should make the same journey, or any part of it, the kindest thing I can wish him is that he may enjoy himself as much as I did, and get as much amusement in off-hours as I have done, in jotting down notes of his doings in Farthest East, and South and West.

APPENDIX.

A FEW NOTES ON HOTELS, DISTANCES, COST, &c.

PENANG.—Oriental Hotel on the beach. Peak Hotel on the hill.

SINGAPORE.—Raffles' Hotel is the best. Ocean Steamship Co.'s boats run every four days to Bangkok, every three days for Deli (Sumatra), weekly for North Borneo ports, fortnightly to Saigon, and fortnightly to Manila and Iloilo. Dutch mail boats fortnightly to Batavia and Javan ports and elsewhere; French mail alternate weeks to Batavia only. Apcar and Holt lines to Penang and Hongkong. Holt and others to Bangkok frequently; B. & S. N. to Australia monthly; to Madras and to Rangoon weekly.

BATAVIA.—Grand Hotel de Java, or Hotel Niederland. Dutch coinage. Five gulden a day.

BUITENZORG.—Hotel de Chemin de Fer; most obliging manager. Hotel Belle Vue better situated. Five gulden a day.

BANDONG.—Hotel Homann. Six gulden a day.

LEMBANG.—Rest-house at foot of Tankoebanprahoe; no food or drink except tea. One horse and syce up hill, four gulden.

TJANDJOER.—Refreshment room at station.

SINDANGLAIJA.—Hotel Leroux. Six gulden a day.

Expenses in Java—all in—easily covered by 20 gulden a day.

HONGKONG.—In town: Hongkong Hotel; Victoria Hotel. On Peak: Peak Hotel and others. $4 a day.

CANTON.—Shameen Hotel (very poor).

MACAO.—Boa Vista Hotel is a new finely situated hotel; there is an older one, where the feeding is said to be better, in the town.

From Hongkong: Many steamers to Chinese treaty ports, to

Haiphong, Manila, Japan. Two lines to Australia (no fixed dates). Also to England, to San Francisco, and Vancouver.

KOBE.—Oriental Hotel; and two others.

YOKOHAMA.—Grand Hotel.

MIYANOSHITA.—Fujiya Hotel. Bachelors will find the Japanese quarters the best.

KIOTO.—Yaami Hotel.

SHANGHAI. ·Central (English); Astor House (American); des Colonies (French). In order of merit.

SYDNEY. Grosvenor Hotel is the best. The Royal (in the town) is commercial. Avoid the Métropole: temperance and uncomfortable.

KATOOMBA. The Carrington: good.

JENOLAN CAVES. Cave House. Take your liquor with you: none to be had there.

MELBOURNE. Scott's is the Squatters' Hotel; it is rather rough. Menzies seems better.

BALLARAT. Craig's Hotel.

INVERCARGILL. Albion Hotel, rather commercial; or Southland Club.

QUEENSTOWN. Eichardt's.

DUNEDIN. The Grand; or Wain's.

CHRISTCHURCH. Coker's (if you are staying some time); Warner's (if you're passing through).

GREYMOUTH. Gilmer Hotel.

NELSON. Masonic.

WELLINGTON. Occidental or Empire.

NAPIER. Criterion (or Masonic).

WANGANUI. Rutland.

NEW PLYMOUTH. White Hart (by Le Grand Jacob).

AUCKLAND. Stay at the Northern Club if you can; it is good, and none of the hotels are.

HONOLULU. Hawaiian Hotel.

ON MANI, Mrs. Yarrow's Boarding House is at Wailuku.

ON HAWAII, the Hilo Hotel at Hilo is sufficiently comfortable.

SAN FRANCISCO.—Palace; or Baldwin's.

LOS ANGELES.—Westminster.

CHICAGO.—Auditorium; or Richelieu.

MONTREAL.—Windsor: very good.

NEW YORK.—I found the Fifth Avenue very good.

Appendix.

GUIDE-BOOKS.

For Singapore and the Straits, and for Java, I don't know of any.

For Hongkong, Canton, Macao, small local guide-books can be obtained in Hongkong; these are quite sufficient.

For Japan. The official Railway Guide, published yearly, and the last edition of Keeling's "Guide to Japan," are sufficient. Both may be got in Hongkong.

For Australia. I don't know of any general guide-book. Cook's Tourist Maps (American folder form) are useful.

For New Zealand. Brett's Handy Guide, to be got in Auckland, and at 147, Queen Victoria Street, E.C. Cook's folders are useful.

For Sandwich Islands. "The Paradise of the Pacific" is obtainable in Honolulu, and is good.

For San Francisco and California. Small books and folders to be got locally.

For Yosemite. The "Yosemite: Where to Go and What to Do" is good (532, Clay Street, San Francisco).

For Canadian Pacific Railway. Folder A and Annotated Time-Table.

For all other places in Canada and the United States of America guide-books and folders got locally are sufficient.

Stanford's Compendium of Travel, "Australasia," gives much information on all countries visited in this tour, except China, Japan, and America.

Appendix.

TABLE OF SEA DISTANCES.

From	To	Miles.	Passage.	By
Singapore	Batavia	550	42 hours	Messageries Maritimes.
Singapore	Saigon	637	37 ,,	,, ,,
Saigon	Hongkong	965	63 ,,	,, ,,
Hongkong	Yokohama	1,802	10½ days	P. and O.
Yokohama	Shanghai	1,085	5¾ ,,	Nippon Yusen Kaisha.
Shanghai	Hongkong	870	3 ,,	P. and O.
Hongkong	Port Darwin	2,352	} 23½ ,,	Eastern and Australian S. N. Co.
Port Darwin	Thursday Island	655 approx		
Thursday Island	Sydney	1,723		
Sydney	Melbourne	576	1¾ ,,	Messageries Maritimes.
Melbourne	Hobart	452	44 hours	Union S.S. Co.
Hobart	The Bluff	933	89 ,,	,, ,,
The Bluff	Port Chalmers	132	12 ,,	,, ,,
Nelson	Picton	85	} 14½ ,,	,, ,,
Picton	Wellington	53		
New Plymouth	Onehunga	135	13 ,,	,, ,,
Auckland	Honolulu	3,836	12 days	,, ,,
Honolulu	San Francisco	2,100	7 ,,	,, ,,
New York	Liverpool	3,100	9 ,,	White Star.

Distances by land, where useful, are given in the various guide-books.

COST.

Rupee at 1s. 6d.; Mexican dollar at 3s. 4d.; American dollar, at 4s.

	£	s.	d.
Through-ticket from Indian port to Singapore, Hongkong, Yokohama, Hongkong, Sydney, San Francisco, New York, Liverpool, London, Rs. 1732	129	18	0
Expenses to and at Singapore (11 days), 34 dols. 50 c.	5	15	0
Return fare to Batavia, 60 dols.	10	0	0
Expenses in Java (8 days), 59 dols. 07 c.	9	16	11
,, ,, Singapore (1½ day), 12 dols. 58 c.	2	1	11
Expenses in Saigon, Hongkong, Canton, Macao (15 days), 91 dols.	15	3	4

Appendix. 343

	£	s.	d.
Expenses in Japan (60 days), 487 dols. 36 c.	81	4	6½
,, ,, Shanghai, Hongkong (19 days), 129 dols. 79 c.	21	12	7
Expenses in Australia (36 days)	45	6	0
,, ,, New Zealand (54 days)	121	14	7
,, ,, Hawaiian Islands (33 days), 167 dols.	33	8	0
Expenses in America (43 days), 490 dols. 70 c.	98	2	9½
Expenses of voyage home (10 days).	3	19	4
Total	578	3	0

This list of expenses includes all charges on account of fares by land and sea, hotel and steamer bills for food, tips, liquor and tobacco, doing oneself comfortably but not extravagantly throughout. It does not include any expenditure on photos, curios, or fancy articles of any kind. It will be seen, therefore, that even allowing a margin of £21 17s., the trip can be done well for £600. But it certainly adds greatly to the enjoyment of one's tour if one can allow a further margin for extravagances, not necessities. A couple of hundred pounds would cover a reasonable expenditure under this head ; say, £800 in all.

www.ingramcontent.com/pod-product-compliance
Lightning Source LLC
Chambersburg PA
CBHW020301240426
43673CB00039B/668